EMPLOYEE PARTICIPATION IN GOVERNANCE

A Legal and Ethical Analysis

Catholic Social Thought is a branch of moral theology. There is now a unified corpus of official Catholic teaching that focuses the resources of moral theology and natural law theory on important social issues of the day. The rights of the employee and the themes of employee ownership and participation have been central and recurring themes as this body of teaching has developed.

This description and explanation of the essential elements of Catholic Social Thought and its relationship to these themes helps the reader think about the place of the corporation in the economy and whether British and European corporate governance and labour law do what they should to put the employee at the centre of corporate governance.

MICHAEL LOWER is an Associate Professor in the Faculty of Law at the Chinese University of Hong Kong.

EMPLOYEE PARTICIPATION IN GOVERNANCE

A Legal and Ethical Analysis

MICHAEL LOWER

CAMBRIDGE UNIVERSITY PRESS
Cambridge, New York, Melbourne, Madrid, Cape Town, Singapore,
São Paulo, Delhi, Dubai, Tokyo

Cambridge University Press
The Edinburgh Building, Cambridge CB2 8RU, UK

Published in the United States of America by Cambridge University Press, New York

www.cambridge.org
Information on this title: www.cambridge.org/9780521862844

First published 2010

Printed in the United Kingdom at the University Press, Cambridge

A catalogue record for this publication is available from the British Library

Library of Congress Cataloguing in Publication data
Lower, Michael associate professor.
Employee participation in governance : a legal and ethical analysis / Michael Lower.
p. cm.
ISBN 978-0-521-86284-4 (hardback)
1. Management–Employee participation. 2. Corporate governance. 3. Labor laws
and legislation. 4. Christian sociology–Catholic Church. I. Title.
HD5650.L78 2010
658.3′152–dc22
2010009137

ISBN 978-0-521-86284-4 Hardback

To Tao and Lewis

CONTENTS

ACKNOWLEDGEMENTS

The author is grateful to *The Journal of Catholic Social Thought* and the *Notre Dame Journal of Law, Ethics & Public Policy* for allowing him to use in this monograph material that first appeared in articles published by them.

LEGAL INSTRUMENTS

Table of cases

Centros Ltd v Erhverus-og Selkabsstyrelsen (C 212 / 97) [1999] ECR I – 1459 (ECJ)
Fulham Football Club Ltd v Cabra Estates plc (1993) 65 P & C.R. 284
Gas Lighting Improvement Co Ltd v Commissioners of Inland Revenue [1923] AC 723, HL
Re Saul D Harrison & Sons plc [1994] BCC 475
Uberseering BV v Nordic Construction Baumanagement GmbH (NCC) (C 208 / 00) [2002] ECR I – 9919 (ECJ)

Table of statutes

Companies Act 2006
  s. 168
  s. 172
  s. 415
  s. 416
  s. 417
  s. 942
  s. 1273
Trade Union and Labour Relations (Consolidation) Act 1992
  s.178
  s. 181
  ss. 183–5
  Sch. A1

EC treaties

art. 138
art. 139
art. 257
art. 262

Table of European material

Council Directive 77/187/EEC on the approximation of the laws of the Member States relating to the safeguarding of employees' rights in the event of transfers of undertakings, businesses or parts of businesses.

Council Directive 80/987/EEC on the approximation of the laws of the Member States relating to the protection of employees in the event of the insolvency of their employer.

Council Directive 94/45/EC of 22 September 1994 on the establishment of a European Works Council or a procedure in Community-scale undertakings and Community-scale groups of undertakings for the purposes of informing and consulting employees.

Council Directive 97/74/EC of 15 December 1997 extending, to the United Kingdom of Great Britain and Northern Ireland, Directive 94 / 45 / EC on the establishment of a European Works Council or a procedure in Community-scale undertakings and Community-scale groups of undertakings for the purposes of informing and consulting employees.

Council Directive 98/50/EC of 29 June 1998 amending Directive 77 / 187 / EEC on the approximation of the laws of the Member States relating to the safeguarding of employees' rights in the event of transfers of undertakings, businesses or parts of businesses.

Council Directive 98/59/EC of 20 July 1998 on the approximation of the laws of the member states concerning collective redundancies.

Council Directive 2001/86/EC of 8 October 2001 supplementing the Statute for a European Company with regard to the involvement of employees.

Directive 2002/14/EC of the European Parliament and of the Council on of 11 March 2002 establishing a general framework for informing and consulting employees in the European Community.

Directive 2004/25/EC of the European Parliament and of the Council on of 21 April 2004 on Takeover Bids.

Council Regulation (EC) No 2157/2001 of 8 October 2001 on the Statute for a European Company.

Table of foreign legislation

Bertriebsverfassungsgesetz ("Industrial Constitution Act")
Gesetz fur Kleine Aktiengesellschaften und zur Derelegierung des Aktienrechts ("Law for Small Stock Companies and to Deregulate Stock Law")

Table of statutory instruments

Companies (Tables A to F) Regulations 1985/805

Table A, regulation 78
Table A, regulation 79
Companies (Model Articles) Regulations 2008/3229
Schedule 3, articles 20 and 21
Transnational Information and Consultation Regulations 1999/3323

1

Introduction

Employee participation as an ethical issue

Catholic Social Thought ('CST') is often said to begin with Leo XIII's 1891 encyclical *Rerum novarum*. Written in response to the inhumane treatment of labour during the industrial revolution, it spelled out the fundamental rights of workers. While it stressed the importance of respect for private property rights for a well-ordered society it set out the ethical parameters within which these rights should be exercised. In a sense, the need for capital-labour relations to be governed by ethically legitimate rules is at the heart of CST. *Rerum novarum* does not mention employee participation specifically but the theme emerged several times in later magisterium (official teaching).

CST is used in this book to refer to the official teaching of the Catholic Church on social matters. It can be distinguished from the attempts of individual scholars either to critique CST or to apply their understanding of CST to particular issues. The first part of this book attempts an explanation and exposition of CST. It sometimes prays in aid non-CST sources (natural law theorists and moral theologians) with a view to providing a fuller explanation of CST. It attempts neither to critique CST nor to defend it from criticism, but simply to explain it. The second part of the book uses CST to carry out an ethical evaluation of the status of employee participation in UK (and EU) corporate governance law and practice. It considers whether they adequately respond to CST's calls for employee participation and, hence, whether or not improvements are possible which might make the corporate governance environment more conducive to the integral human fulfillment of those affected by it.

CST's exclusive focus is on the integral human fulfilment of each individual human person. Integral human fulfillment is a very expansive concept. Grisez, Finnis and Boyle explain that:

ideally the freely chosen actions shaped by moral truths would bear fruit in the fulfillment of all persons in all the basic goods. This *ideal community* is what we mean by 'integral human fulfillment'.[1]

Clearly, there is a limit to the extent to which any individual human being (or even all humans of all times) can achieve this goal. Grisez, Finnis and Boyle suggest, though, that the morally good will is a will towards integral human fulfillment.[2]

CST is concerned with social phenomena because it is convinced that human communities exist to serve the individual (though they can legitimately make great demands on him or her) and that the way that communities are organised has a profound impact on individual well-being. The 'social' in CST should not mislead one into imagining some kind of breach between individual ethics and social ethics; each are concerned with the integral human fulfillment or flourishing of each individual person. Healthy social structures are important because they facilitate the lives and moral growth of individuals.

CST looks at corporate governance, and at social phenomena in general, from the point of view of human self-development (or 'happiness', 'flourishing' or 'integral self-realisation'). The point of any social institution is that, usually in a variety of ways, it meets the needs of individuals. Clearly, the corporation exists to meet the needs of customers or clients. It also meets the needs of its employees and shareholders as well. In a sense, it provides services to employees and shareholders to allow them to meet their own needs, for work and a return on capital respectively. Much of the first half of this book is devoted to an ethical exploration of the relevant needs. Some are obvious, others are less so (though just as real and just as important).

Charity, properly understood,[3] is at the heart of CST and this point should be made from the outset. In modern parlance, charity is seen as a matter of personal taste and disposition and certainly not a factor to be counted on in the 'real world'. Benedict XVI emphasised in *Caritas*

---

[1] G. Grisez, J. Boyle and J. Finnis, 'Practical principles, moral truth and ultimate ends', *The American Journal of Jurisprudence* 32 (1987), p. 128.

[2] Grisez, Boyle and Finnis, 'Practical principles', p. 128.

[3] See the discussion in J. Messner, *Social ethics. Natural law in the western world*, (St Louis and London, B. Herder Book Co, 1965), pp. 334–341, J.-Y. Calvez and J. Perrin, *The Church and social justice. The social teaching of the Popes from Leo XIII to Pius XII*, (Chicago, Henry Regnery and Company, 1961), pp. 162–173 and in G. Grisez, *The way of the Lord Jesus. Living a Christian life*, (Quincy, Illinois, Franciscan Press, 1983), pp. 306–320.

in veritate that charity is very much a factor in human nature and in all inter-personal relations. Charity, he argues, is not something at the margins of the human personality but is rather, 'the principal driving force behind the authentic development of every person and of all humanity'.[4] An impulse to love authentically is built into every human person.[5] For this reason, charity is at the heart of the Church's social doctrine.[6]

CST urges that social structures should be at the service of the integral self-realisation of the individual. It insists that effective communities can only be constructed on the basis of an adequate anthropology (understanding of human nature). Since the need to love and be loved is so central to the human person, any sound system of social ethics must take it into account. Thus, charity, 'gives real substance to the personal relationship with God and with neighbour; it is the principle not only of micro-relationships (with friends, with family members or within small groups) but also of macro-relationships (social, economic and political ones).'[7]

Charity might seem an alien concept to the reader of a book about corporate governance. Corporate governance is, however, principally about the organisation of relationships between the people who engage with each other within the firm. If charity truly is such an important human need and such an important driver of behaviour and relationships then a respect for truth demands that it be taken into account.

Benedict XVI highlighted the link between truth and charity. Charity is not simply a sentiment but is a central aspect of human nature that can be thought about and understood. Charity 'can be recognised as an authentic expression of humanity and an element of fundamental importance in human relations, including those of a public nature.'[8]

One of the major ideas in CST, that this book will seek to explain, is that capital and labour are mutually interdependent (again for a range of reasons some of which are economic but others of which belong to the realm of moral theology). One of the most pressing tasks for societies in general, and for corporations in particular, is to bring about an alignment of the interests of capital and labour. Old images of them as two impersonal (and often mutually hostile) forces need to be discarded, for the right to own private property and work each play a vital role in human self-development. Indeed, in the last analysis private property ownership both serves work and represents work. Employees and shareholders work together in the corporate community.

---

[4] Benedict XVI, *Caritas in veritate*, para. 1.   [5] Benedict XVI, *Caritas in veritate*, para. 1.
[6] Benedict XVI, *Caritas in veritate*, para. 2.   [7] Benedict XVI, *Caritas in veritate*, para. 2.
[8] Benedict XVI, *Caritas in veritate*, para. 3.

Employee participation can be seen as an important strand in a programme that puts respect for the individual human person at the heart of economic, political and civic society. CST's ultimate aim is to humanise communities and institutions with pride of place being given to the workplace and to the economy. It seeks, where necessary, the transformation of the workplace so that the employee is always in some sense in charge of his or her own work and is never a commodity, never a mere object to be manipulated.

Catholic Social Thought

Catholic Social Thought (CST) is primarily to be found in a series of papal encyclicals beginning with Leo XIII's *Rerum novarum* in 1891. The timing of the encyclical is significant; it was the Catholic Church's response to the problems faced by workers at the time of the industrial revolution. Leo XIII lamented that, 'a small number of very rich men have been able to lay upon the teeming masses of the labouring poor a yoke little better than slavery itself'.[9] At the same time, he was concerned to point out the inadequacies of the socialist response to the 'worker question' which saw the abolition of the institution of private property as the solution. *Rerum novarum* proposed an understanding of the question that avoided the excesses of individualistic, *laissez faire* capitalism and the collectivist approach of socialism. CST proposes a much more subtle, and much more realistic understanding of the relationship between the individual and the various communities of which he or she forms part.

John Paul II gave this concise summary of CST's essential nature:

> The Church's social doctrine is not a "third way" between liberal capitalism and Marxist collectivism, nor even a possible alternative to other solutions less radically opposed to one another. Nor is it an ideology, but rather the accurate formulation of the results of a careful reflection on the complex realities of human existence, in society and in the international order, in the light of faith and of the Church's tradition. Its main aim is to interpret these realities, determining their conformity with or divergence from the lines of the Gospel teaching on man and his vocation, a vocation which is at once earthly and transcendent; its aim is thus to guide Christian behaviour. It therefore belongs to the field, not of ideology, but of theology and particularly of moral theology.[10]

---

[9] Leo XIII, *Rerum novarum*, para. 3.   [10] John Paul II, *Centesimus annus*, para. 41.

This is an extremely rich passage. It classifies CST as a branch of moral theology; that is to say that it is practical (rather than speculative) and aims to shape Christian life.[11] It draws its primary data from faith and the Church's tradition. It interprets social realities 'determining their conformity with or divergence from the lines of the Gospel teaching on man and his vocation'. This vocation or call is to human self-development or integral self-realisation or holiness. CST is not addressed to Catholics alone, as other Christian denominations share at least some of the same theological sources as Catholics and are also concerned with how to lead a Christian life. CST is addressed to everyone for everyone sees the point of pursuing the goal of integral self-realisation, has it inbuilt so to speak. And, in natural law, CST has a philosophical vocabulary that allows it to speak to anyone, believer or not.

The passage also makes the point that CST is not a 'third way' between capitalism and socialism. First, extreme forms of each of these systems are constructed on materialistic premises that are incompatible with Christian faith. Second, moral theology cannot be thought of in terms appropriate to political or economic discourse for it is a fundamentally different activity. It is an error to try to place CST somewhere on the left-right political axis (though it can be embraced by people who themselves espouse left-wing or right-wing views).

Although theology is a distinct discipline the boundaries between it and other disciplines, such as economics and politics, are not water-tight. Economic and political choices always have a moral element[12] for any purposeful human choice (whether it results in action or not) neces-sarily determines one to some extent for or against the goal of integral self-realisation. Catholic theology is attached to the notion that there is a unity of knowledge; there can be no truth or knowledge in one discipline that conflicts with the truth or knowledge in any other. And this propos-ition equally holds where one of the disciplines is theological.[13]

Rerum novarum dealt with the ethics of the employment relationship and with the legitimacy of private property as an institution. The capital – labour relationship in general, and employee participation in particular, has been a central theme of CST throughout its history. 'Employee par ticipation' is to be understood in a very broad sense to include employee participation in management, in corporate governance, in profits and in

---

[11] G. Grisez, *The Way of the Lord Jesus. Volume One. Christian moral principles*, (Quincy, Illinois, Franciscan Press, 1983), p. 10.

[12] John Paul II, *Sollicitudo rei socialis*, para. 36.

[13] Grisez, *Christian moral principles*, p. 10.

ownership. CST has also called for employees to play a part in the governance of the broader economy. At stake is the human self-development of
the employee. CST is convinced that putting the employee in charge of his
or her work and making the employee at least a partial owner of the workplace are of central importance.

CST's call for employee participation, in the variety of senses just mentioned, has profound theological and philosophical roots. John Paul II
devoted an entire encyclical, *Laborem exercens*, to an ethical analysis of
human work (and its relationship to capital). This analysis draws upon
the Book of Genesis in which man is called upon to work and to exercise a stewardship over the earth's resources. Work has a central and
indispensable part to play in a person's life; it would be difficult, probably
impossible, to grow as a person without a commitment to work. Employee
participation is important because it creates the conditions in which one's
work makes a contribution to one's development as a person.

Human self-development or integral self-realisation and work

Catholic moral theology proposes the concept of human self-development
or integral self-realisation as the goal or vocation of each human life. The
primary moral criterion is whether any given choice, and the more fundamental commitments that underlie one's choices, are consistent with a
will to human self-development. Christian anthropology sees the human
person as having an inner urge to pursue human self-development and the
human intellect as able to discern the goods that are fulfilling for human
persons. Human self-development is the fruit of an effective commitment
to integrate those goods into one's life; this is the essence of ethics.

Catholic moral theology focuses on the free choices that one makes
and enquires whether or not they are consistent with a will to human self-
development. One develops one's humanity through a pattern of choices
and of commitments that are so consistent. If one's choices form part of
a coherent whole (a life plan anchored in certain core commitments) and
are consistent with a will to human self-development then they will contribute to the formation of a mature, well-rounded personality. Christian
anthropology sees the human person as having an inner urge to pursue
human self-development. The intellect, through reflection on the inbuilt
inclinations that it apprehends, can grasp the goods that are fulfilling for
human persons. These goods will be discussed at greater length in the
next chapter.

The foregoing is the account of human self-development given by the natural law school of philosophical ethics. Catholic moral theology makes use of natural law but its primary sources are theological (the Christian scriptures, Tradition in its technical theological sense and the Church's magisterium). Catholic moral theology holds that everything necessary for salvation (a theological version of human self-development) can be found in Scriptures. Revelation then confirms the central findings of natural law theory so that no-one is left without the guidance they need to allow them to pursue the goal of human self-development. But it goes much further for it also gives a picture of human self-development that builds on and enriches the philosopher's vision of the flourishing personality.

John Paul II's treatment of human work in his encyclical *Laborem exercens* provides an illustration of the interaction between faith and reason in moral theology. *Laborem exercens'* theme is the role that human work plays in the development of the human personality. It identifies work as one of the basic goods that are fulfilling for human persons. This truth, obvious to unaided human reason, is confirmed and deepened by Scripture. John Paul II recalls God's command to Adam and Eve to work and to subdue the earth. Theologically speaking, work is part of man's calling from God and is a way for the human person to act as co-creator. The attributes that separate the human person from non-rational animals (reason and free will) are brought to bear in the process of making the earth's material resources fruitful. Reason and free will are the most specific reflection of the divine image in the human person and in work they are brought to bear on the process of meeting human needs. Thus, work has both an external dimension (the change produced by work) and an internal dimension (the development of the human personality brought about by work).

It may seem that these ideas are other-worldly and that they lack practical importance when compared with the hard facts proposed by, say, economic analyses of corporate governance. Nothing could be further from the truth! Catholic moral theology claims that it can help us to understand who we are, the purpose of our lives and the point of human communities. It does so with a view to helping individuals to build successful lives. Further, an adequate understanding of the human person and the nature of human communities is the foundation on which any discipline committed to the study of human affairs must build.

The corporation and corporate governance

CST has only rarely mentioned the corporation as such. The first such mention was in *Quadragesimo anno*.[14] There Pius XI expressed his concern that its structure would lead to a certain anonymity; the fear was that no person or group within the corporation would accept moral responsibility for the overall well-being of the corporation, its members and those it dealt with.

It is obvious that any study of corporate governance has to begin with an understanding of what the corporation is for. CST assumes that the purpose of the corporation is to meet some range of human needs (a newspaper publisher responds to a need to be informed, a supermarket responds to the need for food and so on). It also has to meet the needs of its employees for jobs that pay reasonable wages and are fulfilling. It has to make enough profit to sustain itself and to pay the market price for any outside capital that it uses. Management's job is to run the corporation with at least these core goals in mind (other tasks may be imposed upon it because of the political and legal environments in which it operates). Achieving these goals will require enormous skill, effort and ingenuity on the part of management (and employees in general). It will require a constant effort to build up the knowledge and competence of the organisation and its members and a search for human needs that the organisation can meet profitably. This vision of the corporation is very compatible with a dynamic society in which the ways in which human needs are met and the constellations of group and individual preferences and ways of doing things is constantly changing. CST nowhere assumes that a job or an organisation will last forever.

The quality of management and of corporate governance is important to employees because it plays a significant role in determining whether the corporation meets its responsibilities to its employees. Those in charge of the organisation are responsible for finding opportunities that the organisation can exploit (human needs that it can profitably serve). They are primarily responsible for enhancing the capabilities of the organisation and of its people. They are responsible for securing the financial and other resources that the corporation requires. In the last analysis, management and corporate governance are responsible for securing the survival of the organisation so long as there are human needs that it can usefully and profitably meet.

---

[14] Pius XI, *Quadragesimo anno*, (1931), (available at www.vatican.va/holy_father/pius_xi/ encyclicals/documents/hf_p-xi_enc_19310515_quadragesimo-anno_en.html, last accessed on 28th July 2009).

The corporation is a community; management, employees and shareholders pursue a common goal at the same time as they seek to meet some of their own needs. One of CST's core principles is that of participation. The members of a community should play as full and active a part as is reasonably possible in the governance of their communities. This is how the design of social institutions pays its respects to the intelligence and free will of their members. Participation is especially important when it comes to a community that organises human work. Work can only play its part in the development of the human personality if the worker is an active subject. CST is concerned with the practical impact of governance arrangements; it asks whether a given arrangement amounts to a reasonably effective way of promoting the cause of human self-development. If co-determination (worker representation) allows the organisation to secure its goals including the goal of making employees into the active subjects of the production process then *prima facie* there is a case to be made for adopting it. But it may be that better solutions can be found to achieve the same goals. CST is concerned with the impact of social structures on human self-development and not to promote a particular form of governance arrangement for its own sake.

To say that the corporation is a community is to say that it has a reality of its own that is to some extent independent of its members. The corporation has a personality that is distinct from its members. But there is more to it than that. The corporation has its own knowledge, memory and capacity to adapt to changing circumstances. The corporation has its own culture (a particular way of addressing fundamental human issues such as interpersonal relations and the organisation of the production process). The corporation has its own purpose.

It is important, however, not to press this idea of the separateness of the corporation (or of any human community) too far. Communities arise because individuals choose to co-operate with each other. As we have seen, employees, shareholders and management work together in the corporation, each with a view to meeting certain of their needs (such as a decent wage and fulfilling jobs). Looked at in one way, the corporation exists because it meets the needs of its employees and shareholders. Further, the corporation as an institution bears the impress of the personality of the people who form part of it. The development of the corporation is in the hands of those who form part of it. One purpose of the principle of participation is to make it possible for every member of a community to shape it in some way.

CST sees the corporation as forming an integral part of a much broader whole. The corporation is an intermediate association that sits between the state on the one hand and the individual and the family on the other hand. CST sees the corporation as forming part of a system of interconnected vessels that have a shared responsibility to meet human needs within the societies of which they form part. Each intermediate association makes its own specialised contribution to meeting the full range of needs within the society. This social purpose, the goal of meeting some specialised needs of its customers or clients, is not one imposed from outside by the state but is in large measure the organisation's *raison d'etre* and its means of making a profit and meeting the needs of employees and shareholders. Each organisation makes its contribution to the common good of the state or states that it operates in.

This does not, however, turn the corporation into a public sector (state-owned or state-controlled) organisation. By pursuing its own private aims, the corporation necessarily helps to meet the goals of the state. The corporation makes its own specialised contribution to meeting the human needs of the members of a particular society. In doing so, it enhances the state's ability to promote the cause of human self-development within its borders.

CST's principle of subsidiarity is a staunch defence of the (permeable) boundaries between the state and private organisations. According to the principle of subsidiarity the state's primary role is to encourage individuals, families and intermediate associations to bear the brunt of meeting human needs and promoting the cause of human self-development. If some important human needs are going unmet and state intervention seems necessary then this intervention should, preferably, take the form of helping (providing *subsidium*) to a private sector actor. Only as a last resort (or in exceptional cases that are peculiarly the province of the state) should the state act directly. When the state does take direct responsibility for some activity that families or intermediate associations could meet, it should try to keep its intervention as brief as possible.

Maritain proffers an explanation of the good sense of the principle of subsidiarity:

> The fact remains that the State has skill and competence in administrative, legal and political matters, but is inevitably dull and awkward – and, as a result, easily oppressive and injudicious – in all other fields.[15]

[15] J. Maritain, 'The people and the state', reprinted in *Logos* 11 (2008), p. 180.

Within the borders of the nation state are to be found a vast range and number of organisations each striving to meet some specialised needs of the citizens of that state. The state's primary responsibility is not to meet those needs itself but, rather, to co-ordinate the activity of individuals, families and the intermediate associations (such as the corporation). One aspect of this co-ordination is simply to create social arrangements that allow one person or group to pursue its activities without unreasonably interfering with the activities of others. The analogy of organising a road traffic system comes to mind. There need to be people who take responsibility for making traffic flow safely and smoothly. But the state's co-ordinating responsibility goes further than this since it has a positive responsibility for ensuring that at least the core needs of its citizens are met. The state will foster the activities of individuals and groups with a view to ensuring that this is the case; it will only take direct responsibility for meeting the needs of its citizens where this is absolutely necessary.

Maritain, again, explains the essential role of the state within the society that it serves:

> The final step would take place … when prodding by the State would no longer be necessary and all organic forms of social life and economic activity, even the largest and most comprehensive ones, would start from the bottom, I mean from the free initiative of and mutual tension between the particular groups, working communities, cooperative agencies, unions, associations, federated bodies of producers and consumers, rising in tiers and institutionally recognised. Then a definitely personalist and pluralist pattern of social life would come into effect in which new societal types of private ownership and enterprise would develop. And the State would leave to the multifarious organs of the social body the autonomous initiative and management of all the activities which by nature pertain to them. Its only prerogative in this respect would be its genuine prerogative as topmost umpire and supervisor, regulating those spontaneous and autonomous activities from the superior political point of view of the common good.
>
> So perhaps it will be possible, in a pluralistically organised body politic, to make the State into a topmost agency concerned only with the final supervision of the achievements of institutions born out of freedom, whose free interplay expressed the vitality of society integrally just in its basic structures.[16]

---

[16] Maritain, 'The people and the state, p. 181.

The transnational dimension

In the last analysis there is a universal common good, a bond that creates a single worldwide community. Openness to human self-development excludes an attitude of indifference to the well-being of others. As communications, tourism and international business shrink the globe they open up an awareness of the needs of people in countries far from one's own. The activities of people in, for example, developed western countries have a discernible impact on the lives of the citizens of developing countries. The territorial reach of the concept of the common good has expanded accordingly. We now appreciate the need to co-ordinate activities across national boundaries. We understand that there is a real sense in which people in every part of the globe have, at least potentially, some right to expect us to behave reasonably towards them. The extent of what they can reasonably demand of us, and we of them, varies according to the importance and the frequency of our interaction with them. So the boundaries of every other community, including the individual state, have a certain instability and contingency about them. We see this today as nations co-operate through international organisations to achieve political, economic or humanitarian goals. The multinational corporation can be seen as an intermediate association not only with respect to the individual nation state but also with respect to broader transnational and even global communities.

Economic activity's transnational dimension creates a need for supranational governance mechanisms. Although the economy and the communities that form part of it should be, so far as possible, self-governing, there is an evident need for some political authority to ensure that economic activity serves the broader goals of human self-development. There is a need for a political authority capable of operating across national borders with the same facility and effectiveness as international businesses. The need for some such authority has been very thoroughly discussed by corporate governance scholars. This is because of the fear that capital will be able to exploit its mobility and political and financial muscle to pressure national governments to further its interests at the expense of labour (and corporate stakeholders).

In principle, the transnational body should have the same essential characteristics as traditional governments. It should have the goal of co-ordinating activity within its jurisdiction with a view to promoting the cause of human self-development and it should respect the principle of subsidiarity. Although democratic accountability may not be possible, the principle of participation suggests that those affected by the decisions of the transnational body should have some way of making their voice heard (perhaps through representative mechanisms). At the very least, the supranational government has to avoid being captured by the representatives of management and finance. The transnational governing body's ability to intervene, to coerce and impose sanctions will, practically speaking, be weaker than in the case of a national government. Provided, however, that the supranational body can effectively achieve its goals this does not detract from its ability to act as a form of government.

The EU experience provides an interesting, and highly relevant, case study. The member states of the EU take divergent approaches to the question of employee participation in corporate governance. Germany, for example, requires its largest businesses to implement a mandatory co-determination system. By contrast, the United Kingdom has firmly committed itself to oppose any attempt to impose mandatory co-determination on British businesses. As it becomes easier for businesses to shop around for the corporate governance regime that suits them, there is clear pressure to follow the line of least resistance and embrace the solution that appeals to the representatives of finance and management. CST has rejected the proposition that employees have a right to a co-determination system. But the battle over co-determination illustrates the need for the sort of transnational political body just discussed. This body has to find a way of resolving the sort of differences of opinion just mentioned within a framework that seeks the common good and human self-development. These are the challenges that have faced the EU.

The economy is not a machine but rather a community of free and rational persons seeking to meet the needs of themselves and of others. The interplay of human freedom and the contingent nature of real life combine to make a mockery of the idea that the economy or the market is a machine that inexorably works towards the creation of the best of all possible worlds. This image fails to give sufficient credit to the influence of human freedom and ingenuity. So a *laissez faire* approach to economic management that entrusts human self-development to the market implies an unacceptable leap of blind faith that no-one would be prepared to make in practice. The principle of subsidiarity suggests, however, that, provided the necessary political safeguards are in place, as much decision-making as possible should be left to economic actors themselves.

Share ownership

A defence of private property rights has been a constant theme of CST. It vehemently rejected the notion that employee rights could only be secured through a transfer of the ownership of the means of production into state hands. Indeed, CST sees private property rights as being at the service of work and as being in most cases a necessary prelude for work to be humanly fulfilling. One of the hallmarks of an ethically just way of organising productive activity is that it should reflect the profound harmony between the interests of capital and labour.

One would have thought that conditions were ripe for this to occur in the United Kingdom. For one thing, employees are, directly and indirectly, the principal owners of British listed companies. The indirect form of ownership occurs through their pension schemes that collectively own large stakes in Britain's biggest companies. As a result, a large proportion of corporate profits is destined for the pockets of employees whether in the form of salaries or as dividends paid to pension funds and other shareholders. Drucker argued that countries like Great Britain are employee societies, where employees are the capitalists. He went on to note that this creates a challenge because managerial power and responsibility did not reflect this reality:

> Professional management may be competent, responsible and performing. But it still faces a severe crisis of legitimacy because it is no longer grounded in yesterday's economic power, that of the capitalist owner, and is not grounded in anything else so far.[17]

Drucker called for the economic interest of the employee to be institutionalised but saw grave difficulties in the way of achieving it. This interest was a true asset of the employee but it had to be made compatible with the ability of the economy to adapt to changing needs and circumstances and with clear, effective governance.[18] The former is, as we will see, is a challenge that company law / corporate governance and labour law have each had to grapple with.

And there are other challenges in the way of governance institutions that reflect and harmonise the interests of employees as workers and as investors. One of these distorting factors is the rise of a shareholder value mythology that puts the emphasis on the financial aspects of the

---

[17] P. Drucker, *Managing in Turbulent Times*, (London, William Heinemann Ltd, 1980), p. 191.
[18] Drucker, *Managing in Turbulent Times*, p. 195.

corporation. Even management that is keen to focus on the broader picture might be distracted by the short-termist demands of investors; pension fund managers have their own incentives and pre-occupations that are potentially at odds with the interests of those whom they are supposed to serve. Many have argued that the problem is compounded by the incentive structures faced by senior management that exacerbate the propensity to pursue strategies that maximise short-term profitability.

There is a growing trend to think of the needs of the corporation as being synonymous with the financial interests of its shareholders. British company law and corporate governance codes have promoted the conception of the corporation as being a system both having shareholder value at its core and resistant to the claims of employees as such. Efforts to integrate employees into management and governance have had to occur outside the sphere of corporate governance properly so-called. This book seeks to describe this process and to consider its ethical implications.

The plan of the book

This book begins by seeking to explain CST (and especially the aspects most relevant to the present study) to readers who have not studied it in depth or who may even have been unaware of its existence. CST's call for employee participation has to be understood in its theological and philosophical context. One has, to some extent, to get inside CST if one is to appreciate what it has to say about specific issues such as employee participation. This does not imply that CST is accessible only to believers; it seeks to engage with everyone, Catholic or not and it should be possible for any thinking person to understand and consider what it has to say whether or not they share the Catholic world-view. But CST's calls for employee participation form part of a broader picture and rest on a particular anthropology and understanding of the nature and purpose of human communities (or society). Understanding CST on employee participation requires some familiarity with this broader context.

The early chapters of this book explain that CST is a branch of moral theology. They explain the sources of CST and explain its relationship to other disciplines. They provide an account of the Christian anthropology (the Christian understanding of the human person) that is at CST's heart. CST asserts that this anthropology is one of its most important contributions to social ethics. They explain the concept of 'community' that is so fundamental to understanding CST's approach to, among other things, corporate governance. The early parts of this book outline CST's principal tools for evaluating social phenomena such as the firm and the economy.

The later chapters of this book critique UK (and to a lesser extent EU) corporate governance arrangements from the perspective of the framework established in section one. This part of the book considers the importance of the theory of the firm underpinning thinking about corporate governance. It then moves on to think about the general theme of employee participation from an ethical perspective. The book then assesses UK corporate governance (including labour law) from a CST perspective before looking at the transnational dimension (taking the EU as its model).

2

Catholic Social Thought: nature, sources and core principles and values

Introduction

This chapter introduces CST, its sources, nature and fundamental concepts. It will try to explain how CST works and how it relates to other disciplines. It attempts to persuade the reader that, even though it is a branch of moral theology, CST can be understood and constructively engaged with by everyone. CST's employee participation prescriptions are a logical consequence of the anthropological and ethical framework within which it operates. This chapter tries to give a clear account of that framework.

The central point to grasp about CST is that it is concerned about the well-being of each and every individual; its central theme is human self-fulfilment[1] and, viewed from the perspective of moral theology, this demands a desire for God's friendship and openness to the self-fulfilment of each and every human person. This chapter will have failed if it does not leave behind it a clear understanding that concern for the welfare of the human person (each and every actual person) is CST's driving force and *raison d'etre*. It will also try to explain the meaning of 'human self-fulfilment' and analogous phrases (such as John Finnis' 'flourishing'). If CST concerns itself with employee participation (or the lack of it) it is especially because of the deep impact that employee participation can have on the development of the humanity of the worker.

Many will find it strange that the Church sees fit to pronounce on worldly or political issues such as corporate governance. Would it not be appropriate for the Church to confine its pronouncements to spiritual matters that are in the purely personal and private domain? The Church rejects this view because, in reality, the human person is a unity of the spiritual and the material. An absolute, clinical separation of human life into watertight compartments labeled 'spiritual' and 'material' is a fallacious concept. If the Church is to promote human self-fulfilment then it

---

[1] Paul VI, *Populorum progressio*, para. 14.

17

will have to engage with the whole person. Since life in community is at the service of human self-fulfilment, since the whole point of any type of human grouping is the pursuit of some element or elements of human self-fulfilment, the Church's concern must extend to social, political and economic societies. The theme of this book illustrates the point. CST advocates employee participation because of a judgment that this will favour the cause of human self-fulfilment.

The Church insists on its own right to speak about anything that might have an impact on human welfare. At the same time, however it is equally insistent on the limitations on its right to speak. It applies to itself Christ's injunction to render unto Caesar the things that are Caesar's and unto God the things that are God's.[2] Benedict XVI put it this way in *Caritas in veritate*:

> If development were concerned with merely technical aspects of human life, and not with the meaning of man's pilgrimage through history in company with his fellow human beings, nor with identifying the goal of that journey, then the Church would not be entitled to speak on it.[3]

If human self-fulfilment is at stake then the Church must speak. It is not, however, equipped to contribute to debate on any subject except from the perspective of human self-fulfilment. So, for example, the Church has no right or ability to contribute to the economic aspects of the employee participation debate provided that the economists' approach and solutions are compatible with human dignity. If CST were to transgress these limitations then it could legitimately be accused of meddling in affairs that are not its concern. These considerations are, it is submitted, the basis for fruitful co-operation between CST and other sciences.

It would be a source of grave confusion to try to analyse CST in terms of a left/right dichotomy. Assuming that the demands of human dignity are respected, there is room for legitimate technical options some of which might be left wing and others of which might be right wing. If one does not appreciate this fact, one will be puzzled to find that CST both accepts that state ownership might be a licit though, it is hoped, temporary phenomenon at the same time as it has been a staunch defender of the individual's right to own private property.

It is important to understand both what CST recommends and why it does so. If followed through, its approach can make an enormous difference to individual fulfillment in the workplace, to our understanding

---

of the relationship between ethics and economics, of the nature and social importance of the corporation and of the appropriate relationship between the corporation and the state. Each of these issues is of the utmost importance.

Nature and sources of Catholic Social Thought

Although CST is a branch of moral theology drawing on both Revelation and natural law theory, it is accessible to believers and non-believers alike. It deals with questions that are the concern of every human person and has a strongly philosophical flavour (both because of the questions that it is concerned with and because of the language that it uses). CST insists that every social institution should be analysed from the perspective of concern for the individual human person; it is founded on a distinctive understanding of what makes for human self-realisation and builds its social ethics on the foundations of Christian anthropology.

CST's purpose is to analyse social institutions in the light of what Revelation has to say about the nature and vocation of the human person.[4] CST is practical rather than speculative; it seeks knowledge for the sake of guiding decision-making and action rather than knowledge for its own sake. Moral theology is the systematic effort to discover who we are and what we are to do if we are to be fully the beings we are meant to be.[5] CST looks at the principles that ought to govern life in society and the construction and operation of institutions (such as the firm) if social life is to facilitate the self-realisation of the individual.

CST critiques social institutions (such as the state, private property and the firm with its associated governance arrangements) from the perspective of the integral self-realisation of individuals. If CST interests itself in employee participation it is not because it claims any competence in finance and economics; rather, it is because of a conviction that work has an absolutely indispensable part to play in every aspect of the well-being of the employee (material, social, psychological, spiritual and so on). Further, part and parcel of being a human person is an intense desire to be in control of one's own life (especially in its most fundamental and character-forming dimensions). Thus, employee participation (as defined earlier) is of critical importance if the workplace is to make the

---

[4] John Paul II, *Sollicitudo rei socialis*, para. 41 and *Centesimus annus*, paras. 54–55.
[5] W. May, *An introduction to moral theology*, (2nd ed), (Huntington, In: Our Sunday Visitor Publishing Division, 2003), pp. 23–24.

contribution that it can, and should, make to the overall well-being of the worker.

CST is rooted in Revelation but modern CST is principally found in a series of papal encyclicals.[6] Modern CST began with Leo XIII's promulgation of *Rerum novarum* in 1891 although the way for it was prepared by the practical efforts of concerned clergy and laypeople to create Christian and humane responses to the industrial revolution that swept Europe in the late nineteenth century.[7] Leo XIII's successors contributed to the development of CST through a series of encyclicals and radio messages. Many of the encyclicals were written to commemorate anniversaries of *Rerum novarum*. *Laborem exercens*, for example, came 90 years after *Rerum Novarum* while *Centesimus annus* marked the centenary of Leo XIII's encyclical. Also of the greatest significance for John Paul II's social magisterium, as Gregg has shown,[8] was *Gaudium et spes*, one of the principal documents to issue from the Second Vatican Council.[9] Benedict XVI's encyclicals, *Deus caritas est* and *Caritas in veritate* are the most recent contributions to the social magisterium.

CST is a unified corpus that is updated from time to time to incorporate reflections on the most pressing needs of the human family. A number of the social encyclicals consciously refer to *Rerum novarum* while *Sollicitudo rei socialis* and *Caritas in veritate* take Paul VI's *Populorum progressio* as their inspiration. Nevertheless, it is clear to an attentive reader of the social encyclicals that they form part of a unified whole. Further, CST has to be understood in the broader context of the Catholic Church's teaching as a whole.[10]

CST conceives of itself as making a contribution to a multi-disciplinary effort to understand the human person and to evaluate life in society

---

[6] For a history of CST see R. Charles, SJ, *Christian social witness and teaching. The Catholic tradition from Genesis to Centessimus annus* (two volumes), (Leominster: Gracewing, 1998). For a shorter account showing the development of CST in both historical and conceptual terms see J. Schall, S.J., 'Catholicism, Business and Priorities', in O. Williams. and J. Houck (eds.), *The Judea-Christian vision and the modern corporation*, (Notre Dame, Ind, University of Notre Dame Press, 1982), pp. 107–140.

[7] See, for example, P. Misner, *Social Catholicism in Europe. From the onset of industrialization to the First World War*, (New York: Dartford, Longman and Todd, 1991).

[8] S. Gregg, *Challenging the modern world. Karol Wojtyla/John Paul II and the development of Catholic Social Teaching*, (Lanham, Maryland: Lexington Books, 1999).

[9] Second Vatican Council, *Pastoral Constitution On The Church In The Modern World, Gaudium et spes* (1965) at www.vatican.va/archive/hist_councils/ii_vatican_council/documents/vat-ii_cons_19651207_gaudium-et-spes_en.html (last accessed 7 September 2006).

[10] Benedict XVI, *Caritas in veritate*, para. 12.

(aware that social phenomena change rapidly). It offers its own services as an 'expert in humanity'.[11] At the same time, it is open to the contributions of the human and social sciences and understands itself as having an important part to play in gathering together and organizing those contributions.[12] So, for example, CST offers its own insights into the significance of the corporation for its participants and for the societies to which the corporation contributes. A CST-based evaluation of the corporation is, however, open to contributions from a wide range of other sciences and has a part to play in filtering, organising and co-ordinating those contributions. A commitment to the idea of truth makes it possible for people of diverging world-views to talk to each other respectfully. Relativism separates peoples, cultures and disciplines into cocoons that are insulated from each other.[13] CST is committed to working with other sciences in a search for a 'new humanistic synthesis'.[14] There is an urgent need for 'an orderly interdisciplinary exchange' that will generate a form of knowledge that is true wisdom and that is inspired by charity (a genuine sense of fraternity, solidarity and desire to serve the common good).[15]

In 2004, the Pontifical Council for Justice and Peace published its *Compendium of the Social Doctrine of the Church*.[16] At a local level, Bishops' conferences have also made contributions to CST. *Economic Justice for All*, the 1986 Pastoral Letter of the US Bishops, is one example of such a contribution.[17] It explains CST principles, analyses policies and institutions in the light of them and then offers suggestions as to the sorts of reforms that might be needed to overcome injustices in US economic life. CST develops through its application to changing historical circumstances. It has developed as it was applied to the challenges and upheavals of the twentieth century. In other words, it has been driven by pastoral rather than by purely theoretical concerns.[18]

[11] John Paul II, *Sollicitudo rei socialis*, para. 7.
[12] Benedict XVI, *Caritas in veritate*, para. 9.
[13] Benedict XVI, *Caritas in veritate*, paras. 4 and 9.
[14] Benedict XVI, *Caritas in veritate*, para. 21.
[15] Benedict XVI, *Caritas in veritate*, paras. 30–32.
[16] Pontifical Council for Justice and Peace, *Compendium of the Social Doctrine of the Church*, (Vatican City, Libreria Editrice Vaticana trans., 2004) (hereinafter *Compendium*).
[17] US Conference of Catholic Bishops, *Economic justice for all*, at www.osjspm.org/economic_justice_for_all.aspx (last visited August 31 2006). See also The Catholic Bishops' Conference of England and Wales, *The common good and the Catholic Church's social teaching*, (1996), (available at www.catholic-ew.org.uk/ccb/catholic_church/publications, last accessed on 25th July 2009).
[18] *Compendium*, para. 104.

CST's aim is:

> the *accurate formulation* of the results of a careful reflection on the complex realities of human existence, in society and in the international order, in the light of faith and of the Church's tradition. Its main aim is to *interpret* these realities, determining their conformity with or divergence from the lines of the Gospel teaching on man and his vocation, a vocation which is at once earthly and transcendent; its aim is thus to *guide* Christian behaviour.[19]

In the last analysis, CST is eminently practical since it aims to shape not merely thought but also behaviour. In our context, it aims to shape the behaviour of all those who participate in the life of the corporation.

CST draws principally on biblical revelation and on the Church's tradition. But faith interacts with reason. The understanding of what revelation and tradition contain is structured by reason.[20] It draws on natural law theory but its theological sources enrich and strengthen some of the contents of natural law. Faith and reason support and enrich each other. One of the effects of this is that CST can be understood by any thinking person, whether or not they are Christian.[21] This chapter seeks to illustrate this point by juxtaposing the Christian humanism of CST with a natural law account of human choices and of what makes for ethical behaviour.

Philosophy is part of the very fabric of CST and many of its basic concepts are philosophical.[22] Some knowledge of natural law theory is indispensable for an understanding of CST. Further, CST sees itself as being open to dialogue with other disciplines; these can enrich CST's knowledge of the human person, of society and of human affairs[23] while CST can help to provide those other disciplines with its own knowledge of the human person. The Church has, however, explained why it is opposed to consequentialist and proportionalist approaches to ethics.[24] John Paul II also rounded on economistic approaches to thinking about human work that would reduce it to a purely material level and threaten the dignity of the worker.[25]

---

[19] John Paul II, *Sollicitudo rei socialis*, para. 41.   [20] *Compendium*, para. 74.
[21] *Compendium*, para. 75.   [22] *Compendium*, para. 77.
[23] *Compendium*, para. 78.   [24] John Paul II, *Veritatis splendor*, paras. 71–83.
[25] John Paul II, *Labourem exercens*, paras. 7 and 13.

Christian anthropology

Catholic moral theology, including CST, is built on the foundations of Christian anthropology. CST's principal contribution to social ethics is derived from its understanding of the human person and the purpose of human life. CST focuses on integral human development and builds on its insights into the human person and the human vocation. It starts from the conviction that 'man is constitutionally oriented "towards being more".'[26]

It draws on natural law but its deepest and most characteristic insights come from Revelation and especially from reflection on the person and teaching of Christ.[27] An understanding of Christian anthropology (the Christian vision of the nature and purpose of human life) is absolutely vital if CST is to be understood. John Paul II's magisterium is full of reminders of the need to avoid reductive understandings of the human person (approaches that would reduce the human person to a series of social relationships or focus on the material and economic aspects of human well-being or that would concentrate on the human person as consumer or as one who experiences pain or pleasure).[28] These reductive anthropological starting points have unhelpful implications for individual and social ethics.

CST is a system of social ethics; it seeks to describe the conditions that societies and their institutions need to possess in order to help individuals to live fruitful and effective lives. Christian anthropology describes who the human person is and the vocation of the human person. CST builds on this to develop a system of social ethics; it provides the ethical foundations on which any human society (including the firm) has to build if it is to be successful. CST is careful to spell out its anthropological basis because it is convinced that there is a profound and organic link between the individual and the societies of which he or she forms part. Communities exist to facilitate the efforts of each individual member to achieve integral self-realisation. Thus, it is natural that the central focus of CST is to ask whether societies and social relations are so structured

---

[26] Benedict XVI, *Caritas in veritate*, para. 14.
[27] For concise summaries of Christian anthropology see *Gaudium et spes*, paras. 12–22 and *Compendium*, paras. 105–151.
[28] John Paul II, *Centesimus annus*, para. 13 and John Paul II, *Redemptor hominis*, (1979), at www.vatican.va/holy_father/john_paul_ii/encyclicals/documents/hf_jp-ii_enc_04031979_redemptor-hominis_en.html (last accessed on 31st August 2006), para. 14.

as to facilitate these efforts. It is also clear that this inquiry cannot begin unless one has a clear picture as to what a human person is like and what the elements of integral self-realisation of the human personality are. This is why CST is built on Christian anthropology.

Christian anthropology is theological in nature. The first account of the creation of man is found in the Book of Genesis:

> So God created man in his own image, in the image of God he created him: male and female he created them.[29]

This is the text that lies at the heart of Christian anthropology and it imparts fundamental lessons about the dignity and the social nature of the human person. The notion that each individual human person is created in the image and likeness of God[30] and so has an immense dignity is central to Christian ethics: what characterises the human person is precisely the fact that he or she is an 'I', a unique and unrepeatable individual.[31] Further, this text suggests that the human person is inherently social and is driven by a need to experience communion with other persons. God is a Trinity of Persons in communion with each other and we, likewise, are designed for life with others. In *Economic Justice for All*, the US Bishops put it like this:

> Christian theological reflection on the very reality of God as a Trinitarian unity of persons – Father, Son and Holy Spirit – shows that being a person means being united to other persons in mutual love.[32]

This idea is reinforced by the fact that God created man, 'male and female'; this reference to the complementarity of the sexes, with the echoes of marital communion, highlights the fact that there is something incomplete about the individual person (paradoxical as this may seem given what we have just said about the dignity of the individual). The human person is called to transcend himself or herself and this transcendence, if it is to be satisfying, has to take the form of self-giving to another person (another human person such as one's spouse). In the last analysis, the human person, like it or not, is called to enter into the most thoroughgoing communion with God himself; human life is a search for God.[33] The human person is designed not merely to co-exist with others, but to

---

[29] *Genesis* 1:27.   [30] *Genesis* 1:27.
[31] *Compendium*, para. 131.   [32] *Economic justice for all*, para. 64.
[33] John Paul II, *Evangelium vitae* (1995), *at* www.vatican.va/holy_father/john_paul_ii/encyclicals/documents/hf_jp-ii_enc_25031995_evangelium-vitae_en.html (last accessed on 31st August 2006), para. 35.

transcend himself or herself and to be open to communion with God and others. The reference to the human person as having been created as 'male and female' points to marriage as the primary, most thorough-going form of interpersonal communion (at the human level). But every dimension of human life and growth is necessarily played out in a social context and these social bonds are, themselves, an irreplaceable source of enrichment for the human personality.[34] One can speak of a law of the gift written on the human heart; we are made to give ourselves to other persons (God in the first place).[35]

Reason and experience confirm the validity of this insight; not only do we need human communities to help us meet the whole range of human needs but we also need social relationships for their own sake. The human person is inherently social. As Canavan puts it, 'Community is as natural to man as is individuality.'[36]

Christian anthropology sees human nature as being flawed (but not completely undermined) as a result of original sin. The Book of Genesis describes a sin of rebellion by Adam and Eve that had profound consequences for the human race and for the whole of creation. The *Catechism of the Catholic Church* explains the results of original sin for Adam and Eve:

> The harmony in which they had found themselves, thanks to original justice, is now destroyed: the control of the soul's spiritual faculties over the body is shattered; the union of man and woman becomes subject to tensions, their relations henceforth marked by lust and domination. Harmony with creation is broken: visible creation has become alien and hostile to man. Because of man, creation is now subject 'to its bondage to decay'. Finally, the consequence explicitly foretold for this disobedience will come true: man will 'return to the ground', for out of it he was taken. *Death makes its entrance into human history.*[37]

Original sin and its consequences are transmitted to the whole human race[38] but they are overcome as a result of Christ's Redemption.[39] So, CST is not utopian; it takes account of the flaws in human nature and the tendencies to selfishness, laziness and general back-sliding that are just as

---

[34] *Gaudium et spes*, para. 12.   [35] *Gaudium et spes*, para. 24.
[36] F. Canavan SJ, 'The Popes and the Economy', *Notre Dame Journal of Law Ethics and Public Policy* 11 (1997), pp. 429–444.
[37] *Catechism of the Catholic Church*, available at www.vatican.va/archive/ENG0015/_INDEX.HTM (last accessed on 31st August 2006) No 400 (hereinafter *Catechism*).
[38] On original sin generally, see *Catechism*, numbers 385–421.
[39] *Catechism*, numbers 599–623.

much part of the human experience as self-giving and the search for fulfilment and union with God. A workable system of social ethics has to take the whole truth about the human person, with its light and darkness, into account. Self-interest, in forms both reasonable and unreasonable, is part and parcel of daily experience. John Paul II made this comment in *Centesimus annus*:

> [M]an, who was created for freedom, bears within himself the wound of original sin, which constantly draws him towards evil and puts him in need of redemption. Not only is *this doctrine an integral part of Christian revelation*; it also has great hermeneutical value insofar as it helps one to understand human reality. Man tends towards good, but he is also capable of evil. He can transcend his immediate interest and still remain bound to it. The social order will be all the more stable, the more it takes this fact into account and does not place in opposition personal interest and the interests of society as a whole, but rather seeks ways to bring them into fruitful harmony. In fact, where personal interest is violently suppressed, it is replaced by a burdensome system of bureaucratic control which dries up the wellsprings of initiative and creativity.[40]

The human person feels called to integral self-realisation; to develop his or her potencies (bodily, intellectual, emotional, spiritual and so on). Each human person feels impelled to pursue their integral self-realisation and this finds its ultimate expression in union with God. In *Laborem exercens*, John Paul II explained:

> Man has to subdue the earth and dominate it, because as 'the image of God' he is a person, that is to say, a subjective being capable of acting in a planned and rational way, capable of deciding about himself, and with a tendency to self-realisation.[41]

The human vocation is a call to self-realisation. This point is clearly and succinctly made by Paul VI in *Populorum progressio*:

> In God's plan, every man is born to seek self-fulfilment, for every human life is called to some task by God. At birth a human being possesses certain aptitudes and abilities in germinal form, and these abilities are to be cultivated so that they may bear fruit. By developing these traits through formal education or personal effort, the individual works his way toward the goal set for him by the Creator.[42]

---

[40] John Paul II, *Centesimus annus*, para. 25.   [41] John Paul II, *Laborem exercens*, para. 6.
[42] Paul VI, *Populorum progressio*, (1967), *at* www.vatican.va/holy_father/paul_vi/encyclicals/documents/hf_p-vi_enc_26031967_populorum_en.html (last accessed on 31st August 2006), at para. 15.

A little later, the passage continues:

> Self-development, however, is not left up to man's option. Just as the whole of creation is ordered towards its Creator, so too the rational creature should of his own accord direct his life to God, the first truth and the highest good. Thus human self-fulfilment may be said to sum up our obligations.
>
> Moreover, this harmonious integration of our human nature, carried through by personal effort and responsible activity, is destined for a higher state of perfection. United with the life-giving Christ, man's life is newly-enhanced; it acquires a transcendent humanism which surpasses its nature and bestows new fullness of life. This is the highest goal of human self-fulfilment.[43]

In other words, heeding the call to 'human self-fulfilment' expresses the essence of one's moral or ethical duty. The next section of this chapter looks at this idea in greater detail. It provides an interesting example of a notion that can be largely understood in natural law terms but, so far as Christian ethics is concerned, can only be adequately grasped in the light of revelation.

The concept of development is closely related to that of integral self-realisation: 'authentic human development concerns the whole of the person in every single dimension.'[44] Development in this sense is the task of everyone. It is not a task that can be left to institutions, however well-designed but, rather, depends on the exercise of personal responsibility.[45] CST is sceptical about utopian promises and of ideologies.

Bainbridge has expressed dissatisfaction with the concept of self-realisation. He points out that Christianity speaks of virtue[46] and self-denial[47] and argues that CST's insistence on the importance of the human urge to pursue self-realisation is incompatible with these Christian ideals. Bainbridge goes so far as to say that Christians ought to view the search for self-actualisation as quite sinful.[48] But the concept of self-realisation is firmly embedded in Christian anthropology; the human tendency to realise oneself through the pursuit of goods such as communion with others, work and so on is taken as given. It is this tendency which drives all human actions. Moreover, this view of human nature and the meaning

[43] Paul VI, *Populorum progressio*, paras. 14–15.
[44] Benedict XVI, *Caritas in veritate*, para. 11.
[45] Benedict XVI, *Caritas in veritate*, para. 17.
[46] S. Bainbridge, "Corporate decision-making and the moral rights of employees", *Villanova Law Review* 43 (1998), p. 780.
[47] Bainbridge, 'Corporate decision-making', p. 782.
[48] Bainbridge, 'Corporate decision-making', p. 783.

of human actions are highly compatible with the concepts of virtue and the Christian practice of self-denial. Human virtues are habits that facilitate the pursuit of self-realisation. Self-denial plays a number of important roles in the Christian life; it is both a type of prayer (an aspect of the effort to achieve union with God) and a form of discipline that helps to keep unruly passions in check. In this latter respect, self-denial makes it easier for the reason and will to take charge of the pursuit of self-realisation.

Bainbridge's unease about 'self-realisation' does, however, suggest some important problems. There is, in fact, a danger that self-realisation could be conceived as a type of moral body-building and acquire narcissistic overtones. In other words, the danger of an excessive preoccupation with the self is a real one and this may be at the heart of Bainbridge's concerns. But Christian ethics avoids this danger (though individual Christians may not always do so). Each person is primarily responsible for the direction of his or her own life. At the same time, the Commandment to love one's neighbour as oneself prohibits one from valuing one's own self-realisation above that of others and calls for a positive effort to do what one reasonably can to help them. Further, communion with others and making a gift of oneself to others is an aspect of one's own self-realisation.

Rationality and free will are central to our understanding of what it is to be human. Freedom is a fundamental human value and an essential element of human dignity. Although the human person may be conditioned in many ways (by heredity, upbringing or social factors), this conditioning is not so absolute as to do away with free will. Freedom or autonomy is an absolutely central feature of the human personality. This has profound implications for social ethics. According to the Christian vision of the human person, freedom and rationality are intimately intertwined in human decision-making. Reason provides freedom with a compass and (all being well) directs it towards those choices that are consistent with human dignity and the integral self-realisation of the human person. The *Compendium of the Social Doctrine of the Church* explains that freedom:

> determines the growth of [man's] being as a person through choices consistent with the true good.[49]

In other words, the human personality is built up and enriched by certain types of choices. Christian anthropology is committed to the notion that there are certain goods that it is fitting for human beings to pursue,

---

[49] *Compendium*, para. 135.

that these goods are (essentially) the same for all people and that reason is capable of discovering those goods. But these goods are capable of being integrated into a life that is successfully tending towards self-realisation in myriad ways and combinations. Human freedom is best regarded as the scope for the exercise of creativity and personal taste and style as one endeavours to give effect to the tendency to self-realisation through responsible and intelligent choices of actions and values.

In *Centesimus annus*, John Paul II draws out the link between one's anthropological understanding and one's vision of life in society. His comments are specifically directed at socialism (*Centesimus annus* was written at the time of the retreat of communism in eastern Europe) but are clearly relevant to a wider set of approaches to social life (including one-sidedly economic approaches):

> [T]he fundamental error of socialism is anthropological in nature. Socialism considers the individual person simply as an element, a mol-ecule within the social organism, so that the good of the individual is completely subordinated to the functioning of the socio-economic mech-anism. Socialism likewise maintains that the good of the individual can be realised without reference to his free choice, to the unique and exclusive responsibility which he exercises in the face of good or evil. Man is thus reduced to a series of social relationships, and the concept of the person as the autonomous subject of moral decisions disappears, the very subject whose decisions build the social order. From this mistaken conception of the person there arise both a distortion of law, which defines the sphere of the exercise of freedom, and an opposition to private property. A person who is deprived of something he can call 'his own', and of the possibility of earning a living through his own initiative, comes to depend on the social machine and on those who control it. This makes it much more difficult for him to realise his dignity as a person, and hinders progress towards the building up of an authentic human community.[50]

To summarise the foregoing sketch of Christian anthropology, the human person, made in God's image, is called to a life of friendship with God and, makes himself or herself fit for that friendship by responding to the call to human self-development. There is great scope for creativity and self-expression in choosing precisely how to pursue the good and the human person shapes himself or herself through the exercise of this freedom. The human person is called to interpersonal communion; only the relation-ship with God is capable of fully satisfying this yearning for communion and self-transcendence. Original sin has introduced disorder into human

---

[50] John Paul II, *Centesimus annus*, para. 13.

nature but has not utterly vitiated the human capacity to take meaningful steps towards self-realisation.

CST seeks to explain the social conditions that make it possible for the human person to pursue the ends of human nature. On the basis of what Christian anthropology has to say, it is logical that CST should emphasise the need for social structures that facilitate social friendship, autonomy (the freedom to make one's own decisions as to how human goods are to be pursued) and creativity/self-expression (that social structures should make it possible for individuals to express their own personality creatively in their social interactions). These are indeed amongst the guiding values of CST.

The human person and society

The human person is inherently social. We need the help or co-operation of others for survival, for education, for play and for successful participation in all of the other human goods. We also need the society of others, and to form part of society for its own sake. Calvez and Perrin put it this way:

> Society is the world where each finds the means to recognise the other as a person, thus assuring his own interior richness of an exteriorization which is adequate to it. That is why society rests on the essential equality of persons between themselves ... [T]he dignity of the human person has as its consequence the equality in dignity of all persons. The person is of so great a value that he can find nowhere in nature anything adequately responding to himself, not even among the objects which he has made and marked with his personality. To one person, none can adequately respond save another. This correspondence, which consists in mutual recognition, necessary to a being which who is altogether the image and the reflection, self-consciousness and reason, *is* society, the equality of persons ... Society, we could say, is the equality of nature, that is, to say, the recognition that another is as good as or equal to oneself. Human nature ... is wishful to share itself and goes out to other spiritual beings. Man seeks to meet man, nature seeks nature equal to itself.[51]

A factor at play in human communities is a human need to give oneself to another person, a spiritual being like oneself.

---

[51] J. Y. Calvez SJ and J. Perrin SJ, *The Church and Social Justice: The Social Teaching of the Popes from Leo XIII to Pius XII 1878–1958*, (tr J. Kirwan), (London: Burn and Oates, 1961), pp. 111–112.

Natural law theory and human self-development

John Finnis'[52] account of the choices open to the human person, his account of human flourishing and of the requirements of practical reasonableness are consistent with CST and can help to shed light upon it. This is not to suggest any formal debt owed by CST to John Finnis or *vice versa*. But natural law can be thought of as providing the philosophical underpinnings of CST. Catholic Social Thought relies on natural law theory but may take an understanding of it for granted. Further, natural law theory, since it relies on reason alone rather than on any form of revelation, provides a philosophical medium through which CST can engage in dialogue with non-Catholics. John Finnis is the natural law theorist whose work is most likely to have been read by someone trained in a British law school. This is a further reason for using his account of natural law to help explain Christian anthropology and ethics.

Natural law theory dwells on practical reason;[53] it looks at what reason suggests to us as being goods or goals to pursue when we decide how to act and when we form our aspirations and plans. Reason discerns that certain goods fulfil us as human beings and that there is an inner tendency or drive to desire those goods. Finnis argues that all such goods can ultimately be reduced to one (or some mixture) of certain basic goods or values: life, knowledge, play, aesthetic experience, sociability / friendship, practical reasonableness and religion. There is nothing moral about these goods; they are, simply, goods that a mature, sensible person would recognise as having a positive role to play in a well-rounded human life. Thus, such a person would acknowledge, for example, that it is better to be well-informed than ignorant or sociable than selfishly individualistic[54]. Put another way, Finnis is arguing that any purposeful human activity must inevitably be interpreted as a pursuit of one or a mixture of these goods. They are, in a sense, the raw material available to us when we set out to act. They are the paths that are open to us.

The validity of the list of goods proposed by Finnis cannot be demonstrated by argument; they are in a technical sense, self-evident. Finnis puts it thus:

> What are the basic aspects of my well-being? Here each of us ... is alone with his own intelligent grasp of the indemonstrable (because self-

---

[52] J. Finnis, *Natural law and natural rights*, (Oxford: Oxford University Press, 2003).
[53] Intellectual activity directed to action rather than to the acquisition of knowledge for its own sake.
[54] Finnis, *Natural law and natural rights*, pp. 59–99.

evident) first principles of his own practical reasoning ... [T]here is no
inference from fact to value ... the proper form of discourse '... is a good,
in itself, don't you think.?'[55]

Natural law does not work by comparing one's choices or behaviour with
the demands of an idealised human nature. Nor does it require a process
of inferring values directly from the experience of inner urges. Rather, it
asks each of us to reflect on our own practical experience and to consider
whether, for example, a well-informed person is (by virtue of being well-
informed) better off than they would otherwise be. From this practical
judgement, we draw the further practical conclusion that knowledge is a
good worth pursuing. This reflection provides one of the first, pre-moral
principles of natural law.

Reason does not only demand that we recognise Finnis' suggested
list of goods (or some similar goods or values) as being goods or values
that are fitting for us, as humans, to pursue; that can almost be taken for
granted in any reasonably mature person. It goes further to discover rules
that allow us to incorporate these goods into our lives in a practically reasonable (or ethical or moral or effective) way. Careful reflection allows us
to see how we can successfully integrate the pursuit of the basic goods or
values into our lives so as to advance towards what some natural law texts
refer to as self-constitution, self-realisation or self-fulfilment or human
flourishing (these and similar terms can be taken as synonyms in this
book). No-one can ever hope to exhaust all of the possible ways in which
the basic goods (or goods constitutive of the human person) can be integrated into a human life. We have finite time, resources and talents and
so choices have to be made. Each good is capable of being lived out in an
almost endless number of ways (think of all of the possible approaches to
knowledge and branches of learning, for example). We can only hope to
participate in the basic goods or values and to find some way of integrating them into our lives with reasonable success. Thus, human life can be
seen as a quest to participate *effectively*, and in ways that accord with our
circumstances and tastes, in the goods or values that are constitutive of
human persons. Practical reasonableness,[56] or ethics, tries to establish the
ground rules for setting about this task. This requirements of practical
reasonableness include such considerations as; the need to have a coherent plan for one's life, avoiding arbitrary preferences amongst the basic
goods and between persons, a commitment to pursuing one's plan of life

---

[55] Finnis, *Natural law and natural rights*, pp. 85–86.
[56] The fruits of the efforts of reason directed towards action.

and having reasonable concern for the consequences of one's actions.[57] These requirements of practical reasonableness are derived from mature reflection on what makes for a well-rounded human life. They are the ethical or moral principles proposed by natural law. Ethics seeks to explain which approaches to integrating the pursuit of the basic goods have generally been thought reasonable.[58]

Someone who manages to build his life around the practically reasonable pursuit of the basic goods hopes:

> for 'happiness' in the deeper less usual sense of that word in which it signifies, roughly, a fullness of life, a certain development as a person, a meaningfulness of one's existence.[59]

This 'happiness' can be thought of as 'inclusive all-round flourishing'. It goes a long way towards explaining CST's concept of human self-development.

Finnis also points out that, although coherent and validated by experience, there is ultimately something unsatisfying about his account of practical reasonableness and flourishing. We can only participate in the basic goods in some very limited measure and we notice the succession of persons. We might ask whether my good (or that of any other individual) has any further point (beyond that already explained) and whether it forms part of any more comprehensive good. Or, again, practical reasonableness might demand considerable self-sacrifice for the sake of friendship, our family or our country; although we see the sense of the self-sacrificing action we might be keenly aware of the conflict of opportunities that it occasions. Does the self-sacrifice have any further point beyond the well-being of one's friend, family or country? The lack of answers to these questions would weaken the attractiveness or appeal to reason of the basic goods.[60]

In the end, Finnis speculates, friendship with God (whose perspective on the point of human flourishing is not limited as ours is) may be the answer to these questions:

> For if the uncaused cause were revealed to favour the well-being of every-man, for no other reason than its (D's) own goodness ... the common good could be pursued by us for a new reason, viz out of love or friendship for the personal being ('God') who not only makes possible whatever

---

[57] Finnis, *Natural law and natural rights*, pp. 100–133.
[58] Finnis, *Natural law and natural rights*, p. 101.
[59] Finnis, *Natural law and natural rights*, p. 96.
[60] Finnis, *Natural law and natural rights*, pp 371–373.

well-being of persons there can be and actually is, but also positively favours (though in ways often unintelligible to us) that common good.[61]

The requirements of practical reasonableness, if this speculation is true, would have a point beyond themselves and would not need to be regarded as a quest for self-perfection. That point would be the game of co-operating with God.[62]

Catholic moral theology, of course, is built on the notion that God has revealed some truths about Himself. What for the philosopher is a question of speculation is a starting point for Catholic moral theology. Germain Grisez discusses the natural law approach to ethics in rather similar terms to those just described. At a critical point he formulates the primary moral norm in these terms:

> The basic principle of morality might best be formulated as follows: *In voluntarily acting for human goods and avoiding what is opposed to them, one ought to choose and otherwise will those and only those possibilities whose willing is compatible with a will toward integral human fulfilment.*[63]

Finnis points out that practical reasonableness is somehow unsatisfactory unless it is open to some further point beyond one's own flourishing and that of one's family and friends and the member's of one's own communities. Practical reasonableness has to be filled out by placing it in a context where it requires a will towards flourishing on a broader scale. Human fulfilment involves successful participation in the basic goods. In the end, however, integral human fulfilment goes further:

> Integral human fulfilment is not individualistic satisfaction of desires; it is the realization of all the human goods in the whole human community. But in the course of human history – even in the course of each person's life – new dimensions of human goods unfold and new possibilities of serving them emerge. Moreover, the human community is not some limited group, but all human persons, past, present and future. Thus, integral human fulfilment is an ideal corresponding to total human responsibility. Like the ideal of perfect love, it is something toward which one can work but which one can never reach by human effort. In other words, "integral human fulfilment" does not refer to a definite goal to be pursued as a concrete objective of cooperative human effort.[64]

---

[61]   Finnis, *Natural law and natural rights*, p. 406.
[62]   Finnis, *Natural law and natural rights*, pp 407–410.
[63]   G. Grisez, *The Way of the Lord Jesus. Volume One. Christian moral principles*, (Quincy, Illinois: Franciscan Press, 1983), p. 7.
[64]   Grisez, *Christian moral principles*, p. 186.

This is as far as philosophy and natural law theory can take us. Integral human fulfilment in this broad sense is the goal to be pursued but it appears unattainable. Grisez returns to the question, however, when he begins his account of Christian morality according to which 'integral human fulfilment is fulfilment in Jesus'.[65] Christ is both God and man. As God, he has divine fullness; as man he achieved fulfilment by living a perfect human life. Human persons can be united with Jesus to find fulfilment in him.[66] The Christian perspective fills out the concept of flourishing, integral self-realisation or human development. Revelation confirms that God does indeed regard the effort to participate in the human goods in a practically reasonable way as pleasing and as a precondition to friendship with Him. At the same time, the whole point of moral theology is to give a useful account of how this friendship is to be achieved and how one is to develop one's humanity most fully.

Homo Economicus

Contemporary corporate governance scholarship, policy and practice is heavily influenced by economic theories of the firm (such as agency theory). This book does not set out to catalogue and evaluate these theories. It does, however, want to suggest the need to be alert to simplifying or reductionist assumptions made by economic theorists (or anyone else) since they have the capacity to mislead by proposing misleading conceptions of the human person and of human communities. At the very least, one ought to have a critical awareness of these assumptions and of their possible shortcomings. This section looks at the concept of *homo economicus* and contrasts it with the Christian humanism explained above.[67]

The first assumption is that human beings are utility maximisers; we are driven to act by a desire to maximise the pleasure, happiness or satisfaction to be obtained by that action.

The rational consumer is at the core of economic theory. This rational consumer, *homo economicus*, ranks alternatives according to the extent to which they meet his or her preferences. This allows preferences to be assigned a numeric value and allows an individual's utility function

---

[65] Grisez, *Christian moral principles*, p. 459.
[66] Grisez, *Christian moral principles*, pp. 462–471.
[67] Economic theory is not value-free but has its own philosophical position about human nature and society. See C. Wilber, 'Economics and ethics: The challenge of the bishops' pastoral letter on the economy', *Notre Dame Journal of Law, Ethics & Public Policy* 2 (1985 – 1987), p. 107.

(ranking of possibilities according to the individual's preferences) to be created and depicted on a graph.

One of the most significant differences between CST's understanding of the human person and that of neoclassical economics concerns the intelligibility of human preferences. CST sees them as necessarily reflecting the urge to self-realisation and the goods that are the building blocks of that self-realisation. For law and economics scholars, there is no way of knowing where these preferences come from. As Sargent puts it:

> Preferences are what they are, and an individual's well-being depends entirely on legal rules' ability to enable individuals to realise their preferences.[68]

For law and economics, rationality simply involves being able to rank those preferences in an internally consistent way.

A second core concept in economic theory is that of 'equilibrium' defined as:

> a pattern of interaction that persists unless disturbed by outside forces.[69]

The rational consumer strives to maximise the satisfaction of his or her consumer preferences; this maximising impulse drives us to action. We are in a constant state of flux or desire, the theory suggests, until we have achieved the best package of goods and services that our budget constraint allows. The rational consumer considers the effect of a marginal change from his or her current situation and asks whether the marginal benefit exceeds the marginal cost. The consumer will make changes until the marginal cost equals the marginal benefit. If we were ever to achieve that state then we would stop striving and we would come to rest. Economists describe this state of perfection as equilibrium. Although we are never likely to achieve equilibrium, we are always tending towards it.

The third basic concept is that of efficiency which is applied to the evaluation, *inter alia*, of production processes (and, for this purpose, a firm or an entire economy might be viewed as a production process). One version of efficiency is Pareto efficiency. An interaction, or series of interactions or potential interactions, would be Pareto efficient if no change to the *status quo ante* could be made without making at least one person worse off (in his or her own estimation) as a result. Thus, for example,

---

[68] M. Sargent, 'Utility, the good and civic happiness: a Catholic critique of Law and Economics', *Journal of Catholic Legal Studies* 44 (2005), p. 36.

[69] R. Cooter and T. Ulen, *Law and Economics*, (4th edn), (Boston: Pearson/Addison Wesley, 2004), p. 16.

one could consider a possible change to corporate governance (such as the introduction of mandatory employee representation on the corporate board) and ask whether any affected actor is likely to be made worse off. If, for example, shareholders could complain that they fear that a reduction in the value of their shares will be the likely result of the change then that reform will not be Pareto efficient and should not be made. The condition associated with Pareto efficiency, that no-one should feel worse off as a result of the change, is so strict, however, that it would probably rule out the making of any change no matter how desirable it appears to be. It is hard to imagine any possible change that would please absolutely everybody affected by it.

A more relaxed version of efficiency is that of Kaldor-Hicks (or potential Pareto) efficiency. Here the criterion is whether the gain to those who benefit from the change exceeds the loss to those who suffer as a result. This would allow the winners to compensate the losers, though the Kaldor-Hicks criterion does not demand that they actually do so. Kaldor-Hicks efficiency does allow for interpersonal comparison. It allows wealth to be used as a kind of common denominator. It relies on an ability to translate all of the relevant gains or losses (whether material or immaterial) of those affected into financial terms. This allows the necessary interpersonal comparison to be made, as Cooter puts it:

> The measuring rod of money makes different goals, material and nonmaterial, commensurable.[70]

Efficiency is a goal worth striving for. To the extent that an economy promotes efficient exchanges, it is said to be productively efficient. This means that the greatest possible output is achieved with a specified amount of input or, put another way, a specified level of output is achieved with the lowest possible level of output. Corporate governance mechanisms can, it is thought, make a contribution to productive efficiency by reducing the costs associated with the bringing together of the firm's inputs (such as labour and capital). An efficient economy also ensures that goods and services are produced of the type and in the quantities that consumers desire (allocative efficiency).

The three core economic concepts; utility-maximisation, equilibrium and efficiency can also be applied to suppliers (firms). Firms are understood to be engaged in a process of seeking to maximise profits. To state

---

[70] R. Cooter, 'The best right laws; value foundations of the economic analysis of law', *Notre Dame Law Review* 64 (1989), p. 817.

the obvious, they do this by increasing their income and reducing their costs. The currently dominant theories of the firm claim that appropriate governance structures help firms to maximise their profits by reducing their governance costs. They seek to explain the existence of the firm, its inner workings and the behaviour of those who interact with it (such as the board, shareholders and employees) predominantly in economic terms.

Pareto efficiency grew out of utilitarian philosophy. It has been argued, however, that while it retains certain of the characteristic assumptions of utilitarian philosophy, it is no longer committed to it.[71] It understands itself as a policy science that is capable of being used in conjunction with a wide range of approaches to law and governance. Implicit in this understanding is the consideration that the economic analysis of law is capable of being put to good or bad use; it does not understand the economic analysis of law to be a complete system of social ethics (or, at least, not all of its adherents do). The economic analysis of law can be understood as a tool to be used to determine the efficiency of laws. It adheres to the belief that efficiency is a positive value and that it would be perverse to promulgate inefficient laws (to choose a more costly rather than less costly route to a proposed end). But it is not committed to the view that efficiency is the *raison d'etre* of all laws or that efficiency is the end of individual or social life.

That said, the economic analysis of law does retain certain of the central characteristics of utilitarian philosophy: it is only concerned with the present or future effects of a proposed change; it characteristically takes a strictly individualistic view of value and it thinks purely in terms of self-interest (and self-interest that is narrowly conceived in terms of the individual as a locus of pain or pleasure). There is clearly the danger of losing sight of the fact that these assumptions have been made for special purposes and that they are artificial, and in many senses unreal, characterisations of human nature and society. As will be seen (when considering the economic theory of the firm and the system of corporate governance built upon it), there is the danger that these assumptions will (when they come to shape law, self-regulatory systems and market based transactions) come to shape the inner world of the actors most affected by the relevant systems. We will see that this might not only be ethically corrupting but, perversely, might lead to very significant inefficiencies. Thus, it is certainly unsafe to cast the burden of providing a conceptual framework

---

[71] Cooter, 'The best right laws'.

for corporate governance theory exclusively on economic theories of the firm; economic theory necessarily leaves important truths about organisations and their participants to be studied by other disciplines.

At this stage, it is possible to make a brief comparison of the human person as understood by Christian anthropology and *homo economicus*. The former sees the human person as being radically inclined to interpersonal communion (and thus readily able to see co-operation with others as not only useful but as a good thing in its own right); *homo economicus* looks at social relations through the prism of an atomistic individualism (even game theoretic approaches seem to rest on this understanding). According to Christian anthropology, human choices are rational when the choices made are directed towards goods that are fitting for human beings and that tend to enhance human dignity. Economic rationality treats the sources of human preferences as being unknowable; it involves the choice of least-cost means to achieve given ends. Economics does not inquire into the fittingness or otherwise of those ends for human dignity. On the face of it, both Christian anthropology and economic thought emphasise freedom. To an extent this is true and it might well be a genuine meeting point between the two approaches. The freedom of *homo economicus* does, however, have certain nuances: it is a freedom to consume and a freedom to make choices through market-place exchanges insofar as one has the means to participate in the market. So it is a restricted form of freedom. Christian anthropology is, as we have seen, at the heart of CST as a system of social ethics. The concept of *homo economicus* shapes the economist's evaluation of social institutions, including the firm and its governance mechanisms.

3

Catholic Social Thought and work

Introduction

CST is committed to employee participation because it is convinced that work is a basic good for the human person. Work builds up the human personality and human communities. Work can only play its proper part, however, if it is carried out under properly human conditions; CST has made it its business to explain what these conditions are. At their most basic, they aim to prevent outright exploitation of the worker. But that is not all there is to it. The relationship between the worker, the tools of his or her work and the 'object' worked upon has to be properly structured to ensure that the worker is the active subject of the work process. Otherwise, the worker is, more or less, reduced to the status of a cog in a machine and is alienated from his or her work. CST's calls for employee participation are its attempt to explain the principles for a well-ordered relationship between the worker and the work process. CST looks at work (and the institutions that surround it) through the prism of the integral self-realisation of each and every worker.

Laborem exercens deals with the question of employee rights; the worker has rights corresponding to his duty to work; the right to access to employment opportunities, to a fair wage, reasonable rest and the right to join a trade union. CST, as we have seen asserts that employee participation is highly desirable and, in some sense, is a right that states have a duty to promote. At the same time, it has never committed itself to the proposition that there is a right to any particular form of participation (such as co-determination arrangements).

Work as a recurring theme of Catholic Social Thought

Work and the rights of the worker have always been CST's central theme. *Rerum novarum* was sparked by the miserable condition of the working classes in the newly industrializing economies of western Europe in the latter part of the nineteenth century. In those circumstances there was an urgent need to emphasize the dignity and rights of the worker and to make it clear that those rights cannot be put at the mercy of market forces. Ninety years later, *Laborem exercens* continued to make the same point in changed circumstances. It described work as the key to the whole social question.[1] It seemed to John Paul II that, in 1981, the world was on the brink of a new wave of changes that would work transformations every bit as profound as those of the industrial revolution. These included greater automation, an increase in the cost of raw materials used in production, growing ecological sensitivity and the emergence of developing countries as a force in international affairs. John Paul II predicted that these changes would 'require a reordering and adjustment of the structures of the modern economy and of the distribution of work'; there was also the prospect of unemployment (temporary, it was hoped) and of a need for retraining for some in the western world. If there was the prospect of a tailing off in the economic growth of developed countries, the other side of the coin was the prospect of a brighter future for many of the world's poorest.[2]

A careful comparison of *Rerum novarum* with *Laborem exercens* will reveal that they share the same central themes and the same concerns; both encyclicals are concerned to show the contribution of human work and the institution of private property to the development of the human personality and to society in general. John Paul II's contribution in *Laborem exercens* was to provide a sustained and explicit treatment of work as a human good and of the relationship between work and private property; in doing so, he drew out ideas that were present in *Rerum novarum* and the social magisterium between 1891 and 1981. *Laborem exercens* sees itself as being 'in organic connection' with prior CST documents. Reviewing its predecessors, it detects a shift in focus. While the earlier documents had been concerned with the 'social question' within the framework of the nation state, the later encyclicals looked at the worldwide dimension of the problem.

John Paul II provided a detailed ethical analysis of human work, primarily in *Laborem exercens* but also in some of his other encyclicals. He does not draw any new conclusions; a personalist understanding of the significance of human work is present from *Rerum novarum* onwards. But *Laborem exercens* gives sustained, explicit attention to the question in a way that previous encyclicals had not. Similarly, it dwells on the

[1] John Paul II, *Veritatis splendor*, para. 3.
[2] John Paul II II, *Laborem exercens*, para. 1.

relationship between human work and the technological and financial instruments that it uses, and creates the new distinction between the 'subjective' and 'objective' dimensions of work. Previous magisterium had given detailed attention to employee rights[3] and *Laborem exercens* sought to add to our understanding of them and of the source of these rights. It makes a novel contribution to CST when it considers the location of the corresponding duties; it casts the net wider than just the traditional employer and, in the process, introduces into CST the categories of 'direct employer' and 'indirect employer'.

Work as a basic human good

CST proposes human self-development as the principal ethical criterion.[4] Purposeful human action inevitably involves the pursuit of one or more of the basic human goods and purposeful human action is the route to human self-development. We shape ourselves through the choices that we make. Human self-development involves a quest for the basic goods conducted in a practically reasonable way. CST identifies work as a basic human good[5]: it has 'an ethical value of its own, which clearly and directly remains linked to the fact that the one who carries it out is a person, a conscious and free subject, that is to say a subject that decides about itself.'[6]

Work is, in several ways, a means of achieving other goods.[7] Most of us work to feed, clothe and house ourselves and our family. It is usually done with and for others and so has an element of friendship to it. In addition, however, work is a good thing in its own right. A life without a serious and stable commitment to work is impoverished and incomplete. There is something missing from a Bertie Wooster existence; the lack of any meaningful work leaves a vitally important aspect of the personality undeveloped.

CST has never attempted a definition of work. The opening lines of *Laborem exercens* describe it as 'any human activity that can and must be described as work'. We know it when we see it (or do it)! Work usually involves bringing about some change, taking things as they are and

---

[3] See, for example, *Rerum novarum*, paras. 41– 46, Pius XI, *Quadragesimo anno*, paras. 66–76 and John XXIII, *Mater et magistra*, paras. 70–79, 135–136 and 248–253.

[4] Paul VI, *Populorum progressio*, para. 14.   [5] John Paul II, *Laborem exercens*, para. 9.

[6] John Paul II, *Laborem exercens*, para. 5.

[7] See S. Stabile, 'Workers in the vineyard: Catholic Social Thought and the workplace', *Journal of Catholic Social Thought* 5 (2008), pp. 371–411 for a reflection on work and the working environment from a CST perspective.

changing them for the better. If the activity in question did not have an end product then it would be difficult to think of it as work. Work usually leads to the production of something that can be of use to oneself or others. Thus, an element of creativity lies at the heart of human work.

Laborem exercens points out that one can speak of work in two senses; it has both an objective dimension (it results in some output or change)[8] and a subjective dimension (it brings about a change in the worker and has the capacity to promote human self-development). The objective dimension of work, then, refers to the work done, to the specific ways in which the worker (or communities or humankind in general) achieve dominion over the world's natural resources.[9] The subjective dimension refers to the effect that working has on the worker; it focuses on the fact that work is a way for the human person to 'realise his humanity, to fulfil the calling to be a person that is his by reason of his very humanity'.[10]

Each dimension is essential to the idea of work but the subjective dimension is the more important[11] for the subjective dimension looks at work from the perspective of the very purpose of the human person. Clearly, however, the objective and subjective dimensions must be intimately linked with each other; they are two facets of the same reality. So, for example, the subjective dimension is promoted more successfully by good work than by bad work. Any other conclusion would empty the idea of human work of something that lies at its core. Work is not play; it is done to achieve some effect and this effect can be achieved with greater or lesser perfection.

In *Laborem exercens*, John Paul II discerns three spheres of the subjective dimension of work. The first is that work, as already explained, is a means of self-realisation. Second, work is the foundation of family life: it provides the means to support one's family and work and industriousness should be learned in the family.[12] The third sphere of the subjective dimension of work refers to its broader social context:

> The third sphere of values that emerges from this point of view – concerns the *great society* to which man belongs on the basis of particular cultural and historical links. This society – even when it has not taken on the mature form of a nation – is not only the great "educator" of every man, even though an indirect one (because each individual absorbs within the family the contents and values that go to make up the culture of a given nation), it is also a great historical and social incarnation of the work of

---

[8] John Paul II, *Laborem exercens*, para. 5.   [9] John Paul II, *Laborem exercens*, para. 5.
[10] John Paul II, *Laborem exercens*, para. 5.   [11] John Paul II, *Laborem exercens*, para. 6.
[12] John Paul II, *Laborem exercens*, para. 10.

all generations. All of this brings it about that man combines his deepest human identity with membership of a nation, and intends his work also to increase the common good developed together with his compatriots, thus realising that in this way work serves to add to the heritage of the whole human family, of all the people living in the world.[13]

Human work has an inherently social dimension. Society educates us for work and in the process we imbibe a particular culture. At the same time, each generation's work contributes to the building up of society. New technology, new ways of doing things and educational processes emerge. A society develops particular strengths and a particular style through the work of its citizens.

The Bible and work

Laborem exercens roots its understanding of work in Genesis:

> When man, who had been created 'in the image of God … male and female', hears the words: 'Be fruitful and multiply, and fill the earth and subdue it, even though these words do not refer explicitly to work, beyond any doubt they indirectly indicate it as an activity for man to carry out in the world. Indeed, they show its very deepest essence. Man is the image of God partly through the mandate received from his creator to subdue, to dominate the earth. In carrying out this mandate, man, every human being, reflects the very action of the Creator of the universe.[14]

Work, in both its objective and subjective dimensions, relies upon the idea of man as exercising dominion over creation.[15] The human person dominates the earth so as to work on it and to improve it and, in the process, to build up his or her own humanity. Through work, the human person 'reflects the very action of the Creator'; work can be seen as a kind of co-creation and the human person participates in God's creative activity. It is a mistake to think of work as a punishment imposed on man for original sin. Work itself is something characteristically human. Work is a participation in God's creative activity. Original sin, however, adds the element of toil that so often accompanies our work.[16]

The Christian outlook on work is also shaped by the fact that Christ himself was a worker; this fact constitutes a 'Gospel of Work'.[17] Christ

[13] John Paul II, *Laborem exercens*, para. 10.
[14] John Paul II, *Laborem exercens*, para. 4.
[15] John Paul II, *Laborem exercens*, paras. 4 and 6.
[16] John Paul II, *Laborem exercens*, para. 9.
[17] John Paul II, *Laborem exercens*, para. 9.

is perfect man he provides a living model to show what human self-development or integral self-realisation looks like in practice. He provides a model on which Christians can reflect as they try to pursue the ideal of integral self-realisation in their own lives.

The primary purpose of work, then, is to allow the worker to fully realise his or her humanity. At the same time, he or she acts as a co-creator and helps to build up and prefect the raw material supplied by creation. The toil associated with work can be united to the suffering that Christ suffered on the Cross and, because of the Resurrection, point the way to a new life and a new good.[18] Thus, one can speak of a spirituality of work.[19] It can also have a profound spiritual significance for the worker. It is a way for the Christian worker to live out the call to be a co-creator and co-redeemer.[20]

Employee participation

In modern industrialised societies, it can easily appear that work is done by machines and that the worker is only there to serve the technology used in the production process. In these circumstances, it is more important than ever before to insist that 'the proper subject of work is man'.[21] Only thus can the worker realise his humanity and 'fulfil the calling to be a person that is his by reason of his very humanity'.[22] Thus, CST has generated the principle of the priority of labour over capital: labour, the worker, is the primary efficient cause in the production process while the means of production are merely instruments.[23] Inherent in the principle is the effective participation of labour in the whole production process.[24] So the Church strives 'always to ensure the priority of work and, thereby, man's character as a *subject* in social life and, especially, in the dynamic *structure of the whole economic process*.'[25]

---

[18] John Paul II, *Laborem exercens*, para. 27.
[19] John Paul II, *Laborem exercens*, para. 26.
[20] John Paul II, *Laborem exercens*, paras. 24–27. See G. Schultze SJ, 'Work, Worship, Labourem Exercens and the United States Today', *Logos* 5 (2002), p. 25 and J. Bethke Elshtain, 'Work and its Meanings', *Logos* 5 (2002), p. 15 for commentaries.
[21] John Paul II, *Laborem exercens*, para. 5.
[22] John Paul II, *Laborem exercens*, para. 6.
[23] John Paul II, *Laborem exercens*, para. 12.
[24] John Paul II, *Laborem, exercens*, para. 13.
[25] John Paul II, *Laborem exercens*, para. 14.

Gronbacher and Sirico expain that work is part of man's original vocation and dignity. The ability to develop our subjectivity through work
means that work can be part of the genuine development of the human
person. They explain that participation is the person acting in communion with others and is necessary for human flourishing. The workplace
is where most of us make our most significant contribution to the common good. Participation, they argue, means that, when possible, workers
should have their own reasonable autonomy and decision-making ability
regarding their own position and tasks. At the same time, they should
respect the authority of the employer provided that the employer seeks
to maintain a workplace ecology that affirms the human dignity of each
employee.[26]

Murphy and Pyke point out the importance of careful job design that
allows the employee, where possible to play a part both in the design and
execution of tasks. This is more conducive to their growth as people than
simply carrying out tasks assigned by managers. Work should be designed
in such a way as to respect the employee's capacity for self-direction and
self-development.[27]

Capital and labour

The importance of work for human self-development is one of *Laborem
exercens'* central themes. Closely linked to it is a consideration of the relationship between capital and labour. Private property ownership is justified principally because it facilitates human work. Private property rights
establish a stable relationship between the worker and the object worked
on. Thus, the worker exercises the dominion that is the necessary prelude
to the work of co-creation that he or she is called on to carry out.

Private property, capital, is at the service of labour. Work is a basic
human need and it presupposes some capital (tools, know-how, finance
and raw materials). CST speaks of a universal destination of goods; in the
last analysis, everyone (at least everyone who is prepared to work) is entitled to access to the capital they need for at least the most basic aspects of
their human self-development. An allocation and use of private property

---

[26] G. Gronbacher and R. Sirico, 'Towards a personalist workplace ethic', in T. Machan (ed.),
Morality and work. Philosophic reflections on a free society, (Stanford, Hoover Institution
Press, 2000).

[27] J. Murphy and D. Pyke, 'Humane work and the challenges of job design', in S. Cortright
and M. Naughton (eds.), *Rethinking the purpose of business. Interdisciplinary essays from
the Catholic Social Tradition*, (Notre Dame, Ind. University of Notre Dame Press, 2002).

rights that fails to respect this principle is unjust; 'the right to private property is subordinated to the right to common use'.[28] There is an intimate relationship between capital and labour; human work is the source of the creation of capital. Proposals for joint ownership and for participation in management and profits take on special significance in the light of these considerations. If the worker is to be the active subject of the production process, the way will have to be paved by adapting the ownership rights in the means of production. This does not, however imply greater levels of state ownership (which might simply add waste and bureaucracy). Rather it is a call for ownership structures that, in some sense, make the worker 'a part owner of the great workbench at which he is working with everyone else'. Share ownership is one possible way that could be conceived of for giving effect to this call.[29]

Workers' rights

Rerum novarum dealt at length with the rights of employees. *Laborem exercens* takes up the theme and locates workers' rights within the broader framework of human rights as a whole. The starting point, however, is the duty to work; this duty is imposed by the demands of human self-development as well as by the need to sustain one's family and to contribute to the life of the nation. *Laborem exercens* spells out the rights to adequate education and training, to a job, to a just wage (and to adequate sickness and pension arrangements). It also mentions the right to Sunday rest (and to holidays) and to a working environment that both is physically safe and respects the worker's moral integrity.

Primary responsibility for ensuring that most of these rights are respected falls primarily on the 'direct employer'. *Laborem exercens* also articulates the concept of the 'indirect employer'. This includes:

> both persons and institutions of various kinds, and also collective labour contracts and the principles of conduct which are laid down by these persons and institutions and which determine the whole socioeconomic system or are its result.[30]

The state is the primary indirect employer but *Laborem exercens* also mentions, 'all the agents at the national and international level that are

---

[28] John Paul II, *Laborem exercens*, para. 14.
[29] John Paul II, *Laborem exercens*, para. 14.
[30] John Paul II, *Laborem exercens*, para. 17.

responsible for the whole orientation of labour policy'.[31] The indirect
employer also has a part to play in shaping a just labour system. Creating
such a system cannot be left to the market, guided by the profit motive,
alone. The direct and indirect employer have a responsibility to ensure
that the whole economy (domestic and international) respects the objective rights of the worker.

Unions have a vital part to play in defending these rights. The right to
join a union is an exercise of the right of freedom of association. There is a
community of 'those who work and those who own the means of production'; the economy itself is a kind of community and unions have a vital
part to play in building it up. This community itself is part of the broader
political community with a responsibility to contribute to the common
good:

> Social and socioeconomic life is certainly like a system of 'connected ves-
> sels', and every social activity directed towards safeguarding the rights of
> particular groups should adapt itself to this system.[32]

This is a pithy statement of the view of society that underlies CST's principle of subsidiarity.

Economism

CST sees capital and labour as being mutually complementary and
involved in a dynamic process of capital creation. This capital is, in various ways, a store of human work and a platform on which future generations of workers can build. The human person establishes dominion
over a certain parcel of material creation with a view to working on it
and improving it. In this way, making use of God's original creation, the
human person acts as co-creator. Work generates capital and capital is at
the service of further work. Capital and labour are inseparably united.
In this image, capital refers especially to technology and know-how, to
the skills, knowledge and tools that are both the product of human work
and intended to facilitate further work. Capital and labour combine in the
production / creation process but work and the interests of workers have
priority. CST promotes the primacy of persons over things.

The problem is that this harmony has been shattered so that it is now
common to think of capital and labour as being opposed to each other

---

[31] John Paul II, *Laborem exercens*, para. 17.
[32] John Paul II, *Laborem exercens*, para. 20.

in some sense. Labour has come to be thought of as an impersonal force and as being on the same level as the impersonal factors of production. This is the economism that *Laborem exercens* condemns; the principle of the priority of persons over things is no longer respected. It has its roots in a materialistic philosophy that sees spiritual realities as superfluous phenomena. It is also rooted in the economic and social practice of the earliest days of the Industrial Revolution. The remedy lies in reforms that overcome the opposition between capital and labour; employee participation in ownership, management and profits are amongst the reforms that could turn the economistic tide.[33]

Conclusion

Conflict between capital and labour marked the Industrial Revolution. *Rerum novarum* spelled out and condemned the inhumane abuses that resulted. CST can largely (though by no means exclusively) be seen as an attempt to articulate the proper relationship between the two. Work is central to human identity; God's original call to each human person is a call to work and so to act as co-creator. Work is both a central element of human self-development and a means by which other aspects of self-development can be attained. Work demands that the worker dominate what is worked on through some form of ownership. The worker must be recognised as the active subject of the production process. These ideas underlie CST's call for employee participation in its various forms. CST's defence of work, and of the rights of the worker, relies on a vigorous defence of the right to own private property.

[33] John Paul II, *Laborem exercens*, paras. 12–13.

4

Catholic Social Thought, private property and markets

Introduction

The social question confronted by *Rerum novarum* was the conflict between capital and labour. Leo XIII's response combined a vigorous defence of the human rights of the worker with an insistence on the natural right to property ownership. It would be superficial (to say the least) to imagine that this was an attempt to strike a political balance between left and right. It would be equally superficial to imagine that the Pope saw this as a defence of two unrelated sets of rights that happened to have come into conflict. Rather, he saw work and private property as being mutually complementary. Substituting state for private ownership would both harm the worker and distort the role of the state.[1] Private property ownership is (for most people) an indispensable precondition for fulfilling work and for being able to bring rationality and free will to bear on planning their own lives and providing for their families. This chapter outlines what CST has to say about the right to private property ownership. It also examines the roles of the state, markets and of actors such as representatives of capital and labour in a soundly-functioning economy and society.

Private property and human dignity

CST sees the right to own private property as a natural right that plays a crucial role in the development of the human personality. It is closely linked to work and to freedom. The ownership of private property allows one to play an active part in developing the communities of which one forms a part (especially one's family). The right to private property ownership is, however, conditioned by the fact that, in the last analysis, material creation is intended to meet the needs of each and every human person.

[1] Leo XIII, *Rerum novarum*, paras. 1–7.

Greed and the consumer mentality can lead to property ownership being a corrupting phenomenon. From its inception, CST has insisted that private property ownership is highly suitable for the human person. Theologically, one can point to the Book of Genesis:

> In the very first pages of Scripture we read these words: "Fill the earth and subdue it." This teaches us that the whole of creation is for man, that he has been charged to give it meaning by his intelligent activity, to complete and perfect it by his own efforts and to his own advantage.[2]

The right to own private property can be seen as a requirement of human rationality. Unlike animals, the human being is capable of securing stable and permanent possession of material things.[3] This stable possession allows the human person to make choices as to how property will be used in the future. Private property, by acting as a store of value, can help to secure a zone of autonomy for individuals and families that allows for a more rational and creative exercise of their freedom. The point is obvious, but far from trivial. The person without any capital lives in a relatively precarious position. There is always the worry about how to meet immediate needs. This worry is alleviated, to a greater or lesser extent, by the ownership of private property. John XXIII, in *Mater et magistra*, pointed to the link between private property and human freedom. Ownership of private property is a guarantee of freedom at the individual level and, experience suggests, at the level of society in general.[4] A little later, the Encyclical says the following about the link between the right to own property and economic and political freedom:

> private ownership must be considered as a guarantee of the essential freedom of the individual, and at the same time an indispensable element in a true social order.[5]

One can discern a number of links between private property and freedom. Property can be the object of free choices and these choices can have profound moral implications. Thus, from time to time, CST has talked of the owner impressing his personality on the property that is owned. This can occur through the care that is taken of the property and the ways in which the owner chooses to enhance it. The arguments in favor of a natural right to private property grow stronger when one considers that this

---

[2] Paul VI, *Populorum progressio*, para. 22.
[3] Leo XIII, *Rerum novarum*, para. 6.
[4] John XXIII, *Mater et magistra*, para. 109.
[5] John XXIII, *Mater et magistra*, para. 111.

right facilitates the observance of man's social and domestic obligations.[6] Private property allows the worker to provide for his or her family; a right that is closely associated with the development and continuance through time of the worker's personality.[7] Providing for the family is not, primarily, the role of the state.[8] The state's usual role is to frame property rights adequately and to ensure that the rights can be enforced. The state should respect the working of markets which are an important facility enhancing the usefulness and value of private property rights both for their owners and for society at large.

Private property can also help to meet the needs of the owner's family and, more generally, allow the owner to make a contribution to the common good of the societies of which he forms part. *Mater et magistra* describes private property ownership as:

> a right which constitutes so efficacious a means of asserting one's personality and exercising responsibility in every field, and an element of solidity and security for family life and of greater peace and prosperity in the State.[9]

Private property and efficient use of resources

The connection between private property and the efficient use of resources is the rationale favored by economic theorists. CST, as has been seen, focuses on the more profoundly personalist implications of private property as an institution. CST does not deny the economic efficiency of private property as an institution; nor does it regard it as an irrelevance. Leo XIII mentions the economic justification for private property rights in *Rerum novarum*. In the course of a lengthy and ardent defense of private property, he says that one of the evils that would attend its overthrow is that:

> the sources of wealth themselves would run dry, for no one would have any interest in exerting his talents or his industry.[10]

Detailed exploration of the economic aspects of private property would take CST out of the sphere of moral theology and into the technical realms of economics, politics and law. These are not its areas of competence.

---

[6] Leo XIII, *Rerum novarum*, para. 12.
[7] Leo XIII, *Rerum novarum*, para. 13.
[8] Leo XIII, *Rerum novarum*, paras. 13–14.
[9] John XXIII, *Mater et magistra*, para. 112.
[10] Leo XIII, *Rerum novarum*, para. 15.

The universal destination of goods

The right to own private property is, then, a natural right. It is consistent with human dignity, reflects the divine call to subdue the earth and make it fruitful and plays a well-nigh indispensable role in allowing individuals to achieve their self-realisation. At the same time, it generally leads to a better (more creative and less wasteful) use of resources than communist systems that seek to abolish the right to private property. But it is important to understand that, in the last analysis, the world's resources are intended for the benefit of all mankind and the right to own private property has to be understood with this fact in mind.

Paul VI explained that the right to private property is subordinate to a more fundamental principle:

> Now if the earth truly was created to provide man with the necessities of life and the tools for his own progress, it follows that every man has the right to glean what he needs from the earth. The recent Council reiterated this truth: "God intended the earth and everything in it for the use of all human beings and peoples. Thus, under the leadership of justice and in the company of charity, created goods should flow fairly to all.[11]

Pius XI, in *Quadragesimo anno*, had already insisted on the social obligations attached to private property. The section on private property begins by noting the principle that created goods are intended to meet the needs of the entire family of mankind.[12] Pius XI does not discern a tension between the individual and social aspects of property rights; indeed, it is clear that he regards the two aspects as mutually reinforcing. Thus, it is desirable that as many people as possible own some property. The concept of the universal destination of the world's resources would ideally be met by a system that makes property –owners of as many people as possible rather than by a system that does away with private property rights.[13]

The role of the state concerning private property rights

The right to own property is a natural right and not the product of a concession by the state. At the beginning of *Rerum novarum*, Leo XIII describes as unjust the contention that 'individual possessions should become the common property of all to be administered by the State or

---

[11] Paul VI, *Populorum progressio*, para. 22.
[12] Pius XI, *Quagragesimo anno*, para. 45.
[13] Pius XI, *Quadragesimo anno*, para. 63.

by municipal bodies'.[14] At the same time, it is obvious that the state has a number of important roles to play if a system of property ownership is to emerge and develop in a way that meets the needs of society. This system will have to explain how the owner of a particular bundle of property rights is to be identified and precisely what the bundle consists in. It will have to deal with questions such as the mechanism for transferring ownership of property and for protecting one's property rights against would-be trespassers or infringers. It will have to incorporate some kind of system for resolving disputes between, for example, rival claimants to the same (or conflicting) bundles of property rights.

The state is not the source of the right to private property but it does have an indispensable role to play in shaping the system of private property to meet the needs of a given society. It is a guarantor and enabler of an effective system of private property rights. Calvez and Perrin explain:

> At the level of natural law, or, more exactly, of the innate rights of the human person, there exists in man, independently of any empirical determination, a right to use the goods of this world. At a lower level, there is private property a natural institution designed to give practical effect to this fundamental human right: the step from one to the other being made by a consideration of nature's exiguity and of the difficulties of sharing goods. At the lowest level, there is the positive law regarding property and its effective administration in any given situation: there is no question as to whether or not private ownership should exist – that is settled – but only as to which person should hold which thing for his own.[15]

The state is responsible for ensuring that the use of material resources, and the exercise of the right to private property, is directed towards the common good. *Centesimus annus* puts it this way:

> Economic activity, especially the activity of a market economy, cannot be conducted in an institutional, juridical or political vacuum. On the contrary, it presupposes sure guarantees of individual freedom and private property as well as a stable currency and efficient public services. Here the principle task of the State is to guarantee this security, so that those who work and produce can enjoy the fruits of their labours and thus feel encouraged to work effectively and honestly.[16]

Individuals can legitimately look to the state to facilitate the exercise of private property rights. The system that emerges from this state

---

[14] Leo XIII, *Rerum novarum*, para. 4.
[15] J.-Y.Calvez and J. Perrin, *The Church and Social Justice. The Social Teaching of the Popes from Leo XIII to Pius XII (1878–1958)*, (London, Burns & Oates, 1961), pp. 205–206.
[16] John Paul II, *Centesimus annus*, para. 48.

intervention serves the common good since it facilitates, in the ways that have already been discussed, the integral self-realisation of property owners and the efficient use of a society's resources.

The state is also responsible for ensuring that private property ownership is effectively harmonised with the concept of the universal destination of created goods. This might be done in any one of a very large variety of ways. A real property system, for example, that allows for new property rights to emerge from a long, continuous period of uncontested use is not only economically efficient but also helps to prevent an unhelpful hoarding of assets that hinders a more widespread distribution of property ownership. Systems of taxation can be used to even out the distribution of wealth in ways that might serve social peace. The state can provide subsidies to would-be home-buyers so as to help them assume the mantle of property-owner. Similarly, it could give tax-breaks or other encouragement for employee share schemes. The list of possible tools that the state might use is almost endless. This is not a charter for out-and-out state intervention since the principle of subsidiarity has to be respected. It is to say, however, that private property rights have to be designed with the demands of the entire human family in mind.

Markets

CST analyses markets and the economy from the perspective of human self-development. This analysis shows that free markets have positive features since 'the free market is the most efficient instrument for utilising resources and effectively responding to needs'.[17] But markets only meet the needs of those people with the purchasing power to participate and it only meets needs insofar as a profit can be made. It is obvious, however, that this leaves many people (those too poor to participate) and some important human needs outside the framework of the market.[18] Further, left to themselves the free play of market forces can be positively degrading since it is common for markets to emerge that create false needs that harm the human self-development of those they serve.[19] Economic needs are only one dimension of overall human needs and economic freedom is only one element of human freedom. If we are viewed as mere consumers then economic freedom loses its necessary link to the human person.[20]

---

[17] John Paul II, *Centesimus annus*, para. 34.
[18] John Paul II, *Centesimus annus*, para. 34.
[19] John Paul II, *Centesimus annus*, para. 36.
[20] John Paul II, *Centesimus annus*, para. 39.

The state is responsible for common goods such as the natural and human environments; market forces on their own cannot be relied upon to promote the common good.[21]

In an important passage, John Paul II said:

> Here we find a new limit on the market: there are collective and qualitative needs which cannot be satisfied by market mechanisms. There are important human needs which escape its logic. There are goods which by their very nature cannot and must not be bought or sold. Certainly the mechanisms of the market offer secure advantages: they help to utilise resources better; they promote the exchange of products; above all they give central place to the person's desires and preferences, which in a contract, meet the desires and preferences of another person. Nevertheless, these mechanisms carry the risk of an idolatry of the market, an idolatry which ignores the existence of goods which by their very nature are not and cannot be mere commodities.[22]

The state cannot allow its functions to be usurped or rendered ineffective by the market. This poses significant challenges in the modern context where markets and economic actors transcend national boundaries. So there will be a need for new methods and legal frameworks to ensure that markets do not operate in a legal and moral vacuum. Laws cannot always take contractual exchange as their ideal since the lawmaker must be guided by a concern for human self-development; markets generally take the search for profit as their guide. There is no reason why a quest for profit should be a constantly reliable guide as to the demands of human self-development and everyday experience provides examples of markets that meet false needs or that are positively immoral. *Centesimus annus* warns against entrusting to markets the task of providing the framework that would put economic freedom at the service of human freedom in its totality; there is a risk of the spread of a radical capitalist ideology that would leave this to the free development of market forces.[23]

Conclusion

CST has always defended the institution of private property. Property ownership is fitting for the human person; it facilitates the call to dominate the earth and so to improve it. It facilitates the exercise of human freedom and the self-interest that arises out of property ownership provides

---

[21] John Paul II, *Centesimus annus*, para. 40.
[22] John Paul II, *Centesimus annus*, para. 40.
[23] John Paul II, *Centesimus annus*, para. 47.

incentives for the efficient use of resources. At the same time, however, private property comes with a social mortgage. Put another way, the legal framework surrounding the right to private property, and the way that that right is exercised, have to respect the principle of the universal destination of created goods.

The state does have a role to play but this is usually one of creating the institutional infrastructure to facilitate the smooth operation of private property rights and to ensure that they are exercised in a way that is compatible with the common good and with the principle of the universal destination of human goods. Exceptionally, the state might have to intervene more directly to meet a society's economic needs but this should be a temporary phenomenon.

Free markets are a useful way of facilitating the exercise of the right to dispose of one's property; in this sense they can be understood as a helpful adjunct to the right to own private property and as facilitating the exercise of freedom in the economic sphere. It would be folly, however, to assume that (by some invisible hand) they will lead to *le meilleur de tous les mondes possibles*. They are only accessible to those with the resources to participate in them and are often blind to the requirements of human self-development (prostitution and the drugs and arms trades provide the most obvious illustrations of this). Economic activity has to be subjected to at least some level of co-ordination and oversight. In the last analysis, this is the responsibility of the political authority. The principle of subsidiarity, however, suggests that so far as possible, the state should leave it to economic actors themselves (such as representatives of capital and labour to regulate markets and economic activity with a view to the common good).

5

The corporation

Introduction

The preceding two chapters have looked at the role that work and private property play in integral self-realisation. The corporation is the community that brings work and private property together. This chapter will explain CST's understanding of the corporation and the philosophical understanding of the ideas of community and the common good that underpin it. One's understanding of the point of belonging to a particular group, such as the corporation, will play a significant part in determining the role that it plays in the pursuit of self-realisation. The theory of the firm that one adopts has practical significance for the all round well-being of employees and (perhaps) shareholders. This chapter will look at the practical importance of the theory of the firm. It will also look at the question of the reality of the corporation: does it have some reality of its own or is the corporation or any other human grouping a mere fiction? This will lead into a discussion of the interaction of CST and the social sciences. Finally, the chapter will consider what the theory of the firm means for employees.

Catholic Social Thought and the corporation

Theories of the firm have to deal with the relationship between the individual and the groups to which he belongs. This philosophical question is very important for corporate governance since it helps us to understand what motivates the members of organisations and how it is that the corporation plays a positive role in the broader economy.

CST conceives of the corporation as being something with a reality and existence of its own. It has its own common good to which its members contribute and from which they benefit. It has an action and operation of its own which, while clearly dependent on its members, cannot simply be reduced to the sum of the actions of its individual members.

John XXIII introduced the idea that the corporation is a community into CST[1]. He referred to the ideal enterprise as one which is 'modeled on the basis of a community of persons working together for the advancement of their mutual interests in accordance with the principles of justice and Christian teaching'.[2] In one short passage that is a powerful summary of CST's position, John Paul II said:

> In fact, the purpose of the business firm is not simply to make a profit but is to be found in its very existence as a community of persons who in various ways are endeavouring to satisfy their basic needs, and who form a particular group at the service of the whole of society.[3]

This is a remarkable passage that conveys a number of crucial points: the firm has an existence; it is a community of persons; it facilitates the individual's effort to meet basic needs and it is at the service of a broader society.

What does it mean to describe a corporation as a community of persons? The essence is that the members of a community have a shared purpose at least in the minimal sense that they need to consciously coordinate their activity if they are to attain the ends that brought each of them to the firm. According to Finnis, common action is the element that creates a group or community: one or more people can be said to be a group or community or society if they share some common purpose:

> a group, in the relevant sense, whether team, club, society, enterprise or community, is said to exist whenever there is, over an appreciable span of time, a co-ordination of activity by a number of persons in the form of interaction, and with a view to a shared objective.[4]

Maritain explains that social relations always centre on some material or spiritual objective.[5] The common good of the firm is intrinsically linked to the good of its individual members. Greenfield (although not writing from a CST perspective) captures some of the central elements of CST's approach to the concept of the corporation well:

> Shareholders believe that buying shares is better than putting money in savings accounts, for example, because shareholders believe that managers can utilise the productive capacity of the firm to make a better, or safer, return than other possible investments. Workers show up to work

---

[1] John XXIII, *Mater et magistra*, para. 91.
[2] John XXIII, *Mater et magistra*, para. 142.
[3] John Paul II, *Centesimus annus*, para. 35.
[4] J. Finnis, *Natural law and natural rights*, (Oxford, Oxford University Press, 2003), p. 153.
[5] J. Maritain, 'The people and the state', reprinted in *Logos* 11 (2008), pp. 164–165.

because they believe that the managers can organise their labour and other resources so that they can be more productive than the sum of their productiveness as individuals, and that they will share in the gain.[6]

The *raison d'etre* of the firm is that it allows its shareholders and employees to get more out of their money or their work than would otherwise be possible.

The common good

Looked at in one way, the community can be said to be formed for the sake of its members. But the relationship is subtler than this would suggest since the human person is inherently social. There is a profound link between the good of the individual and the common good of the communities to which he belongs.

The term 'common good' has several meanings. The well-being of the firm is a good for each of its members. First, if the firm does well it is more likely that its members will achieve the goals that brought them to the firm. Second, the members of the firm may well feel loyalty towards it and rejoice if it does well.

Gaudium et spes proposed this definition of the common good:

> the sum of those conditions of social life which allow social groups and their individual members relatively thorough and ready access to their own fulfilment.[7]

In this sense, the common good of the firm has a material aspect (the financial and physical resources of the firm) but the common good of the modern firm also includes its know-how, intellectual property, managerial prowess, governance structures and reputation. It includes the culture of the firm, its team spirit, its work ethic and its spirit of service. The common good in this final, central, sense clearly does not belong to any individual, although it is of the greatest importance to the individual members of the firm. It is what facilitates their pursuit of their own fulfilment in the social context of the firm.

Speaking of the common good of the political community, Maritain said:

> The common good is not only the collection of public commodities and services which the organisation of common life presupposes: a

---

[6] K. Greenfield, 'The place of workers in corporate law', *Boston College Law Review* 39 (1998) 39, p. 300.

[7] Second Vatican Council, *Gadium et spes*, para. 26.

strong fiscal condition, a strong military force; the body of just laws, good customs and wise institutions which provides the political society with its structure; the heritage of its great historical remembrances, its symbols and its glories, its living traditions and cultural treasures. The common good also includes the sociological integration of all the civic conscience, political virtues and sense of freedom, of all the activity, material prosperity and spiritual riches, of unconsciously operating hereditary wisdom, of moral rectitude, justice, friendship, happiness, virtue and heroism in the individual lives of the members of the body politic. To the extent to which all of these things are, in a certain measure, *communicable*, and revert to each member, helping him to perfect his life and liberty as a person, they all constitute the good human life of the multitude.[8]

This is said of political society but it gives something of a sense of what might constitute the common good of a major corporation.

It is important to note, too, that the common good of the firm is established, kept in being and developed by the firm's members. The firm's common good is an expression of the personality of its members as they work to achieve their own purposes and, in doing so, to build up the organisation for which they work.

The idea of the common good, then, emphasises the separate being of the firm; it has a common good which is not directly the good of any individual member or even of all of its members at any one time. At the same time, there is a real link between the common good of the firm and the good of its individual members; the latter create the common good of the firm and benefit from it. The most profound benefit that the common good offers to the individual is that it allows the individual to express his social nature by making a contribution to the societies of which he forms part. There is something self-interested in this, it is true but it is also a realistic perspective and one that requires a certain generosity.

As an aside, it is worth considering the relationship between the common good of society and the good (integral self-realisation) of the individual. Calvez and Perrin talk of a 'dialectic of the person and society':[9] society is personal since it is oriented to human goods:

> [Society] is a living unity, rich in content, directed as is the person, of whom it is the flowering, towards the highest purposes of human existence, towards the spiritual, even the "eternal".[10]

---

[8] Maritain, 'The people and the state, p. 172.
[9] J.-Y. Calvez S.J. and J. Perrin S.J., *The social teaching of the Popes from Leo XIII to Pius XII*, (Chicago, Henry Regnery Company, 1961), p. 119.
[10] Calvez and Perrin, *The social teaching of the Popes*, p. 111.

This is as true of the economy as it is of society in general. Even the economy should be informed with something of the moral and spiritual life; the common good is a part of the moral order.[11]

Benedict XVI explained that the common good is at the service of the individual. At the same time it is true for each of us that our individual effort and commitment to serve the common good of the communities to which we belong is an important way in which we can build a meaningful charity into our lives:

> [The common good] is a good that is sought not for its own sake, but for people who belong to the social community and who can only really and effectively pursue their good within it. To desire the *common good* and strive towards it *is a requirement of charity and justice*. To take a stand for the common good is on the one hand to be solicitous for, and on the other hand to avail oneself of, that complex of institutions that gives structure to the life of society, juridically, civilly, politically and culturally, making it the *polis* or city.[12]

We see here the realistic, subtle account of the relationship between the individual and the community offered by natural law theory and enriched by CST.

One might ask whether the individual is more important than society or the reverse. Fundamentally, society exists to promote the well-being of the person. Society has a certain pre-eminence because 'not only does it express, realise in outward form, but also truly guarantee the fundamental right of the person to which therefore it remains interior.'[13] Society is personal:

> Society contributes to the full development of the person, but it does so by drawing upon the springs of personal life and personal dignity.[14]

Society is personal since it comes from within the person, exists to serve human self-realisation and has to guarantee the fundamental rights of the person. One can err either by failing to give society its due or by failing to recognise that society is linked to the human rights of the individual.

The foregoing discussion can cast some light on the relationship between the firm and its members. The firm's common good, too, is personal in that it exists to promote certain specialised (though fundamental) aspects of human self-realisation. Clearly, the analogy between the

---

[11] Calvez and Perrin, *The social teaching of the Popes*, p. 115.
[12] Benedict XVI, *Caritas in veritate*, para. 7.
[13] Calvez and Perrin, *The social teaching of the Popes*, p. 119.
[14] Calvez and Perrin, *The social teaching of the Popes*, p. 119.

firm and society in the broad sense should not be pushed too far; society is necessary to human self-realisation to a degree that the firm is not. Nevertheless, what has been said about the personal character of society sheds some light on the personalist significance of the firm.

The idea of the common good can have a significant impact on the attitude of employees towards the corporation since, as Kennedy points out, a mature individual will have the virtue of solidarity: he or she will be committed to acting in such a way as to sustain the common good of any community of which he or she is a member.[15]

Theories of the firm

Theories of the firm have been enormously significant in shaping our understanding of the legal nature of the corporation and corporate law and policy. Millon has charted the interplay between theory, social and economic context and legal policy. Though the relationship between theories of the firm and legal policy is complex and multi-directional, Millon shows clearly that changes in theory have accompanied (and to some extent caused) changes in how the law has regarded the corporation[16]. The basic idea is clear:

> [L]egal theories set forth a positive or descriptive assertion about the world – an assertion about what corporations *are*. Normative implications are then said to follow from the positive assertion. Thus, for example, because a corporation is an artificial entity, the state ought to be free to impose regulations on corporate activity deemed necessary to serve the public interest. Or, because the corporation is nothing but a nexus of contracts among private individuals, the state should not interfere with the parties' autonomy by imposing restrictions on their freedom of contract.[17]

Millon's contention is that the conclusions drawn from any given theory depend on a dynamic interplay between the theory itself, current law and practice and the prevailing orthodoxy as to the normative conclusions to be drawn from that theory.[18]

---

[15] R. Kennedy, 'The virtue of solidarity and the purpose of the firm', in S. Cortright and M. Naughton (eds), *Rethinking the purpose of business. Interdisciplinary essays from the Catholic Social Tradition*, (Notre Dame, Ind., University of Notre Dame Press, 2002), p. 57.

[16] D. Millon, 'Theories of the corporation', *Duke Law Journal* (1990), p. 201.

[17] Millon, 'Theories of the corporation', p. 241.

[18] Millon, 'Theories of the corporation', p. 243.

Discussion about the theory of the firm is abstract but full of practical significance. The theory of the firm adopted by its participants, by markets and by governments shape the life of the organisation and its people. Ghoshal and Moran point out that, '[a]ll positive theories of social sciences are also normative theories, whether intended or not.'[19] One's understanding of human nature and of social relations will have a profound impact on one's opinions and behaviour. Further, the theories that have shaped the life of an organisation will also influence both the external environment of its members and their inner selves. Ghoshal and Moran explain:

> Social sciences carry a special responsibility because of the process of the double hermeneutic. The theories affect the agents who are its subject matter. By assuming the worst, [Williamson's Transaction Cost Economics – discussed below] can bring out the worst in economic behaviour.[20]

The bonus culture that has played such a significant part in our current economic woes can surely be attributed to a pessimistic view of human nature and (which may seem paradoxical) to a strongly negative approach to the role of organisations in the life of individuals and of society at large.

The nexus of contracts approach, Williamson's transaction cost economics conception of the firm and stakeholder theory are each discussed later in this chapter. The first two have in common a pessimistic view of human behaviour. Jensen and Meckling's point of departure is that:

> If both parties to the relationship are utility maximisers there is good reason to believe that the agent will not always act in the best interests of the principal.[21]

Taking this as one's starting point means that the central question for corporate governance is the need to protect shareholders from managerial misconduct. It is assumed that, given the opportunity and the incentive, managers will readily renege on the commitment that they gave to shareholders. Corporate governance is assigned the negative task of providing protection against the darker side of human nature. Similarly, Williamson sees shirking and cheating as the central problems that corporate governance has to contend with.

[19] S. Ghoshal and P. Moran, 'Bad for practice: a critique of the transaction cost theory', *Academy of Management Review* 21 (1996), p. 15.
[20] Ghoshal and Moran, 'Bad for practice', p. 39.
[21] M. Jensen and W. Meckling, 'Theory of the firm: Managerial behaviour, agency costs and ownership structure', *Journal of Financial Economics* 3 (1976), p. 308.

The nexus of contracts view of the firm

CST's approach to the corporation is part of a broader vision of society that runs counter to the view implicit in the nexus of contracts approach. CST does not deal with the question of the reality or otherwise of the corporation. This chapter nevertheless contends that it is implicitly committed to an understanding that social groupings do have some degree of reality; they are not mere fictions. This is implicit, for example, in the principle of subsidiarity. This principle, explained below, is most easily understood if one conceives of human communities as having some real level of being. Only then does it make any sense to talk of society as a system of interconnected vessels. The debate between those who see the corporation as being real and those who see it as being a mere fiction is discussed below.

Catholic Social Thought, and the natural law concepts and approach on which it relies, see the firm as having a reality of its own. One can intelligibly say of some people that they are members of the firm and of others that they are not. This is not the dominant view of how things are. It is common to find corporate governance scholars speaking of the firm as a nexus of contracts or as an especially sophisticated contract. The idea that the firm is a mere nexus of contracts is the foundation of many contemporary theories of the firm. According to this view:

> The private corporation or firm is simply one form of legal fiction which serves as a nexus for contracting relationships and which is also characterised by the existence of divisible residual claims on the assets and cash flows of the organisation which can generally be sold without permission of the other contracting individuals. While this definition of the firm has little substantive content, emphasizing the essential contractual nature of firms and other organisations focuses attention on a crucial set of questions – why particular sets of contractual relations arise for various types of organisations, what the consequences of these contractual relations are, and how they are affected by changes exogenous to the organisation. Viewed in this way, it makes little or no sense to try to distinguish those things which are "inside" the firm (or any other organisation) from those things which are "outside" of it. There is in a very real sense only a multitude of complex relationships (i.e. contracts) between the legal fiction (the firm) and the owners of labour, material and capital inputs and the consumers of output.[22]

---

[22] M. Jensen and W. Meckling, 'Theory of the firm: Managerial behaviour, agency costs and ownership structure', *Journal of Financial Economics* 3 (1976), p. 311.

In other words, the firm is no more than the fictitious counterparty to a collection of contracts. At its core is a set of financial claims on its assets and cash flows. There is no such thing as the firm and any suggestion that some people fall within its boundaries while others do not is a delusion.

This is very different from CST's vision of the firm. CST sees the firm as having a reality of its own, the nexus of contracts view sees it as a pure fiction; only the underlying contracts are real. CST thinks of communities such as the firm in terms of their contribution to meeting human needs while the nexus of contracts view is agnostic as to what motivates individuals to contract with the firm. CST's concept of the common good of the firm has no place in the nexus of contracts approach. If there is no firm, it cannot have its common good in the central sense identified earlier. Each contracting party deals with the firm for his own purposes and, presumably, seeks to take from it as much as possible. There is no reason why the contracting party would want to build up the firm or feel any sense of loyalty towards it. The concept of the common good is replaced by the much thinner concept of welfare maximisation. The nexus of contracts view of the firm distorts our understanding of the nature of human organisations by depriving them of any ability to be and to operate that is separate from the individuals or groups who contract with the firm. The nexus of contracts view that the firm is a fiction is a poor starting point for any attempt to understand the firm as a community with its own common good. It seems to undermine the distinctive role that organisations play in economic life.

A further shortcoming of the nexus of contracts view is that it does not help to locate the firm in the broader social and economic context. CST sees the firm as being a part of a bigger social, political and economic picture. CST's principle of subsidiarity, it is true, emphasises the need to respect the relative autonomy of intermediate associations but, in so doing, implicitly accepts that the corporation is neither isolated from the broader social fabric nor beyond the legitimate reach of the political authority. The corporation has its own part to play in the societies of which it forms part. This is clearly incompatible with the essentially individualistic premises on which the nexus of contracts view rests.

Eisenberg points out that the nexus of contracts theory fails to capture the way in which rules and directions function in the lives of those who are members of hierarchical organisations, such as corporations, the way in which instructions issued by an organisational hierarchy differ (psychologically and economically) from contractual exchange and the organisation's capacity for learning that means that it is more than the sum of its parts. He argues that the nexus of contracts approach is a theory as to why there are no firms rather than a theory of the firm.[23] Eisenberg points out that the nexus of contracts approach provides no basis for understanding (or taking into account) employee loyalty to the corporation and that this would undermine one of the bases on which the corporation's success rests.[24]

Williamson's theory of the firm

Williamson assumes that the firm and market-place contracting are alternative ways of organising economic activity; in essence the firm is just one type of contractual exchange. The need to economise is the decisive factor when deciding on whether to use the firm or some other type of contract to govern a particular exchange. Firms come into their own when the parties to an exchange are making a transaction-specific investment (one where the value of the asset in which one invests has a much greater value in the context of a given exchange than in any alternative context). When such an investment has been made, the fear of being cheated grows because of the loss that would follow from taking the investment and applying it to some other use. Thus, the fear that one's commercial partner will behave opportunistically becomes the dominant factor in the decision to associate in the context of the firm; the firm, and relations within it, are to be structured in such a way as to minimise the risk of loss from opportunism.[25]

Williamson's approach to corporate governance is based on the premise that, 'the relations between each constituency and the firm needs to be evaluated in contractual terms'.[26] The transaction is the basic unit of analysis and one of the principal purposes of economic organisation is to economise on the costs of transacting over time.[27] Williamson uses this framework as the basis for his discussion as to which constituencies should have their interests protected by the corporate governance contract.

---

[23] M. Eisenberg, 'The conception that the corporation is a nexus of contracts, and the dual nature of the firm', *The Journal of Corrporation Law* 24 (1998–1999), p. 832.
[24] Eisenberg, 'The conception that the corporation is a nexus of contracts'.
[25] O. Williamson, 'Transaction-cost economics: the governance of contractual relations', *Journal of Law and Economics* 22 (1979), p. 233 and 'Corporate Governance', *The Yale Law Journal* 93 (1984), p. 1197.
[26] Williamson, 'Corporate governance', p. 1198.
[27] Williamson, 'Corporate governance', p. 1201.

Ghoshal and Moran argue that markets and firms each have their own, distinctive institutional logics.[28] Markets allow for autonomous adaptation under two conditions: (1) prices must be known or be predictable (so that they can offer an effective signal to market participants; and (2) autonomous adaptation is biased towards static efficiency. The distinguishing feature of an organisation is shared purpose.[29] This allows for purposive adaptation. Shared purpose induces co-ordination. This offers the following advantages vis-à-vis markets: first, there is no need for a known price or an organised market; and second it allows organisations to pursue dynamic efficiency. Ghoshal and Moran continue:

> Because organisations' members and routines are repositories of knowledge and skills, they can have an edge over autonomous market participants in co-ordinated adaptation ... Shared purpose permits organisations to relax the binding constraint of current period efficiency and allows the organisations' members and subunits to ignore (ie not select) some allocations and select others, in ways that they could not outside the organisation.[30]

Ghoshal and Moran, with Williamson's transaction cost economics approach in mind, point out the dangers of giving aberrant behaviour too central a place in corporate governance. They argue that corporate governance systems that take opportunism for granted and make it their central concern turn into self-fulfilling prophecies; they lead to systems of hierarchical controls that emphasize monitoring and extrinsic rewards. Evidence suggests that these hierarchical controls send a signal to employees that they are not trusted or trustworthy; they decrease their sense of personal autonomy and of intrinsic motivation.[31] Ghoshal and Moran summarize their concerns thus:

> [M]anagers who pay heed to Williamson's version of TCE will be distracted from the business of generating the collective energy of their organisations and focusing it on the task of running a business. Instead, they would oversee the dissipation of their organisations' energy, or worse, they would witness it being channeled into and consumed by the efforts of each individual to protect himself or herself from colleagues. Because opportunism is difficult to distinguish *ex ante* from entrepreneurship and leadership, in an effort to control the former, they will destroy the latter.[32]

[28] Ghoshal and Moran, 'Bad for practice', pp. 32–36.
[29] Ghoshal and Moran, 'Bad for practice', p. 33.
[30] Ghoshal and Moran, 'Bad for practice', p. 34.
[31] Ghoshal and Moran, 'Bad for practice', p. 13.
[32] Ghoshal and Moran, 'Bad for practice', p. 27.

Those who propose a theory of the firm need to bear in mind that if it is taken seriously it will affect governance and management generally; it will have an impact on the moral ecology of the organisation. Ghoshal and Moran observe that by assuming the worst, Williamson's theory of the firm can bring out the worst in economic behaviour.[33] The sort of environment that the theory helps to create will attract some types of people but may drive others away. It may well have an impact on the integrity of employees and on whether or not they are able to pursue their self-realisation through their membership of the firm.

Teubner, too, emphasises that the contractual view of the firm does away with the specific advantages of corporations[34]:

> Certainly the advantages of contractual arrangements lies in the speed of reactions with which action systems can be built up and demolished in the short term, in accordance with the fluctuations of environmental pressures. The drawback, however, is that contractual solutions cannot exhaust the 'organisational surplus value.' 'Organisational surplus value' arises through (1) the building up of long-term co-operative arrangements which would be continually destroyed by contractual flexibility; (2) through the diffuseness of 'commitments' in the organisation which by comparison with rigid, sharply defined contractual obligations produces more situational flexibility; and finally (3) in the orientation towards the organisation's interest which provides stronger orientation than mere linkage to a contractual purpose.[35]

Teubner, like Ghoshal and Moran, is pointing out the damage that is done when one thinks of the corporation in purely contractual terms. The commitment to the firm's common good ('long-term co-operative arrangements'), the firm's ability to respond flexibly to new environments ('situational flexibility') and loyalty are all diminished. The theory of the firm, apparently abstract, turns out to have very great practical importance.

The stakeholder theory of the firm

Stakeholder theories focus on the mutual interdependence of the firm and other groups and argue that this interdependence ought to be reflected in corporate governance; this could be achieved through a modification of

---

[33] Ghoshal and Moran, 'Bad for practice', p. 39.
[34] G. Teubner, 'Enterprise corporatism: new industrial policy and the essence of the legal person', *American Journal of Comparative Law* 36 (1988), p. 155.
[35] Teubner, 'Enterprise Corporatism', pp. 154–155.

the duty of loyalty, by giving stakeholders a seat on the corporate board or through corporate reporting. Mallin's list of stakeholders represents the usual view:

> Stakeholders include: employees, suppliers, customers, banks, and other creditors; the government; various 'interest groups', for example, environmental groups; indeed anyone on whom the activities of the company may have an impact.[36]

Stakeholder theory might be taken as a call for firms to deal justly with the various individuals and groups that it deals with or who are in some way affected by its decisions and behaviour. No-one could object to this. If, however, stakeholder theory implies an essentially contractual view of the firm then it is open to the same objections as are levelled at the nexus of contracts approach: it discards the reality of the firm and its common good and cannot accommodate the principle of subsidiarity. This type of stakeholder theory would lack an adequate understanding of what it means to say that a human group or community has come into existence.

Does the corporation have a reality of its own that cannot be reduced entirely to the reality of its members and the contracts between them?

Does the corporation, or any other human grouping or society, have a reality or existence that is independent of its members? No-one could doubt that the corporation is brought into being by contract nor that relations within the firm are essentially governed by contract. The questions are, however, whether the corporation can be reduced to the sum of its parts (the individuals and the contracts between them) or is itself no more than a sophisticated form of contract. CST, it is contended, answers both of these questions in the negative. It attributes a reality to the corporation for reasons that are philosophically compelling, capture much more satisfactorily the experience of those of us who work in organisations and provides a generally sounder basis for thinking about corporate governance.

Contractual approaches place heavy emphasis on the will of the individual as the source of life in community. The natural law approach, by contrast, looks at the firm in the context of the flourishing of the individual. Freedom is a part of the picture but not the whole for free choices

---

[36] C. Mallin, *Corporate governance*, (2nd edn), (Oxford: Oxford University Press, 2006).

ought to be directed towards the building up of the human personality. The idea that a community has a being of its own can be said much more convincingly of the state than of the corporation since the state exists to promote flourishing in an open-ended way whilst the firm is more specialised in what it seeks to achieve and in the range of goods that it seeks to promote. Nevertheless, and bearing in mind this important difference, this chapter takes the view that what is said about the reality of the state can be said, analogously, of the corporation.

The corporation is a reality that has a being separate from that of its members. CST talks of the firm as a community of persons. It is a community that allows its participants to combine for their own individual advantage but it is also a community that unites its participants in pursuit of common goods and that allows them to develop their humanity through a sharing of goods.[37]

The corporation has a common good of its own and it cannot be understood as being simply a shorthand way of referring to its members. CST's principle of subsidiarity suggests that social groupings (such as the corporation) have a reality that is independent both of the state and of their individual members. Some major theories of the firm promote, or rest on, the view that the corporation is a pure fiction. According to the nexus of contracts view, only the individuals and the contracts between them have any reality to them.

The terms of the debate between those who think of human communities as really existing and those who deny that position have very deep roots. Fundamentally, it is possible to trace them to a revolution in moral theology that took place in the fourteenth century. Writing after St Thomas Aquinas, Ockham proposed an approach that was radically at odds with that of Aquinas. Pinckaers explains:

> With Ockham we witness the first atomic explosion of the modern era. The atom he split was obviously not physical but psychic. It was the nadir of the human soul, with its faculties, broken apart by a new concept of freedom. This produced successive after-shocks which destroyed the unity of theology and Western thought. With Ockham, freedom, by means of the claim to radical autonomy that defined it, was separated from all that was foreign to it: reason, sensibility, natural inclinations and all external factors. Further separations followed: freedom was separated

---

[37] J.-Y. Calvez and M. Naughton, 'Catholic Social Teaching and the purpose of the business firm', in S. Cortright and M. Naughton (eds.), *Rethinking the purpose of business. Interdisciplinary essays from the Catholic Social Tradition*, (Notre Dame: Indiana, University of Notre Dame Press, 2002), p. 11.

from nature, law and grace; moral doctrine from mysticism; reason from faith; the individual from society.[38]

The consequences of nominalism for moral theology were enormous, as the above extract suggests. For present purposes, it should be noted that:

> According to nominalism, only individual realities exist. They are unique in their singular existence. Universals are simply convenient labels, having no reality in themselves and only nominal value. Within the moral domain, reality lies in the individual decision of the free will.[39]

Thus, the modern view that the corporation is a pure fiction has its roots in this revolution of centuries ago. The individual reality is the employee, the shareholder, the manager. The contracts between these individuals and the firm are similarly accessible to those of a nominalist cast of mind.[40] The firm, however, according to this approach, seems to be nothing more than a mere word or something purely conceptual with no existence or reality outside of the mind. CST, by contrast, sees the firm as something that does, in some sense, have a reality of its own.

The principle of subsidiarity

The principle of subsidiarity requires the political authority, the state,[41] to leave individuals, families and intermediate associations (such as the firm) to do as much as possible for themselves. The state is to refrain from crowding out the individual and intermediate associations. This self-restraint leaves space for individuals to make their own personal contributions to the common good; it makes it more likely that society will bear a personal imprint and less likely that it will be the product of a faceless bureaucracy. In the last analysis, the principle of subsidiarity respects the fact that only freely performed actions can build up the human personality. Freedom is a necessary pre-condition for integral self-realisation.

---

[38] S. Pinckaers, O.P. *The sources of Christian ethics*, (Washington D.C.: The Catholic University of America Press, 1995), p. 242.

[39] Pinckaers, *The sources of Christian ethics*, p. 242. See also, F. Copleston SJ, *Medieval Philosophy*, (New York: Harper & Brothers, 1961), pp. 25–41.

[40] See J. Messner, *Social ethics. Natural law in the western world*, (St Louis and London, B. Herder Book Co., 1964), pp. 107–108.

[41] Nowadays it is unrealistic to think of political power as being vested in a single, all-embracing political unit since political power is now often shared (in a variety of ways) across supra-national institutions. It is, nevertheless, convenient to refer to 'the state' for the purposes of this discussion.

The principle of subsidiarity suggests that one should think in terms of clusters of mutually supportive communities. The cluster includes the family and other, more specialised, communities such as the firm. The state's role in this cluster, is to co-ordinate the activities of the individuals and lesser communities within its jurisdiction with a view to creating the social conditions that make it as likely as possible that those individuals and communities can each achieve their fulfilment. This implies, of course, that the political community has a wider responsibility than do the lesser communities and that it has a certain ability to lay down the law for individuals and lesser communities. The principle of subsidiarity would make little or no sense if the firm did not have a reality of its own. The principle assumes that intermediate associations exist and act and have a reality of their own. They are neither emanations of the state nor a fiction. The principle assumes that there are really existing lesser associations that lie between the firm and the state.

Legal personality of the corporation

Those who believe that the corporation is a fiction presumably think that the legal personality of the corporation is a matter of administrative convenience, a kind of shorthand way of referring to the individual contracting parties. If, however, one believes that the corporation has a reality of its own then the idea of legal personality takes on greater interest and importance. According to Teubner, corporate personality helps to reinforce amongst the participants in a human community the sense that they are a group as well as facilitating attribution of actions to the group.[42] Legal personality is not a necessary attribute of human groups but it is helpful. Legal personality can be thought of as an element of the firm's common good.

The UK confers separate personality on the corporation.[43] Indeed, this seems to be a feature of the corporate law of very many jurisdictions.[44] As a result, it can own property, enter into contracts, be a party to legal

---

[42] G. Teubner, 'Enterprise Corporatism: new industrial policy and the essence of the legal person', *American Journal of Comparative Law* 36 (1988), pp. 154–155.

[43] For a discussion of the point, see, for example, P. Davies, *Gower and Davies' Principles of modern Company Law*, (7th edn), (London: Sweet & Maxwell, 2003), pp. 27–30 or S. Mayson, D. French and C. Ryan, *Mayson, French & Ryan on Company Law*, (2006 – 2007 edition), pp. 155–190.

[44] H. Hansmann and R. Kraakman, 'The basic governance structure?' in *The anatomy of corporate law. A comparative and functional approach*, Reinier Kraakman *et al.*, (New York: Oxford University Press, 2004).

proceedings and so on. Although British corporate governance focuses on the needs of shareholders, British company law has expressly rejected the proposition that a corporation is to be regarded as the property of its shareholders:

> Between the investor, who participates as shareholder, and the undertaking carried on, the law interposes another person, real though artificial, the company itself, and the capital employed is its capital and not in either case the business or the capital of the shareholders ... the idea that [the company] is mere machinery for effecting the purposes of the shareholders is a layman's fallacy. It is a figure of speech which cannot alter the legal aspect.[45]

Davies, too, points out that shareholders own their shares and not the company.[46] Although British company law makes directors accountable to shareholders and seeks to make the board responsive to the interests of shareholders. It does not see the corporation as being simply the property of shareholders although shareholders are given extensive rights of control over the levers of power within the corporation.

Communities can be said, in some sense, to have a personality of their own. In some cases, such as those of the state and the corporation, the community is endowed with legal personality too. Thus, it can own property and enter into contracts. The legal personality of the corporation can be thought of as an element of its common good since it allows the corporation and its members 'relatively thorough and ready access to their own fulfilment.'[47] Teubner makes an interesting suggestion as to the role that legal personality plays in this regard. His argument is that legal personality reinforces the consciousness of the members of the corporation that they are a group (in his terms that they are 'an internal dynamics system, with selections of its own, and with a capacity for self-organisation and self-reproduction.'[48])

Legal personality is not, Teubner argues, a necessary attribute of the corporation as a social actor but it is a highly useful one that links 'legal capacity to the social capacity for collective action'.[49] Thus, legal personality and the underlying collectivity are mutually reinforcing so that

---

[45] *Gas Lighting Improvement Co. Ltd v Commissioners of Inland Revenue* [1923] AC 723 at 741 *per* Lord Sumner.
[46] P. Davies, *Introduction to Company Law*, (Oxford, Oxford University Press, 2002), p. 257.
[47] Second Vatican Council, *Gadium et spes*, para. 26.
[48] Teubner, 'Enterprise corporatism', p. 136.
[49] Teubner, 'Enterprise corporatism', p. 145.

Teubner asks: 'May not the legal person's function indeed consist in making self-reference possible and in increasing self-reference still further in the interest of organisational autonomy?'[50] The corporation as a separate person cannot be reduced to its shareholders (nor to any other group within the corporation) rather, 'the legal person is identical with the collectivity, as the personification of the enterprise.'[51].

Catholic Social Thought and the social sciences

CST is usually taken to refer to a series of papal encyclicals beginning with, and in some way consciously developing, Leo XIII's *Rerum novarum* in 1891 and to include the Second Vatican Council's Pastoral Constitution *Gaudium et spes*.[52] *Rerum novarum* looked at the social question (the problems facing employees as a result of the industrial revolution). It did so, 'so that a proper evaluation may be made in the light of the doctrinal principles founded on Revelation and on natural law and morality.'[53] CST is a branch of moral theology[54] and so its primary data are the bible and Tradition.[55] Thus, it is from these sources, from revelation, that CST derives its anthropology (its understanding of the human person). The Church is concerned about social issues because of their impact on the all-round well-being (or integral self-realisation) of each individual human person.

Philosophy, natural law theory in particular, plays a central role in understanding CST's central concepts such as the person, society, the common good, the state and subsidiarity.[56] CST's ethical appraisal of the firm is supplemented by the specialist contributions from a range of disciplines, notably economics and management. Each discipline brings its own specialised perspective to bear in a multi-disciplinary effort that CST expressly endorses.[57] CST also seeks dialogue with the human and social sciences. It seeks to learn from them but also challenges them to 'open themselves to a broader horizon aimed at serving the individual person who is acknowledged and loved in the fullness of

---

[50] Teubner, 'Enterprise corporatism', p. 148.
[51] Teubner, 'Enterprise corporatism', p. 152.
[52] See Pontifical Council for Justice and Peace, *Compendium of the Social Doctrine of the Church*, (Vatican City, Libreria Editrice Vaticana trans., 2004) (hereinafter "Compendium"), paras. 87–104 for an outline of the historical development of CST.
[53] *Compendium*, para. 89.   [54] John Paul II, *Sollicitudo rei socialis*, para. 41.
[55] *Compendium*, para. 74.   [56] *Compendium*, para. 77.
[57] John Paul II, *Sollicitudo rei socialis*, para. 1.

his or her vocation.'[58] They offer partial-yet true insights into the human person.[59]

CST's broad ethical perspective and its concern with the most fundamental questions facing the human person allow it to help direct the efforts of the human sciences and to integrate them. CST, Catholic theology in general, is committed to the concept of the unity of knowledge. CST offers especially its knowledge of the human person and of the ultimate ends of human existence. It offers this broad focus as a counterbalance to the reductionism to which the social sciences are prone:

> methodological necessity and ideological presuppositions too often lead the human sciences to isolate, in the various situations, certain aspects of man, and yet to give these an explanation which claims to be complete or at least an interpretation which is meant to be all-embracing from a purely quantitative or phenomenological point of view. This scientific reduction betrays a dangerous presupposition. To give a privileged position in this way to such aspect of analysis is to mutilate man and, under the pretext of a scientific procedure, to make it impossible to understand man in his totality.[60]

The contractual view of the corporation offers an example of this reductionism at work. Relations within the firm are, undoubtedly, contractual in nature but this does not mean that the firm is simply a collection of contracts. It is quite possible to think of the firm's governance arrangements as being both contractual and as providing a process for the formation and administration of contracts. Again, however, this is a part of the picture but not the whole. It ignores the separate operation and being of the corporation and the subtle nature of the relationship between the individual and the communities of which he or she forms part: the individual needs the community for self-realisation and building up one's communities is a component of one's self-realisation. An individual might see the sense, the intelligibility or rationality, of making sacrifices (even to the extreme of sacrificing one's life) for the sake of a community to which he belongs. The contractual view is insufficiently alert to the full human context in which the contract is formed: it does not look at the human goods that are being pursued by the participants nor at the role that the organisation plays in helping people to pursue integral self-realisation.

The problem, as *Octogesima adveniens* points out, is that social science theories often have practical implications when they inform policy. The

---

[58] John Paul II, *Centessimus annus*, para. 59.
[59] Paul VI, *Octogesima adveniens*, para. 40.   [60] Paul VI, *Octogesima adveniens*, para. 38.

theories, grounded in simplifying assumptions (about human decision-making and the nature of human societies), have an air of scientific objectivity about them. It is all too easy to forget that social science theories have to be interpreted and understood in the light of the limitations imposed by their methodology and assumptions.

Implications for employees

CST interprets social phenomena from the perspective of the integral self-realisation of the individual. When one thinks about the corporation from this perspective, the employee naturally takes centre stage. The corporation is intrinsically linked to human work; it organises work, is built up through work and makes work more productive and fulfilling.

One's theory of the firm will shape one's understanding of who belongs to the firm and of whose interests the firm exists to serve. Jacoby's comparative study of the role and importance of HR directors in Japan and the US, for example, shows how the Japanese conception of the firm as a community has practical implications for board composition (the inclusion of the HR director on the main board of Japanese listed companies) and for employees (greater commitment to security of tenure and to the use of internal labour markets).[61] Edwards' study of the impact of national corporate governance and industrial relations styles on how employees are treated in corporate restructurings also provides evidence of a positive link between corporate governance and the way that employees are treated by the firm.[62]

The theory of the firm has implications for how corporate governance and management should think of their responsibilities. Management is responsible for promoting the common good of the firm which is intimately connected to (though not identical with) the good of its individual participants. This common good has a moral and spiritual dimension even though we are talking about an organisation with an economic purpose. The firm is especially concerned with the organisation of work with a view to enhancing its productive capacity and channelling it towards meeting some range of human needs. But work is not a commodity or impersonal resource; it is one of the core goods that shape a human life,

---

[61] S. Jacoby, *The embedded corporation. Corporate governance and employment relations in Japan and the United States.*, (Princeton: Princeton University Press, 2004).

[62] T. Edwards, 'Corporate governance, industrial relations and trends in company-level restructuring in Europe: Convergence towards the Anglo-American model?' *Industrial Relations Journal* 35 (2004), p. 518.

it is profoundly personal. An appreciation that this is the case is bound to have an impact on how management think of their responsibilities and of the priority that they give to employee concerns.

Contractual views of the firm distance themselves from any consideration of the human values that are at stake in the running of the business organisation. The nexus of contracts view hollows out the whole concept of the human community or organisation. Thus, there is no room for it to accommodate CST's concepts of the common good. Williamson's contractual view of the organisation has been challenged on the basis that it makes dealing with opportunism, self-seeking with guile, the central concern of corporate governance. The focus is not on building up the firm's common good but on something that is essentially negative. Ghoshal and Moran have pointed out the baleful consequences of this approach. Opportunism is, no doubt, a problem to be addressed but it is a question of getting the right balance, of looking for realistic ways of harnessing self-interest within a more positive framework.

On the face of it, stakeholder theory provides a basis for focusing management attention on the interests of employees by diluting the emphasis on shareholder interests promoted by the nexus of contracts view, for example. If, however, a version of stakeholder theory is adopted that sees the firm as essentially contractual then, again, the concept of the common good is under threat and the idea of the firm's common good includes much that is of vital concern to employees.

Contractual approaches to the firm deny that the firm is something that really exists, with a life and operation of its own; they reduce the firm to its individual members and the contracts that they enter into. In this way, they are impoverished accounts of the relationship between the person and the community. They make it difficult to explain how organisations add value and how it is that they are able to command loyalty. Implicitly or explicitly, they focus on the need to control dishonesty and laziness rather than on the positive value to be achieved through collaboration.

6

The firm and society

Introduction

The previous chapter looked at the corporation in a certain sense in isolation from other communities. The chapter was concerned to show that the corporation (like all communities) has a reality of its own. Thus, the firm has its own ability to act and it can continue in being regardless of any change in the composition of its members. Another important concern of the previous chapter was to show that the firm is at the service of certain specialised aspects of the flourishing of its members. The firm enables its members (employees and shareholders) to pursue certain of their goals in collaboration with each other. By working together in the firm, its members can get more out of their work and their investment than they could achieve in isolation. Thus, the firm and its common good can only be understood and evaluated by considering how well it facilitates the flourishing of their members. The perspective provided in the previous chapter has now to be filled out by considering how the firm relates to the broader economy and to society at large. The previous chapter looked inward by asking about the relationship between the firm and its members. This chapter looks outward and places the firm into a broader social fabric.

Society

The previous chapter explained that a group, society or community could be said to exist when two or more individuals agree to co-ordinate their activity for the sake of achieving some common purpose. It might be sensible to go slightly further and to say that this co-ordination should be expected to last for an appreciable time span. Some natural law writers make distinctions between, say, societies and communities, but there does not seem to be any real need for present purposes to pursue this path.

Life in society is a necessity for the human person. Central to Christian anthropology is the idea that the human person is built for communion with other persons (including, and especially, communion with God). Thus, life in society is something to which we tend in any event. Finnis proposes the family as a good model of human community:

> A family can have a special unity in the order of relationships, inasmuch as each of its members (especially the one(s) directing and shaping the common life) is devoted to finding his or her own self-fulfilment (at least in part) in helping the other members to fulfil themselves, by caring for them and helping them to grow in freedom and responsibility and other basic aspects of human flourishing.[1]

Keeping the family as the model is useful, Finnis suggests, if one wants to understand the part that life in community can play in promoting integral self-realisation[2] and therefore to understand how life in community shapes one's practical reasoning.

And life in society is also of the utmost importance to us because every aspect of our own self-realisation depends on co-operation with others. We rely on the associations to which we belong (family, workplace, state, sports team and so on) because we need the help of others for survival and growth. The previous chapter dwelt on the ways in which the firm helps its participants to achieve certain aspects of their life plans. Everyone can draw on his or her own experience to think of how the other communities to which we belong (sporting, cultural or religious communities, for example) play their part in promoting our growth as persons.

Communities can be classified very broadly according to the type of contribution that they make to the promotion of integral self-realisation. Thus, one can make a division between civil and economic society. Civil society is made up of a vast range of voluntary groupings, such as sports clubs, bodies set up to promote education, health or religion, groups set up to promote some hobby or leisure pursuit or to promote some cause such as human rights or environmental protection. The essential point is that they are voluntary associations of individuals. Economic society by contrast is the community the purpose of which is to organise production with a view to meeting human needs. The firm might be thought of as having a foot in both camps and as being both an element of civil society and a participant in economic society.[3]

---

[1] J. Finnis, *Natural law and natural rights*, (Oxford: Oxford University Press, 2003), p. 138.
[2] Finnis, *Natural law and natural rights*, p. 141.
[3] See R. Charles, S.J., *An introduction to Catholic Social Teaching*, (Oxford: Family Publications, 1999). The whole of this work seeks to explain the idea of society and of the distinction between civil, economic and civil society.

Civil society and economic society each have their own specialised contribution to make to integral self-realisation while the family and political society are more open-ended and can be said to be necessary in a way that groups forming part of civil or economic society are not. The latter (groups forming part of economic and civil society) are 'intermediate groups'; they are intermediate groups since they stand in a sort of hierarchy between the individual and family on the one hand and the state on the other. Intermediate groups have some specialised contribution to make to integral self-realisation.

There is a need, however, to belong to a society that, in principle, can take responsibility for promoting integral self-realisation in an open-ended way and this is the political community:

> [T]here emerges the desirability of a "complete community", an all-round association in which would be co-ordinated the initiatives and activities of individuals, of families and of the vast network of intermediate associations. The point of this all-round association would be to secure the whole ensemble of material and other conditions, including forms of collaboration, that tend to favour, facilitate and foster the realisation by each individual of his or her political development.[4]

Political society, then, exists to promote human flourishing in an open-ended way. Society's common good is open-ended in that there is no limit in principle to the scope of its commitment to the promotion of human flourishing. Political society has its own common good in that it has an apparatus of government, a system of law and regulation and control over a range of facilities that can be of use to its citizens.

The political society exists principally to co-ordinate the activities of the individuals and intermediate groups that belong to it. It is these individuals and intermediate groups that are in the front line. Only when intermediate groups leave some important human need unmet might the state intervene. Its aim should be to goad individuals into action and into creating new intermediate groups to meet the need. Only when that cannot be done effectively should the state take direct responsibility. There may of course be special cases (of which policing and defence are the obvious examples) which should be reserved to the state. There are now many creative examples of helpful partnerships between the state and intermediate groups.

The political society draws on the energy and initiative of individuals and of intermediate associations to achieve its own purpose (facilitating the human flourishing of its members). Political society meets the clear

---

[4] Finnis, *Natural law and natural rights*, p. 147.

need for some community that will complement and co-ordinate the specialised contributions made by individuals and intermediate associations. Aquinas thought of organised governments as natural societies; since 'they are necessary for the fulfilment of men's natural needs and for the leading of a full human life.'[5] The state, the political or law-making body in society is responsible for building up society's common good and is endowed with the authority (and the coercive power) it needs to perform this overarching function.

The common good of society, then, should be built up by its members with the state exercising some oversight. For example, schools and universities are intermediate organisations committed to the good of knowledge (learning and research). The firm provides and co-ordinates work and channels it towards the provision of specific goods or services; it provides useful work for capital to accomplish. These private goods of the school, university or firm are so many contributions to the common good of society. Thus, a society's common good is a reflection of the personality of the very many individuals and groups who form part of it. The efforts of previous generations are built upon by those who follow. Society and its common good are personal because they reflect and gather together the personalities of individuals and groups. Society is also personal because it does not exist to serve itself or some abstract ideal but, rather, to serve its citizens.

Catholic Social Thought and corporate social responsibility

The concept of corporate social responsibility, broadly speaking, is that corporations have a responsibility to society at large and not merely to shareholders. Carroll puts it this way:

> For a definition of social responsibility to fully address the entire range of obligations business has to society, it must embody the economic, legal, ethical and discretionary obligations of business performance.[6]

Barnard and Deakin argue that the corporate social responsibility movement has the potential to humanise the shareholder value concept (explained in chapter eight) and to move it in the direction of ensuring greater corporate accountability on social and environmental issues.[7]

[5] F. Copleston, *Medieval philosophy*, (New York: Harper Brothers, 1961), pp. 168–169.
[6] A. Carroll, 'A three-dimensional conceptual model of corporate performance', *The Academy of Management Review* 4 (1979), p. 499.
[7] C. Barnard and S. Deakin, 'Corporate governance, social policy and the single market', *Industrial Relations Journal* 33 (2002), p. 497.

THE FIRM AND SOCIETY

Corporate social responsibility has its critics. Milton Friedman said:

> In a free enterprise, private-property system, a corporate executive is an
> employee of the owners of the business. He has direct responsibility to
> his employers. That responsibility is to conduct the business in accord-
> ance with their desires which generally will be to make as much money
> as possible while conforming to their basic rules of society, both those
> embodied in law and those embodied in ethical custom.[8]

His central point, indeed the title of his article, is that the social responsibility of business is to make a profit. He contrasts this view with what he
regards as the contrary and erroneous view that corporations have a more
general social responsibility to help promote important political goals in
the relevant society. This he regarded as 'pure and unadulterated socialism'. He suggests that the arguments of the corporate social responsibility
camp lack rigour.

The last chapter argued that the board of directors and senior management and the whole of the corporation's governance and managerial
systems are principally at the service of employees and shareholders. In
the next chapter it will be argued that profit is a useful indicator of the
effectiveness of a business and that it is meeting genuine needs but that
it cannot be the sole criterion since a firm might pursue profit in grossly
immoral ways. The closing words of the above extract from Friedman are
an acknowledgement that this is true. It will be appropriate in this chapter to consider briefly whether there are sound reasons for thinking that
businesses do have a social responsibility.

One reason for thinking so is that the individual participants in the
enterprise undoubtedly do have a moral responsibility to contribute to the
common good of the societies to which they belong. Many would consider
it a privilege to have the opportunity to do so. It would be strange if the
firm, which is an extension of the personality of its individual members,
did not also have an ethical duty to make some contribution to the common good of the community or communities in which it is embedded. In
normal times, it will probably make this contribution just by going about
its normal business. But there is no reason in principle to exclude the possibility that in some situations it would be reasonable to expect more of it.
Argandona explains:

> [T]he common good extends beyond the confines of the company. If
> the common good comes from human sociability, all the company's

[8] M. Friedman, 'The social responsibility of business is to increase its profits.' *The New York
Times Magazine*, 13th September 1970.

relationships will carry an element of the common good. We therefore
have to extend the list of stakeholders to include customers and suppliers,
banks and unions, the local community, the authorities (at different
levels), interest groups, competitors and so on, until it encompasses all
men of all times, by virtue of the unity of the human family.[9]

Mele explains that the firm contributes to the common good of society
in a variety of ways: through the products or services it offers; through
the work carried on within it; through its culture and leadership and by
creating channels for investment.[10] Novak makes the point that multinational corporations often make valuable contributions to the host states
in which they operate.[11]

CST's view of human groups and the common good provide the solid
foundation that theories of corporate social responsibility so often seem
to lack. Corporate social responsibility springs naturally from the organic
connection between intermediate associations and the broader civil, economic and political societies. It is not to be explained as a result of some
kind of bargain under the terms of which, for example, the state confers
certain privileges on the corporation (such as limited liability) in return
for a commitment to promote political goals of the state.[12] Further, the
social responsibility of the corporation can be seen as an extension of the
social responsibility of its individual participants. Collaboration in the
firm also enriches the ways in which its individual participants can contribute to the well-being of society at large.

Some employee participation advocates invoke the idea of corporate
social responsibility as the basis for putting the employee at the heart of
corporate governance. It should be clear from this chapter and the previous chapter that the corporation does indeed perform its social function by focusing on the needs of its employees and shareholders. To this
extent, the concept of corporate social responsibility is relevant. It is misleading, however, if it conveys the impression that management's core

[9] A. Argandona, 'The stakeholder theory and the common good', *Journal of Business Ethics* 17 (1998), pp. 1093–1102.
[10] D. Mele, 'Not only stakeholder interests. The firm oriented towards the common good', in S. Cortright and M. Naughton (eds.), *Rethinking the purpose of business: Interdisciplinary essays from the Catholic Social Tradition*, (Notre Dame, Indiana: University of Notre Dame Press, 2002), p. 194.
[11] M. Novak, *Toward a theology of the corporation*, (Washington, The AEI Press, 1990), p. 42.
[12] This view is taken by, for example, J. Parkinson, 'Models of the company and the employment relationship', *British Journal of Industrial Relations* 41 (2003), pp. 481–509. Parkinson explains the company-as-social-institution idea on this basis.

responsibility is to shareholders and that it has a less intense, discretionary duty to employees.

Society as an interconnected system

CST puts the case for the reasonableness of corporate social responsibility another way. It conceives of society as being made up of a collection of human communities that are interconnected. For working purposes, most of us focus our attention on the small number of communities with which we engage most intensely. Typically these will include our family, working community, perhaps a religious, sporting or cultural group and our country and our friendships. Further, we tend to focus on these communities one at a time. So, as in this book, we sometimes focus on our relationship with our employer. At other times, we think of our relationship with the state (perhaps because we are due to vote or pay our taxes). Although this approach is natural and useful the effect is that we think of communities as being more or less isolated from each other. We also tend to think of a fairly simple public / private or state / individual dichotomy.[13]

CST, by contrast, thinks of the political authority and the individuals and groups that it is responsible for as being engaged in a collaborative effort to ensure that by working together they build up society's common good and meet all genuine human needs. Lutz points out that Christian social thought sees corporate management as having a responsibility both for the limited common good of the corporation and for ensuring that the corporation makes its contribution to the common good of the economy as a whole.[14] Even the notion of competitive markets should reflect this concept. Competitive markets should be thought of as a way of allowing firms in a given sector to work together to improve the lot of consumers or clients by spurring each other on to greater efforts; competition is a

---

[13] See L. Harrington, 'Ethics and public policy analysis: Stakeholders' interests and regulatory policy', *Journal of Business Ethics* 15 (1996), pp. 373–383 for a critique of this false dichotomy and an argument that there is no sharp public /private divide but rather a public – private continuum with a grouping's place on the continuum being determined on the breadth and nature of its common good. For the contrary view, drawing a rigid public / private distinction see I. Lynch Fannon, *Working within two kinds of capitalism. Corporate governance and employee stakeholding. US and EC perspectives*, (Oxford: Hart Publishing, 2003).

[14] D. Lutz, 'Christian social thought and corporate governance', in R. Kennedy (ed.), *Religion and public life*, (Lanham, Md., University Press of America, 2001), pp. 125–126.

cum petere (a collaborative search for the best way of serving customers or clients). The idea of competition as having an element of hostility is an aberration.

Globalisation and political authority

Nowadays, firms and market activity are no longer confined by national or regional boundaries. Individuals, firms and other intermediate associations often have transnational (even global) interests and ambitions. The need for a corresponding global vision of the common good and of the political order is obvious. Kofi Annan put the point this way:

> State sovereignty, in its most basic sense, is being redefined – not least by the forces of globalisation and international co-operation.[15]

This has been a theme of CST since the early 1960s[16]. In *Caritas in veritate*, Benedict XVI noted that the new context of international trade and finance imposes limitations on state sovereignty. This has provoked a re-evaluation of the role of public authorities that could be beneficial in the long term since it could allow organisations forming part of civil society to participate in the political life of society.[17]

CST invites us to think of 'society' in broad terms and as encompassing, at least in principle, a global community oriented towards the integral human development of each and every person. Communities of all shapes and sizes take their place in a fabric or system of interconnected vessels. Political authority need not be concentrated in discrete national clusters, nor need it be concentrated in just one body but could be distributed in a variety of ways.

The need for suitably global political institutions is obvious but designing them and bringing them into being is one of the most pressing and difficult challenges facing us today.[18] Our understanding of the common good has to take on a more universal scope.[19] At the same time, it can be argued that the notion of the common good has new relevance in an age

---

[15] K. Annan, 'Two concepts of sovereignty', *The Economist* (18th September 1999), p. 49.
[16] Paul VI, *Populorum progressio* (available at www.vatican.va/holy_father/paul_vi/ encyclicals/documents/hf_p-vi_enc_26031967_populorum_en.html, last accessed on 25th July 2009).
[17] Benedict XVI, *Caritas in veritate*, para. 24.
[18] D. Hollenbach S.J., *The common good and Christian ethics*, (Cambridge, Cambridge University Press, 2002), p. 220.
[19] Hollenbach, *The common good and Christian ethics*, p. 212.

THE FIRM AND SOCIETY

when states (as conceived for the past few centuries) become less able to go it alone.[20]

Subsidiarity and globalisation

In *Quadragesimo anno*, Pius XI formulated the principle of subsidiarity in the following terms:

> Just as it is gravely wrong to take from individuals what they can accomplish by their own initiative and industry and give it to the community, so also it is an injustice and at the same time a grave evil and disturbance of right order to assign to a greater and higher power what lesser and subordinate organisations can do. For every social activity ought of its very nature to furnish help to the members of the body social, and never destroy and absorb them.[21]

This reflects the idea of society as a system of interconnected and interdependent people and organisations working together in a spirit of friendship to achieve common aims. It also has an element of 'power to the people'. Decision-making should come as close to the individual as possible. This will allow individuals an element of control over their own lives compatible with human dignity. It will create opportunities for individuals to make a contribution to the common good.[22] It also makes for operational efficiency for, as *Quadragesimo anno* goes on to say, the state will be overwhelmed if it tries to do too much itself.[23] Carozza suggests that subsidiarity 'purports to affirm a universal common good while still requiring ample room for pluralism in the concrete determination and application of that good.'[24] Carozza's insight is certainly relevant to the question of employee participation.

As chapter 10 will show, the EU has worked hard to find a way for corporations established in any member state to operate throughout Europe without the need to establish a multitude of new corporations as they set up a stable presence in member states other than that in which they

---

[20] Hollenbach, *The common good and Christian ethics*, p. 231.
[21] Pius XI, *Quadragesimo anno*, para. 79.
[22] L. Tavis, 'Modern contract theory and the purpose of the firm', in S. Cortright and M. Naughton (eds.), *Rethinking the purpose of business: Interdisciplinary essays from the Catholic Social Tradition*, (Notre Dame, Indiana: University of Notre Dame Press, 2002), pp. 215–236.
[23] Pius XI, *Quadragesimo anno*, para. 80.
[24] P. Carozza, 'Subsidiarity as a structural principle of international human rights law', *American Journal of International Law* 97 (2003), pp. 68–69.

were first incorporated. It has also created the European Company as a legal structure that businesses can adopt . In doing so, the EU has had to struggle with the question of the impact of greater freedom of movement on existing employee participation structures in some member states. Keller argues that the result is that we are witnessing new modes of regulation with flexibility, voluntarism and subsidiarity to the fore. According to Keller, the European Company reflects a shift towards 'negotiated Europeanisation'. He predicts that the upshot will be the emergence of a variety of voluntaristic, tailor-made, enterprise-specific rules.[25]

The principle of subsidiarity is relevant in many contexts; within the firm, within the state and in the context of supranational governance structures. McCann describes it as a protean statement of CST's understanding of the right ordering of relationships among the various institutions that constitute society. He argues that it is best understood from a theological perspective in that all social relationships have Trinitarian traces. Subsidiarity assumes that people are inherently social and, in the context of the firm, implies a participatory management style.[26] Fort talks of 'mediating institutions':

> The hallmark of a mediating institution is the notion of community. It is a relatively small place in which we meet others face-to-face and thereby learn the direct consequences of our actions on them. We form our identities, develop our affections, and internalise our responsibilities. In short, we acquire the anchor of that expanding chain of solidarity of which [John Paul II] speaks when we collaborate in communal shared tasks.[27]

Fort argues that the corporation should function as a mediating institution, a community that is closer to the individual than is the political authority and that gives scope for individuals to make choices, act and accept responsibility. As a mediating institution, the corporation could open up the way for its participants to get involved in the life of the broader civil and political societies. Lutz, too, applies the principle of subsidiarity to the corporation:

---

[25] B. Keller, 'The European Company statute: Employee involvement and beyond', *Industrial Relations Journal* 33 (2002), pp. 424–445.

[26] D. McCann, 'Business corporations and the principle of subsidiarity', in S. Cortright and M. Naughton (eds.), *Rethinking the purpose of business: Interdisciplinary essays from the Catholic Social Tradition*, (Notre Dame, Indiana: University of Notre Dame Press, 2002), pp. 169–189.

[27] T. Fort, 'Business as a mediating institution', in S. Cortright and M. Naughton (eds.), *Rethinking the purpose of business: Interdisciplinary essays from the Catholic Social Tradition*, (Notre Dame, Indiana: University of Notre Dame Press, 2002), p. 253.

> Christian social thought ... views the subject of corporate governance
> within the context of a broader social philosophy that places a primary
> emphasis upon the multiple roles and contributions of the vast array of
> intermediary economic bodies that contribute to the economic good of
> society as a whole.[28]

Corporations and other intermediate bodies play an important part in
meeting human needs without being subsumed within the state.

There is a practical need for an effective political authority that is capable of directing the global economy. Hollenbach suggests that:

> An accountable form of governance in our world will have to be multi-
> layered, including formal governmental bodies on local, regional, and
> international levels, but also composed of intergovernmental regimes in
> which civil society-based NGOs play a key role.[29]

Quite clearly, globalisation means that the composition and method
of operation of the political authority has to adapt to face the new
challenges.

CST has, of course, no business in trying to suggest the model that
should be followed. Clearly, however, respect for the principle of subsidiarity will become more important in the modern era; the global political
order will have to draw on the efforts of nations and regional groupings,
transnational firms and other bodies equipped to handle the scale and
complexity of the issues that require co-ordination on a global scale.
Corporate social responsibility takes on even greater importance in this
new globalised order. Multinational corporations have the capability and
the power to make an enormous contribution to the promotion of the
common good in its emerging global sense.

The state and markets

Some suggest that it is reasonable to leave it to market mechanisms to deal
with the governance of economic life. Properly functioning markets seem
to them to be the key to ensuring that, so far as possible, scarce resources
are allocated to socially desirable uses. Governments should, it is argued,
concentrate on removing impediments to the efficient functioning of
market mechanisms. To what extent should the political authority adopt
a *laissez faire* approach?

[28] Lutz, 'Christian social thought and corporate governance', p. 126.
[29] Hollenbach, *The common good and Christian ethics*, p. 241.

The relationship between the political order and markets is a very deli-
cate one. In the last analysis, the state is responsible for trying to ensure
that economic activity serves the common good. There are a number of
factors in favour of self-restraint by the state. Markets allocate resources
according to the law of supply and demand and this usually results in
their efficient allocation. Reliance on markets as opposed to regulation
or commands from on high makes it easier for an economy to respond
to shocks or new circumstances and opportunities. The principle of subsidiarity suggests that the state should foster the ability of individuals and
intermediate associations to take decisions for themselves; markets are
mechanisms that facilitate this process. Further, markets reward initiative
and an entrepreneur's ability to organise things and to foresee consumer
demands; they facilitate the exercise of the right of economic initiative.

A tendency to rely on the market, on contractual exchange, is entirely
consistent with the idea of the economy as being at the service of the
human person. This tendency should not, however, be pursued thought-
lessly or with a blind faith that markets will inevitably be consistent with
the common good. Markets lack any inbuilt mechanism to ensure that
they are consistently ordered towards the goal of integral self-realisation.
Thus, they cannot be relied on to give adequate attention to the basic
material needs of those who cannot afford to pay. They have no means
of discriminating between consumer preferences that are consistent with
integral self-realisation and those that are not. The business of an assassin
whose services were available to the highest bidder might be very profitable but it would also be immoral; the same could be said of the business
of a drug-dealer or the business conducted in a brothel.

Markets have no mechanism that would ensure a just distribution of
material resources. Only people with access to the necessary material
resources can participate in markets and very many are excluded from
them. The market has, therefore, to be subjected to rules and regulations
and to a moral code that will supply these deficiencies.

The state and labour markets

CST has always been particularly concerned about the need to regulate the labour market and to establish a set of ethical guidelines for the
relationship between capital and labour. The social question that was
the catalyst for *Rerum novarum* was the inhumane treatment of working people at the hands of their employers. Left to its own devices, capitalism can result in the exploitation of workers. In *Laborem exercens*,

John Paul II noted that workers in the late nineteenth century were frequently exploited by entrepreneurs driven by the principle of the pursuit of maximum profit. Even today, we think in terms of a conflict between capital and labour. The Church, by contrast, proposes the principle of the priority of labour over capital. Work, as we have seen, helps the human person to grow; it has to be understood in terms of personal as well as economic values. Capital (technology, the means of production) is a result of human work and is intended to facilitate and serve it. The fully human view of the meaning of work is threatened by the economistic view that sees human work in exclusively economic terms.[30]

Structures are not enough

Ingenious governance structures are not enough. Good governance depends on the personal qualities and effort both of those in charge of governance and of every member of the relevant community. CST speaks of a virtue of solidarity:

> [Solidarity] is a firm and persevering determination to commit oneself to the common good. That is to say to the good of all and of each individual, because we are all really responsible for all.[31]

The idea that everyone takes responsibility for the common good is entirely in line with CST's calls for the personal character of society and the common good to be protected and enhanced. So far as governance and management are concerned, great skill will be needed to create structures that make it possible for everyone to make a contribution and to give people the relevant knowledge and skills. The education system and the entire culture of the community will need to foster a desire to make an intelligent commitment to playing some part in public life. Kennedy suggests that businesses can practice solidarity by consciously thinking in terms of their contribution to the common good.[32]

---

[30] John Paul II, *Laborem exercens*, para. 13.
[31] John Paul II, *Sollicitudo rei socialis*, para. 38.
[32] R. Kennedy, 'The virtue of solidarity and the purpose of the firm', in S. Cortright and M. Naughton (eds.), *Rethinking the purpose of business: Interdisciplinary essays from the Catholic Social Tradition*, (Notre Dame, Indiana, University of Notre Dame Press, 2002), pp. 61–62.

7

Employee participation in corporate governance: an ethical analysis

Introduction

This chapter outlines the ethical case put forward by Catholic Social Thought ('CST') for giving employees a role in corporate governance and some type of ownership interest in the corporations that they work for. The first section provides some definitions of corporate governance and considers the ethical significance of a corporate governance system and the impact on employees of the theory of the firm (and accompanying approach to corporate governance) that is adopted. The following section offers a definition of employee participation and explains its ethical and economic advantages. It outlines the German system and explains that co-determination has never taken root in the United Kingdom. This section concludes with a brief explanation of some alternatives to co-determination as ways of building employee interests into corporate governance. The third section looks at the question of employee ownership. Again, it notes the ethical and the economic arguments in favour of employee ownership. ESOPs are one possible way forward and they can have a significant impact on employees and on corporate governance. Badly designed forms of employee ownership could harm both the firm and its employees. The article gives some indications as to why this is so. It assumes, nevertheless, that these problems can be surmounted or avoided. The governance structure of the John Lewis Partnership plc is explained in some detail and is offered as a possible model for employee-owned businesses. Finally, the article will look at the case for the introduction of mandatory co-determination systems.

Corporate governance

One of the best-known definitions of corporate governance is to be found in the Report of the Committee on the Financial Aspects of Corporate Governance:

Corporate governance is the system by which companies are directed and controlled. Boards of directors are responsible for the governance of their companies. The shareholders' role in governance is to appoint the directors and the auditors and to satisfy themselves that an appropriate governance structure is in place. The responsibilities of the board include setting the company's strategic aims, providing the leadership to put them into effect, supervising the management of the business and reporting to shareholders on their stewardship. The board's actions are subject to laws, regulations and the shareholders in general meeting.[1]

'Corporate governance', then, as it is usually explained and understood now, refers to the system for setting policy at the highest level, establishing and monitoring management processes and establishing systems of risk control.

The corporation, as is true of any human community of any size, needs a system of governance. 'Corporate governance' describes the system answering the need for a 'political' authority in the corporate community. It identifies the corporation's decision-making bodies and how they interact with each other. It allows the members of the corporation to act collectively. Corporate governance includes arrangements for deciding on the composition of the board, the groups or persons to whom it is accountable and the criteria to be applied when assessing the board's performance.

The Cadbury report definition of corporate governance suggests that it is a system dominated by the board and shareholders: the board administers the corporate governance system and accounts to shareholders for its stewardship of that system (implicitly because the system is managed on behalf of shareholders). It seems from this definition that employees have no role to play in corporate governance and that they have a subordinate claim (or no claim at all) on the board's attention. This is in line with the current orthodoxy that sees the shareholders as being, in practical terms, the owners of the corporation.

There are other explanations as to the nature of corporate governance. Gospel and Pendleton suggest that corporate governance essentially deals with the relationship between capital, management and labour.[2] They say

---

[1] *The Report of the Committee on the Financial Aspects of Corporate Governance*, ('the Cadbury report') (1992), para. 2.5.

[2] H. Gospel and A. Pendleton, 'Corporate governance and labour management: an international comparison', in H. Gospel and A. Pendleton (eds.), *Corporate governance and labour management: an international comparison*, (Oxford: Oxford University Press, 2005), pp. 4–5.

that 'corporate governance is concerned with who controls the firm, in whose interest the firm is governed and the various ways whereby control is exercised.'[3] Kay and Silberston suggest a 'trusteeship' model of corporate governance that emphasises 'the evolutionary development of the corporation around its core skills and activities'.[4] Corporate governance, on this view, aims to build up the corporation so that it is better able to carry out its core activities. To a large extent, their theory of the firm suggests, this will involve refining the structures, routines and organisational structures that are at the heart of the corporation. They also argue that governance involves preserving and enhancing the value of corporate assets and balancing fairly the various claims on the returns generated by those assets.[5] There is much good sense in this explanation of the firm. It emphasises the dynamic aspects of the life of the corporation but also that it has an inner core that should not be lightly gambled away and that decisions affecting it are not exclusively to be considered in terms of the impact on shareholders.

Corporate governance is about finance, about the relationship between employees, shareholders and management and about the evolutionary development of the core skills and activities of the corporation. It is also about ensuring that the corporation plays its part as a responsible citizen. In other words, corporate governance has to deal with all of the aspects of the life of the corporation even though, in some contexts, it may be appropriate to highlight one or other of these aspects (such as shareholder relations).

A natural law approach to thinking about the corporation can help to integrate partial insights into the nature of the firm. It also emphasizes that corporate governance, like any other social reality, should be appraised in terms of human flourishing. A natural law approach to the firm reminds us that the principal question is whether corporate governance makes it easier for the corporation to meet the genuine human needs of clients or customers and, in doing so, makes it easier for employees, shareholders and management to fulfill themselves as human persons. It also asks whether the corporation plays the part it should as an element of the broader fabric of economic and social communities.

[3] H. Gospel and A. Pendleton, 'Finance, corporate governance and the management of labour', *British Journal of Industrial Relations* 41 (2003), p. 560.
[4] J. Kay and A. Silberston, 'Corporate governance' in F. Macmillan Patfield (ed.), *Perspectives on Company Law: 2*, (London: Kluwer Law International, 1997), p. 61.
[5] Kay and Silberston, 'Corporate governance', p. 61.

CST sees the firm as a community of persons. At the heart of the firm is the relationship between its participants (its employees and shareholders). The firm allows them to combine to produce goods or services in ways that would not have been available to each participant as an individual acting alone. Thus, the firm allows its employees to meet a range of needs. It provides a salary and an opportunity to use and develop skills. Many people probably find that their work offers them their greatest opportunity to contribute to the development of society. Shareholders find in the firm an opportunity to put their capital to productive use and to get a return on it. A community's governance is intended to help it achieve its goals; in the end, the community's collective goal is oriented towards helping its members to meet the needs that brought them to the community. The profound link between the good of the firm and the flourishing of its participants is what brings corporate governance into the ethical or moral sphere.

It is obvious that human communities, other than the very smallest, need some formal mechanism to co-ordinate the activities of their participants and to focus them effectively on whatever it is that the community seeks to achieve. Those in charge of governance have a responsibility to work to build up the community's common good. Drawing on the initiative and resources of the governed, they have to develop the infrastructure that will allow the community to achieve its goals more easily and fully. The corporation shares this need. Some person or body has to take responsibility for this task. Otherwise, the firm cannot perform its essential function of enabling its participants to do much more by working together than they could achieve alone. The firm seeks to add value to human work and effective governance is indispensable if this goal is to be achieved. Those in charge of governance have to decide on the projects to be pursued, organise employees and secure the necessary financial and other resources. They have to develop the productive capacity of the corporation and its ability to meet the needs of its customers or clients. Governance arrangements will need to establish who is to take decisions within the firm and who has the authority (and in which circumstances) to act in the name of the firm as a whole. 'Corporate governance' describes the system answering the need for a political authority in the corporate community. It identifies the corporation's decision-making bodies and how they interact with each other. It allows the members of the corporation to act collectively.

From this view of the nature of the firm it follows fairly naturally that employee welfare should be a paramount concern of corporate governance.

Argandona explains that the company's purpose is to enable its members to achieve their personal goals.[6]

It is clear that CST's approach (founded on Christian anthropology and its own principles and values) is markedly different from that of much contemporary corporate governance scholarship (what one may call 'the mainstream'). The latter often looks at economic activity from a materialistic perspective. It tends not to think in terms of human flourishing and of the significance of membership of the firm for its participants; it often has a utilitarian underpinning that consciously rejects any emphasis on goods that are fulfilling for human persons. Implicitly, at least, the mainstream view sees human work (and the worker) as inputs or raw material. Work and the worker rank alongside financial and material resources in terms of importance with special respect being accorded to financial returns. Employee welfare is relevant to corporate governance in the sense that it is a means to an end, in the same way that keeping hens happy might be thought of as leading to more and bigger eggs. Employee welfare, according to this view, is a legitimate concern of corporate governance only to the extent that it enhances profitability. That labour is at the service of capital seems self-evident and this 'axiom' creates a very high burden of proof for those who would want to see employee welfare as a central theme of corporate governance. The concept of shareholder value is an expression of the belief that the corporation is principally a tool to meet the needs of shareholders. CST would suggest that employee value is an equally important concept to develop.

CST sees the economistic mindset (the view that labour is an immaterial commodity) as the ultimate source of practices that degrade the worker.[7] CST comes into its own when it engages with this world-view. Indeed, the idea that the firm exists only to make a profit has not only an ethical but also a religious dimension. Usually implicitly, it suggests a mechanistic conception of the world and a belief that the market is self-governing. The idea of the invisible hand is highly suggestive of a deistic conception of God as a watch-maker who sets the wheels in motion and then withdraws.

[6] A. Argandona, 'The stakeholder theory and the common good', *Journal of Business Ethics* 17 (1998), p. 1097.
[7] John Paul II, *Laborem exercens*, paras. 7 and 11–14.

Agency theory

The work of the board of directors, and any discussion of corporate governance, is shaped partly by the theory of the firm that is adopted. A natural law approach to social ethics emphasises that the corporation has a reality of its own, that it is part of social, economic and political communities that have a more wide-ranging commitment to human flourishing and that it is at the service of its customers or clients as well as of its employees and shareholders. Corporate governance has to help the corporation to meet these objectives and cannot be understood by focusing on just one of these objectives or a sub-set of them.

Contemporary corporate governance has become very preoccupied with the agency problem: agency theory highlights the danger that the directors will abuse their power over the corporation and divert corporate assets to themselves (directly or indirectly). In particular, directors are described as the agents of shareholders (rather than of the corporation). Agency theory emphasises the need for company law and corporate governance to provide shareholders with adequate protection against the risk of expropriation by directors.[8] British company law and corporate governance have developed a range of tools to try to counter this concern.

There is no doubt that the danger is real. The question is whether dealing with it has been allowed to skew corporate governance and to focus excessive attention on one aspect of one relationship within the corporation (the shareholder – director relationship). Some suggest plausibly that the danger is over-stated because directors are motivated by factors such as a desire to do a good job, to be respected and by a sense of professionalism.[9] Others go further and suggest that building corporate governance around agency theory will amount to a self-fulfilling prophecy and create a low-trust environment in which opportunistic behaviour will become the norm.[10] Gospel and Pendleton criticize the agency

---

[8] See, for example, M. Jensen and W. Meckling, 'Theory of the firm: Managerial behaviour, agency Costs and ownership structure'. *Journal of Financial Economics* 3 (1976), pp 305–360.

[9] See, for example, the critique in L. Donaldson, 'The ethereal hand: Organisational economics and management theory', *The Academy of Management Review* 15 (1990), pp. 369–381.

[10] S. Ghoshal and P. Moran, 'Bad for practice: A critique of the transaction cost theory', *The Academy of Management Review* 21 (1996), pp. 13–47 and J. Roberts, 'Trust and control in Anglo-American systems of corporate governance: the individualizing and socializing effects of processes of accountability', *Human Relations* 54 (2001), pp. 1547–1572.

model for its reductionist exclusion of actors other than managers and shareholders.[11]

Concern over the agency problem has spilled over into thinking about employee participation. It has been argued that shareholders are vulnerable to exploitation by directors. This is clearly also true of employees but it is further argued that employees can protect themselves through carefully drawn contracts while shareholders cannot.[12] Some point to the German co-determination system to show that management is able to play shareholder and employee representatives on the supervisory board off against each other. As a result, it is argued, they loosen the system of monitoring and accountability that minority shareholders depend on.[13]

On the other hand, it can be argued that employees cannot usually protect themselves contractually against loss of their human capital investment in the firm and so they are as vulnerable as shareholders;[14] experience and common sense tend to confirm this view. Agency theorists see monitoring of executives as an important role of non-executives yet, as Jacoby points out, outsiders may not be well-placed to make an effective contribution to governance.[15] In principle, employees are likely to be more expert and more keenly interested monitors of senior management. If one accepts that this is true, the challenge is to design governance systems that will, at the same time, allow employees and shareholders to contribute appropriately to governance, allow for strong and decisive management of the corporation and make management accountable to both employees and shareholders.

Corporate governance and employee interests

Gospel and Pendleton suggest that corporate governance deals with the relationship between capital, management and labour.[16] This is a realistic way of thinking about corporate governance: it is impossible to understand

[11] Gospel and Pendleton, 'Finance, corporate governance and the management of labour', p. 560.
[12] O. Williamson, 'Corporate Governance', *The Yale Law Journal* 93 (1984), pp. 1197–1230.
[13] K. Pistor, 'Codetermination: A socio-political model with governance externalities', in M. Roe and M. Blair (eds.), *Employees and corporate governance* (Washington DC: Brookings Institution Press, 1999).
[14] R. Howse and M. Trebilcock, 'Protecting the employment bargain', *University of Toronto Law Journal* 43 (1993), pp. 751–792.
[15] S. Jacoby, *The embedded corporation*, (Princeton, NJ: Princeton University Press, 2004), pp. 162–163.
[16] Gospel and Pendleton, 'Corporate governance and labour management: an international comparison', pp. 4–5.

the central purpose of the firm, and to think about how it adds value, without bringing employees into the picture. Clearly, employee interests cannot be well-served if corporate governance is reduced to a conversation between management and capital. As Jacoby has shown, employee participation in corporate governance can make a radical difference to how employees are treated by the firm.[17]

Jacoby's comparative study of the role and importance of HR directors in Japan and the US shows how the Japanese conception of the firm as a community has practical implications for board composition (the inclusion of the HR director on the main board of Japanese listed companies) and for employees (greater commitment to security of tenure and to the use of internal labour markets).[18] Edwards' study of the impact of national corporate governance and industrial relations styles on how employees are treated in corporate restructurings also provides evidence of a positive link between corporate governance and the way that employees are treated by the firm.[19] More broadly, it is hard to believe that anyone can benefit in the long term from a skewed vision of the firm and of the goals that corporate governance ought to serve.

Lord Wedderburn of Charlton explored the link between the British view of the corporation and the difficulty in finding a place for employee participation in British corporate governance:

> [T]he interests of the employee find little solace in our company law as it has been developed since the repeal of the Bubble Act in 1825. The status of the shareholder and the nature of the share were anchored by the common law firmly into an individualist ideology of proprietorship which ran with the grain of society and especially with the capital market of the day. The shareholder's property in his share and the 'interests of the company' as the shareholders interests alone, became pillars of the modern law with no plurality of other interests acknowledged (such as those of the employees) ... In England, the company law developments did nothing to assuage, and something to sharpen, hierarchic structures of authority. Modern company legislation in Britain has barely addressed these social dimensions of the law, and the next Companies Bill is likely to concentrate on deregulating private companies, not making a contribution to consensus.[20]

---

[17] Jacoby, *The embedded corporation.*   [18] Jacoby, *The embedded corporation.*
[19] T. Edwards, 'Corporate governance, industrial relations and trends in company-level restructuring in Europe: Convergence towards the Anglo-American model?", *Industrial Relations Journal* 35 (2004), pp. 518–535.
[20] Lord Wedderburn of Charlton, 'Companies and employees: Common law or social dimension', *Law Quarterly Review* 109 (1993), pp. 261–262.

Elsewhere, Lord Wedderburn has pointed out that the deeply-entrenched shareholder value approach made it difficult for measures that might have promoted employee interests to gain any ground in the recent reform of UK Company Law.[21]

Rock and Wachter suggest that two governance systems exist side-by-side within the firm: there is employee governance and corporate governance. Corporate governance topics include (1) entering new markets, closing plants and investing in new technology; (2) issues concerning payments to shareholders; and (3) relations between the board and executive officers. Employee governance is concerned with the relationship between the firm and its employees and especially with the pattern of remuneration over the course of the employment relationship. Rock and Wachter acknowledge that these two strands of governance need to be integrated into the overall governance structure of the firm.[22] The idea that employees and shareholders have distinctive concerns, areas of expertise, concerns and modes of contribution to the overall governance of the firm is plausible. It must be remembered, however, that there is no clinical divide between what Rock and Wachter term corporate governance and the legitimate interests of employees; plant closures offer an obvious example of a 'corporate governance' topic as to which employees could reasonably expect to be kept informed and to have their interests taken into account.

Parkinson highlights the link between the prevailing conception of the corporation and the way that employee interests fit into the corporate governance structure. He argues that the firm should be seen as a complex social institution. It is not simply the property of its shareholders nor a mere nexus of contracts; these conceptions of the firm are to some degree impoverished. Rather, he suggests that the firm should be considered as a complex social institution that has a reality of its own and that is not simply the property of its shareholders. This way of thinking about the firm would bring employees (and he believes other "stakeholders") into the centre of corporate governance. The challenge is then to find legal mechanisms to give content and meaning to the firm-as-social-institution approach.[23]

---

[21] Lord Wedderburn of Charlton, 'Employees, partnership and company law', *Industrial Law Journal* 31 (2002), p. 108.

[22] E. Rock and M. Wachter, 'Tailored Claims and governance: the fit between employees and shareholders' in M. Blair and M. Roe (eds.), *Employees and corporate governance*.

[23] J. Parkinson, 'Models of the company and the employement relationship', *British Journal of Industrial Relations* 41 (2003), pp. 481–509.

Blair proposes a view of governance that would give control of corporate assets to those who bear the risks associated with ownership. She argues that employees should be given some control rights to encourage them to make firm-specific investments. Firms that rely on such investments should, she suggests, make use of employee share ownership schemes.[24]

Blair and Stout[25] see the firm's central role as being the organisation of team production. The firm's governance structure can help to overcome the shirking and rent-seeking problems that might plague team production. Corporate assets are controlled by an internal hierarchy under the overall control of the board. The hierarchy's role is to co-ordinate the activities of team members, allocate the resulting production and mediate disputes among team members over that allocation. The board's principal task is to encourage firm-specific investments essential to certain forms of production. The hierarchy's control over corporate assets enables it to play the co-ordinating role that the successful team requires.

Profitability as the central purpose of corporate governance

Corporate governance should include some criterion or criteria to guide decision-making by the board. What has been said already suggests some principles that should guide a CST-inspired approach to corporate governance. First, governance will ensure that customer or client needs and expectations are as fully satisfied as is possible. Second, governance is at the service of the firm's participants; it exists to facilitate their pursuit of the goals that (reasonably) brought them to the firm. Third, those in charge of governance have some responsibility for deciding on how the firm is to contribute to the common good of the societies in which the firm is integrated. Much of this can be summed up by saying that those in charge of governance are responsible for developing the firm so that it is better able to make its specialised contribution to the well-being of its participants and the common good of society at large.

Can profitability provide the necessary criterion to guide corporate decision-makers? To some extent, of course, it must be taken as a

---

[24] M. Blair, *Ownership and control. Rethinking corporate governance for the twenty-first century,* (Washington DC: The Brookings Institution, 1995) and M. Blair, 'Firm-specific human capital and theories of the firm' in M. Blair and M. Roe (eds.), *Employees and corporate governance.*

[25] M. Blair and L. Stout, 'A team production theory of corporate law', *Virginia Law Review* 85 (1999) pp. 247–328.

criterion of central importance. Profit provides the return that investors need and it is needed to pay salaries. It can be a source of the funds that the business needs to sustain itself, grow and contribute to the communities of which it forms part. Profitability also provides a means of assessing whether the corporation's assets have been put to effective use. There is a moral case for choosing the most efficient (or least wasteful) means to achieve given ends and measuring profitability provides a way of checking whether or not the correct choices have been made in this regard. So, profitability is undoubtedly a good measure of the corporation's vitality. At an ethical level, however, it can never be the sole determinant for decision-making. To take obvious examples, a drugs cartel or a protection racket might be extremely profitable but they are not consistent with a will to self-realisation.[26] They will harm the common good and destroy rather than build up lives and communities. As a practical matter, it seems implausible to suggest that directors could routinely take the pursuit of profit as their sole decision-making criterion. It is more likely that in practice they have to juggle a range of concerns that include the development of the products and services offered by the firm, meeting the needs of shareholders (especially those with significant shareholdings), employee concerns and external pressures (such as those imposed by government or by lenders and suppliers). It is doubtful whether telling directors that they have to make a profit (or to maximise shareholder value) provides directors with any guidance at all beyond that which is glaringly obvious to them in any event. As Davies and Lord Wedderburn of Charlton put it:

> [T]here seems to be no mechanism which will guarantee continuous profit-maximising behaviour on the part of controllers of large companies. Neither shareholder control (whether by institutional or private shareholders), the forces of market competition, the market in corporate control via takeovers, nor the threat of liquidation seem ... to be sufficient to impose upon corporate managements the discipline of profit maximization.[27]

The task of those in charge of corporate governance is sophisticated and demanding; they are responsible for building up the business and its common good and this task cannot be adequately explained by saying that the ultimate goal is the pursuit of profit.

---

[26] John Paul II, *Centesimus annus*, paras. 35–36.
[27] P. Davies and Lord Wedderburn of Charlton, 'The land of industrial democracy', *Industrial Law Journal* 6 (1977), p. 201.

Employee participation in governance

'Employee participation' can refer to the range of ways in which employees can participate in the major decision-making fora that affect their working lives and environments. Employee participation can refer to participation at levels of governance higher than the corporation, including employee participation in governance at the level of the economy as a whole or of specific sectors within the economy. Employee participation can also refer to decision-making at levels below the board such as the workplace or within the employee's immediate team. This participation might be direct, with each individual employee participating in the decision-making process. More usually, however, it will be indirect in that employees participate in governance through representatives.

The principal focus of this book is on employee participation in corporate governance. The corporation has an impact that is both extensive and direct on the working life of the employee and, as argued above, the corporation exists to enhance the productive capacity of the individual employee. Codetermination is the best-known form of employee participation in corporate governance. This system reserves seats on the board of directors for employee representatives. It is not, however, the only form of employee participation in governance. In Japan, the human resources director often acts as an advocate for employee interests; he does so within a corporate governance culture that gives a high priority to employee welfare in any event.[28]

From an ethical perspective, there are at least two good reasons for seeking to promote employee participation in corporate governance. The first reason is related to CST's principle of participation.[29] CST is anxious to promote the idea of the subject character of society. We are not simply objects to be governed but rather we are to do what we can to build up the communities to which we belong. A society's common good is built up through the intelligence, commitment and effort of its members. Communities should be 'personal' in that they serve some range of personal values so that they play their part in enhancing the personality of their members. They should also be personal in the sense that they reflect the personality of their members. Each community, each corporation in our case, will have its own style of governance because it will reflect the

[28] S. Learmount, *Corporate Governance – What can be learned from Japan?*, (Oxford, Oxford University Press, 2004), pp. 138–141.

[29] See Pontifical Council for Justice and Peace, *Compendium of the Social Doctrine of the Church*, (Vatican City, Libreria Editrice Vaticana, 2004), pp. 107–109.

unique style of its participants and the way in which the corporation, over time, has managed to harness the energies of its members. One of the cardinal rules for the design of governance structures should, therefore, be that they facilitate the active participation of as many as possible in ways that are compatible with effective collective action. The corporation's governance structure should not be a bureaucratic machine but, rather, should ensure the intelligent and appropriate participation of management, employees and shareholders. Co-determination allows employees to participate indirectly, through representatives, in the life of the corporation. It would, of course, need a supporting structure of mechanisms to allow the individual employee to engage with governance. Otherwise, co-determination might do little to make a reality of the corporation as a community of persons.

In other words, the first justification for employee participation is rooted in the same sort of considerations as the principle of subsidiarity. Kohler says of the principle that:

> It exposes the actions and the rationale of individuals and institutions alike to the widest possible discussion and examination. It thereby activates and makes use of the most valuable of assets: the normativity of the human mind as expressed through common sense and insight. The principle helps to diffuse tendencies towards the totalitarian, the needlessly bureaucratic and the silly by providing endless checks against policies, principles and programs that simply are not reasonable.[30]

Subsidiarity is not restricted to the question of the relationship between the political authority and intermediate groups. It can also help in thinking about relationships within the firm.

Employee participation can also help employees to protect themselves from unjust treatment when the corporation is going through hard times or in the event of a major restructuring. In *Economic Justice for All*, the US Bishops said:

> As a minimum, workers have a right to be informed in advance when such decisions are under consideration, a right to negotiate with management about possible alterations, and a right to fair compensation and assistance with retraining and relocation expenses should these be necessary. Since even these minimal rights are jeopardized without collective negotiation, industrial co-operation requires a strong role for labour unions in our changing economy.[31]

[30] T. Kohler, 'Lessons from the social charter: State, corporation and the meaning of subsidiarity', *University of Toronto Law Journal* 43 (1993), p. 619.
[31] US Catholic Bishops, *Economic justice for all*, 1986, para. 303.

Employee participation is a theme that emerged gradually in CST. *Rerum novarum* does not explicitly mention employee participation. Its emphasis on the dignity of the worker, however, could be said to imply that this is a theme that would be developed later. Some Catholics argued that employee participation was a natural right that should be enshrined in law.[32] Pius XI rejected this view of employee participation as an entitlement in *Quadragesimo anno* but stressed the desirability of a partnership approach to relations within the firm[33]. This idea was developed in various ways in *Mater et magistra* which spoke of employee participation in decision-making both within the firm and at the level of the economy in general. Since employees were affected by policies developed at levels higher than the firm, they ought also to be allowed to participate in developing those policies. *Mater et magistra* also called for employees to be allowed to share in the profits of the businesses that they work for.

CST's stance on employee participation was summed up in this passage of *Gaudium et spes*:

> In economic enterprises it is persons who are joined together, that is, free and independent human beings created to the image of God. Therefore, with attention to the functions of each – owners or employers, management or labour – and without doing harm to the necessary unity of management, the active sharing of all in the administration and profits of these enterprises in ways to be properly determined is to be promoted. Since more often, however, decisions concerning economic and social conditions, on which the future lot of the workers and of their children depends, are made not within the business itself but by institutions on a higher level, the workers themselves should have a share also in determining these conditions-in person or through freely elected delegates.[34]

CST claims no competence when it comes to devising technical solutions for the implementation of employee participation in its various forms. There is obviously a range of acceptable solutions and each firm and each economy will have to work out approaches that suit it best. *Laborem exercens* points the way. The goal to be achieved is that 'on the basis of his work each person is fully entitled to consider himself a part-owner of the great workbench at which he is working with every one else.'[35] The passage continues:

[32] J. Newman, *Co-responsibility in industry: Social justice in labour-management relations*, (Cork, Cork University Press, 1954), p. 3.

[33] Pius XI, *Quadragesimo anno*, paras. 64–65.

[34] Second Vatican Council, *Gaudium et spes*, para. 68.

[35] John Paul II, *Laborem exercens*, para. 14.

> A way towards that goal could be found by associating labour with the ownership of capital, as far as possible, and by producing a wide range of intermediate bodies with economic, social and cultural purposes; they would be bodies enjoying real autonomy with regard to the public powers, pursuing their specific aims in honest collaboration with each other and in subordination to the demands of the common good.[36]

It is for the direct employer (the firm) and the indirect employer (anyone with a say in the terms of employment such as the state) to reach workable and just solutions.

Maritain's explanation of the concept of 'socialisation' is to the point here:

> [T]aken in its genuine sense [socialisation] refers to that process of social integration through which association in a single enterprise extends not only to the capital invested, but also to labour and management, and all persons and various groups involved are made participants in some form or other of co-ownership and co-management. This process is not an attack on, but an expansion of private ownership. It depends on the search of free initiative for new economic modalities and adjustments, the more successful of which will one day be sanctioned by the law. It rises from the natural growth of the system of free enterprise, when common consciousness becomes aware of the social function of private property and of the necessity of giving organic and institutional forms to that law of the 'common use' on which Thomas Aquinas laid particular stress.[37]

Rerum novarum was inspired by concern over the material poverty of the working classes in the industrialised nations at the end of the nineteenth century. It was also a response to an economic system and a way of looking at things that saw work as a mere commodity so that no respect was accorded to the subjective dimension of work. CST has emphasized the importance of allowing employees to exercise their initiative and to play a part in the governance of the firm and of the economy but it has not committed itself to any specific model of employee participation since a range of ethically acceptable approaches exists.

CST is, of course, not alone in making the ethical case for employee participation in corporate governance. Axworthy makes the moral case for employee participation in these terms:

> Employees are denied any meaningful degree of control over their working lives. This stems from their lack of power in their corporations. If control over one's life is seen as being important, it would seem that

---

[36] John Paul II, *Laborem exercens*, para. 14.
[37] J. Maritain, 'The people and the state', reprinted in *Logos* 11 (2008), p. 180.

some power should be conferred on employees. The solution should be to ensure mechanisms which permit employees to be the effective decision-makers in their places of work. Only then can meaningful strides be taken towards participatory democracy at the workplace.[38]

Klare calls for a recasting of corporate governance and labour law to promote workplace democracy. He argues that the main goal of labour law should be to expand and enhance democracy at every level of the experience and organisation of work. This is a demand both of a respect for self-realisation and of the practical needs of the firm operating in a modern economy. Employees increasingly look to their work as a source of self-realisation in a deep sense (as presenting opportunities for learning and expression, challenging work and an improvement in their technical skills and personal capacities).[39] McCall argues that employee participation rights should operate at every level. He considers that rationality, fairness, self-respect, health and democracy are all promoted by employee participation rights. Rationality and freedom are core aspects of human identity and they are incompatible with the idea that employees should be the passive objects of management; this is especially important because work is a central aspect of our lives. Fairness rests on the conviction that human beings all enjoy equal dignity. The nature of work relationships can have a profound impact on an individual's sense of self-respect. Finally, he suggests that corporate democracy can lead to greater participation in the political process.[40]

There is also an economic case to be made for employee participation. Indeed, there is no shortage of commentators who point out the economic benefits of making credible commitments to employees that their interests will be given reasonable consideration in times of crisis. Armour *et al.* make the point that takeovers may have the effect of expropriating employees by reneging on implicit promises made to them. The takeover threat would then make it very difficult for management to make credible commitments to employees.[41] Howse and Trebilcock consider the risk of

[38] C. Axworthy, 'Corporation law as if some people mattered', *University of Toronto Law Journal* 36 (1981), p. 423.

[39] K. Klare, 'Workplace democracy and market reconstruction: An agenda for legal reform', *Catholic University Law Review* 38 (1988), pp. 1–68.

[40] J. McCall, 'Employee participation in corporate governance: a defense of strong participation rights', *Business Ethics Quarterly* 11 (2001), pp. 195–213.

[41] J. Armour, S. Deakin and S. Konzelmann, 'Shareholder primacy and the trajectory of UK corporate governance', *British Journal of Industrial Relations* 41 (2003), pp. 531–555. See also S. Deakin, 'The coming transformation of shareholder value', *Corporate Governance: An International Review* 13 (2005), pp. 11–18 and S. Deakin, R. Hobbs, D.

employee dislocations in the event of major restructurings.[42] They point out that workers invest human capital in their employers and that there is a need for mechanisms to protect these stakes in the firm. Howse and Trebilcock note that it is difficult to craft ex ante contractual commitments that adequately protect employees. Earnings are often set below an employee's contribution to productivity in the early years but rise with seniority. Shareholders can engage in rent-shifting by reneging on the implicit agreement about employee entitlements. They ask how participation could function to protect the employment bargain. Employee representation on the board could be useful, even if the employee representatives were in a minority, because of the information that the representatives would gain about the economic condition and strategy of the firm. The employee representatives could also act as whistle-blowers and raise an early warning about management proposals that have the potential to harm employee interests. Employee representatives would also be able to add a new dimension to boardroom discussions by pointing out difficulties or strategies that management had simply not considered. Howse and Trebilcock make the point that it is possible to design arrangements for useful employee participation at board level that would not involve employees in the governance structure for worker-management relations. The alternative might be an obligatory, ongoing consultation process about events or proposals that threaten job security. Even if major restructuring and job losses are inevitable, such an arrangement might allow an orderly and humane transition.

Co-determination

Co-determination is the most obvious example of a system of employee participation in corporate governance. A co-determination system gives one or more employee representatives a formal place at the boardroom table. Germany is an example of a jurisdiction with mandatory co-determination rules. Its system of company law specifies the size of the supervisory board of any *Aktiengesellschaft* ('AG') and of a *Gesellschaft mit beschraenkter Haftung* ('GmbH') with more than 2,000 employees. An AG established after 1994 with fewer than 500 employees is exempt

Nash and G. Slinger, 'Implicit contracts, takeovers and corporate governance: in the shadow of the City Code', ESRC Centre for Business Research, University of Cambridge Working Paper 254.

[42] R. Howse and M. Trebilcock, 'Protecting the employment bargain', *University of Toronto Law Journal* 43 (1993), pp. 751–792.

from the co-determination rules.[43] Above these thresholds, German law requires minimum levels of employee representation on the supervisory board[44] although, ultimately, shareholder representatives have a majority of the voting rights. In addition, Germany has a system of national Works Councils and these may apply even to quite small businesses.[45]

The German approach to co-determination has been summarised by Jackson, Hopner and Kurdelbusch thus:

> Employee voice is institutionalised through the legal institution of codetermination at the level of the supervisory board and works councils … Employee representatives on the supervisory board provide a counterweight to shareholders in the appointment of management, as well as involving employees in monitoring of strategic business decisions. In certain companies, the appointment of a labour director to the management board by the employees reinforces the consensus nature of decision-making within the board.[46]

Hopt points out the need for ways of monitoring board performance (through audit mechanisms, for example or the use of market-based mechanisms such as the market for corporate control). Labour representation at board level could be seen as a further tool for monitoring board performance and can be seen as similar to the use of outside directors. He argues that co-determination has not been economically inefficient (despite the fact that it slows down decision-making). Indeed, he suggests that co-determination has positive economic effects because it reduces strategic behaviour and improves the flow of information to the board. He acknowledges that having employee representatives on the board poses challenges in terms of the need to ensure that they respect their duties of confidentiality and loyalty to the corporation; he believes, however, that these challenges can be met.[47]

---

[43] *Gesetz fur Kleine Aktiengesellschaften und zur Derelegierung des Aktienrechts* ('Law for Small Stock Companies and to Deregulate Stock Law').

[44] *Bertriebsverfassungsgesetz* ('"Industrial Constitution Act').

[45] See D. Sadowski, J. Junkes and S. Lindenthal, 'Employees and corporate governance: Germany: The German model of corporate and labour governance', *Comparative Labour Law & Policy Journal* 22 (2000), pp 33–66 for an explanation of the German system, an evaluation of the economic efficiency of the German insistence on compulsory rather than voluntary co-determination.

[46] G. Jackson, M. Hopner and A. Kurdelbusch, 'Corporate governance and employees in Germany: Changing linkages, complementarities and tensions', in H. Gospel and M. Pendleton (eds.), *Corporate Governance and Labour Management: An International Comparison*, (Oxford: Oxford University Press, 2005, p. 89.

[47] K. Hopt, 'New ways in corporate governance: European experiments with labour representation on corporate boards', *Michigan Law Review* 82 (1983–1984), pp. 1338–1363.

Dinh argues that co-determination, works councils and collective bargaining are part of a package that allow management and labour to carry on a continuous negotiation process. Having several channels allows for issues to be divided up between those that are best dealt with at firm level and those that can be dealt with at industry level.[48] The co-determination aspect of the package has come in for criticism but it is more likely that Germany will continue with a reformed version of co-determination than that it will abandon it altogether.[49] Goodijk argues that Germany's model can help to build a participative company where there is worker involvement in the implementation of policy, the design of the workplace and the improvement of work processes. Direct participation by employees in some levels of decision-making could, he suggests, be complemented by indirect or representative participation at corporate level. He recommends improving the links between works councils and the board and between works councils and trade unions.[50]

Jackson *et al.* note that Germany is becoming more open to shareholder value management practices and consider what this is likely to mean for co-determination. Despite the pessimistic claims of some, co-determination has proven able to justify itself in terms of shareholder value. It has not resulted in a loss of managerial accountability; quite the reverse is true. Co-determination and a shareholder value approach to governance, in combination, lead to a partnership approach being taken to industrial relations; this works well for employees with stable positions within the firm. They observe a trend towards firm-by-firm negotiation of the details of co-determination; it is becoming less politically guaranteed and more contractually negotiated.[51]

The United Kingdom flirted with the idea of co-determination in the late 1970s. The Bullock Report[52] proposed that there should be a system of employee participation on the boards of companies with more than 2,000 employees. There were to be equal numbers of shareholder and employee representatives and a third group selected by the first two groups. The third group would both provide expertise and act as a tie-breaker in the event

---

[48] V. Dinh, 'Codetermination and corporate governance in a multinational business enterprise', *Journal of Corporation Law* 24 (1999), p. 982.

[49] J. Du Plessis and O. Sandrock, 'The rise and fall of supervisory codetermination in Germany', *International Company and Commercial Law Review* 16 (2005), pp 67–79.

[50] R. Goodijk, 'Corporate governance and workers' participation', *Corporate Governance* 8 (2000), pp. 303–310.

[51] Jackson, Hopner and Kurdelbusch, 'Corporate governance and employees in Germany: changing linkages, complementarities and tensions', pp. 115–118.

[52] Command Paper (Cmnd.) 6706, London: HMSO.

of deadlock. The system would only apply to businesses once employees had voted in favour of its introduction. Bullock recommended that certain functions (appointment of senior management, changes in capital structure and major disposals) would be reserved to the board regardless of the wishes of shareholders. The report recommended that there should be a statutory statement of directors' duties and that one of these should require directors to take employee interests into account. The principal proposals of the Bullock Report were never implemented.

There is no guarantee that co-determination would turn an enterprise into the sort of participatory community that CST calls for:

> Only if there is parity of employees on the board of directors, only if they have support staff answerable to them to advise them, and then only if the employee directors do not become co-opted can the scheme have any chance of being effective. Merely permitting employee representatives to sit on the board of directors will do little to ensure that appropriate attention is paid to employee interests.[53]

At the very least, co-determination has symbolic value in that it gives employees a constitutionally recognised place in corporate governance. Employee representatives can act as advocates for employee interests and help to improve the flow of information between the board and employees.

It has been argued that some forms of co-determination are harmful in that they allow managers to play employee and shareholder representatives off against each other. As a result, management may be able to free itself from effective scrutiny.[54] The indirect result of this would, presumably, be to raise the company's cost of capital (assuming that minority shareholders felt that there was a significant agency risk).

An alternative (or complementary) strategy to co-determination would be the reformulation of the directors' duty of loyalty so that it includes a duty to promote employee welfare. O'Connor is among those calling for this approach to be taken. She laments the fact that the shareholder-value approach fails to acknowledge the importance of human capital. But she suggests that this failure will be corrected as economic systems are forced to ackowledge the importance of human capital. She argues for the imposition of a fiduciary duty on directors to keep employee representatives

---

informed about the business and to have regard to any representations that they may make.[55]

Even without a co-determination system, indeed even without structural reform of corporate governance, it would be possible to bring employees into the corporate governance system. Jacoby has argued that a human resources director in the boardroom could do much to ensure that directors have regard to employee welfare[56] (though this would rely on the human resources director understanding that his role was, in part, to act as an advocate for employees). Gospel and Pendleton argue that even in shareholder-centred systems like the UK, managers can secure a very considerable degree of discretion to handle matters as they see fit.[57]

Deakin *et al.* also contend that it is important not to get too carried away with the idea that there is a single approach to corporate governance common to all UK listed companies. UK company law and corporate governance are, it is true, strongly attuned to the needs of shareholders. At the same time, there is empirical evidence to show that unions can play a significant role, even in UK listed companies. Goodwill is not enough, however. Management will only be able to persuade key investors of the benefits of a partnership with employee representatives where there is a clear link between financial returns to shareholders and product or service quality. The human factor also has a part to play: effective management-employee partnerships depend on the quality and vision of management at all levels as well as of union representatives. Finally, it is important that there is an effective human resources director playing a part in board-level decisions; this person can argue the case for investment in human capital.[58]

Employee share ownership

CST's interest in employee share ownership (or some functional equivalent) is principally based on its reflection on the relationship between the human person and material creation. The Church's thought on this

[55] M. O'Connor, 'Employees and corporate governance: United States: Labour's role in the American corporate governance structure', *Comparative Labour Law & Policy Journal* 22 (2000) p. 97.
[56] Jacoby, *The embedded corporation*, pp. 161–2.
[57] Gospel and Pendleton, 'Finance, corporate governance and the management of labour: a conceptual and comparative analysis'.
[58] S. Deakin, R. Hobbs, S. Konzelmann and F. Wilkinson, 'Partnership, ownership and control. The impact of corporate governance on employment relations.', *Employee Relations* 24 (2002), pp. 335–352.

matter is rooted in reflection upon the account of creation given in the opening chapters of the Book of Genesis. God made His initial gift of the created world to the entire human race. The human person, each individual, has, in the Christian view of things, a unique vocation to play a part in cultivating the earth's resources so that it is enhanced and so that it meets human needs. *Laborem exercens* puts it this way:

> When we read in the first chapter of the Bible that man is to subdue the earth, we know that these words refer to all the resources contained in the visible world and placed at man's disposal. However, these resources can serve man only through work. From the beginning there is also linked with work the question of ownership, for the only means that man has for causing the resources hidden in nature to serve himself and others is through his work. And to be able through his work to make these resources bear fruit, man takes over ownership of small parts of the various riches of nature: those beneath the ground, those in the sea, on land or in space. He takes all these things over by making them his workbench. He takes them over through work and for work.[59]

The following passage occurs a little later:

> ... it is clear that recognition of the proper position of labour in the production process demands various adaptations in the sphere of ownership of the means of production.[60]

The institution of private property, that is, plays an indispensable part in establishing an appropriate, properly human link between the worker and the part of creation worked upon. The worker achieves the stable form of possession that sustained work (with its enormous significance for the self-realisation of the worker at a range of levels) demands and the profit he makes by his work provides him with an incentive to put the property to good use.[61]

Centesimus annus did not deal directly with employee rights, nor with the question of employee participation. The need to give employees some stake in their work, to make an appeal to a legitimate form of self-interest is, however, reinforced by this extract from *Centesimus annus*:

> Man tends towards good, but he is also capable of evil. He can transcend his immediate interest and still remain bound to it. The social order will be all the more stable the more it takes this fact into account and does

[59] John Paul II, *Laborem exercens*, para. 12.
[60] John Paul II, *Laborem exercens*, para. 14.
[61] J.-Y. Calvez and J. Perrin, *The social teaching of the Popes from Leo XIII to Pius XII (1878 – 1958)*, (Chicago, Henry Regnery Company, 1961), pp. 190–225.

not place in opposition personal interest and the interests of society as a whole, but rather seeks ways to bring them into fruitful harmony. In fact, where self-interest is violently suppressed, it is replaced by a burdensome system of bureaucratic control which dries up the wellsprings of initiative and creativity.[62]

The idea of an alignment between self-interest and the well-being of one's communities is obviously relevant to the theme of employee participation. This provides another, very pragmatic, reason for giving employees some kind of financial participation in their own firm: this participation (if well-designed) can reinforce their commitment to the common good of the firm.

CST urges those involved in corporate governance to look for specific and effective ways of strengthening the concept of the mutual complementarity of capital and labour. One could say that CST calls for a more work-oriented vision of the corporation to complement and correct the finance-driven view of the corporation that currently prevails. Employee share ownership is the most obvious way of aligning the interests of shareholder and employees. Properly structured, it could give employees a way of participating in governance as well as the other benefits of ownership (financial and psychological).

Gates[63] points out that the capitalist system as currently constructed has set in train a dynamic that tends to concentrate wealth in the hands of a few people. This process results in more and more wealth becoming concentrated in the hands of an elite. He calls for a financially engineered reponse that would enable more people to acquire significant capital. ESOPS, for example, could be encouraged through the right tax incentives. Turning employees into owners would benefit the organisation, he argues, since it would enhance feedback mechanisms and give employees a way of having their voices heard. There would be obvious financial benefits to employees but Gates hopes that there would be wider benefits too:

> Fundamentally, we need organisational structures enlivened with *spiritus* ('life-breath'). That requires commercial relationships that foster a sense of belonging while providing avenues for exercising personal responsibility according to a self-perceived sense of place, commitment and community. That new context will, in turn, awaken people to their opportunities

---

[62] John Paul II, *Centesimus annus*, para. 25.
[63] J. Gates, 'Reengineering ownership for the common good', in S. Cortright and M. Naughton (eds), *Rethinking the purpose of business. Interdisciplinary essays from the Catholic Social Tradition*, (Notre Dame, Indiana, University of Notre Dame Press, 2002), p. 264.

to serve (both inside and outside the firm) and provide them (through ownership) an institutionally empowered means for taking up those opportunities. My hope and expectation is that a renaissance in service would evoke in its turn a renaissance in commitment to the democratic process, as those who have gratitude for the opportunities accorded them will be eager to extend those opportunities to others.[64]

Employee ownership is capable of conferring economic benefits on the firm. Employee participation and ownership can align the interests of owners with those of employees and, properly structured, can provide employees with additional incentives to work well. Employee participation engenders loyalty and commitment and so reduces the need for supervision costs. Incentives for individual effort do not reward contributions to a team effort. Employee commitment to the firm is especially important in sectors that rely on innovation.

Njoya has shown that the idea that employees have a proprietary interest in their jobs has had judicial approval in the UK and the US. The question, though, is how the concept can be given practical meaning: clearly, economic reality means that no-one has a guaranteed job for life. Njoya, for good reasons, focuses on protecting employees when the firm is restructuring or approaching insolvency. The promotion of employee share ownership is another avenue that could be explored; it is another possible way of operationalising the job-as-property concept.[65]

Shareholders do not own the corporation as such. Davies comments:

> The old argument that the shareholders have [control rights] because they are the owners of the corporation now carries little sway, because its premise is false: shareholders own their shares, not the company.[66]

Shareholders are, however, almost invariably granted extensive rights of control over the corporation's management, constitution and economic surplus.[67] It could be argued that in practical terms, those control rights amount to ownership of the corporation.

The vast majority of corporations in the United Kingdom are, at least in principle, run for the benefit of their shareholders. Gospel and Pendleton highlight the ways in which the corporation's financing arrangements

---

[64] Gates, 'Reengineering ownership for the common good', p. 285.

[65] W. Njoya, *Property in work. The employment relationship in the Anglo-American firm*, (Aldershot: Ashgate Publishing, 2007).

[66] P. Davies, *Introduction to Company Law*, (Oxford: Oxford University Press, 2002), p. 257. See also *Gas Lighting Improvement Co. Ltd v Commissioners of Inland Revenue* [1923] AC 723 at 741 per Lord Sumner.

[67] Davies, *Introduction to Company Law*, pp. 15–16.

have an impact on management policies. Finance and governance, they suggest, affect the interests pursued by managers, the time horizons that they adopt in their decision-making processes and the strategies that they pursue (whether the focus tends to be on profit or on incremental product improvement). It also has an impact on whether the firm tends to rely on market-based incentives to secure employee commitment.

The influence of finance and governance specifically on labour management occurs at system level. It has an impact on job security and internal labour markets. Further, a shareholder value system of corporate governance forces firms to break implicit contracts with employees. Then there is an effect in terms of employees' willingness to acquire firm-specific skills. Finance and governance may have an impact on the nature of firms' demand for skills. It may be difficult to promote flexible forms of work and teamwork in the UK / US.[68]

There are some well-founded objections to employee ownership. Some suggest that investor-owned firms are the norm because they enjoy significant efficiencies that employee-owned firms cannot replicate. It has been argued that shareholders can play the governance function more efficiently. Unless the employee-owned firm's governance and management structure are well-designed and unless they can find ways of financing the business, employee owned and managed firms will fail. Dow and Putterman suggest that capital usually hires labour because: the owners of capital have better incentives to monitor the use of physical assets; workers could not finance the firm; workers are risk averse and need to diversify some of their wealth away from their employer; labour-managed firms cannot cope with highly specialised physical assets and because labour-managed firms find it difficult to reach collective decisions because of the diversity among employees in terms of appetite for risk, personal situations and attitudes.[69] No doubt there is substance in many of these objections. They are not, however, lethal to the arguments put forward here.[70] Rather, they show the need for careful attention to detail when trying to design participatory workplaces.

[68] Gospel and Pendleton, 'Finance, governance and the management of labour: a conceptual and comparative analysis, p. 557.

[69] G. Dow and L. Putterman, 'Why capital (usually) hires labour: An assessment of proposed explanations', in Blair and Roe (eds.), *Employees and corporate governance*. See also H. Hansmann, 'When does worker ownership work? ESOPs, law firms, codetermination and economic democracy', *The Yale Law Journal* 99 (1989–1990), pp. 1749–1816.

[70] See R. Oakeshott, *The case for workers co-ops*, (Basingstoke, MacMillan Press Ltd, 1990) for a frank acknowledgement (illustrated in a set of case studies) of the difficulties that arise when the economic problems associated with employee control are not adequately

Employee share ownership plans (ESOPs) are one possible way of meeting CST's aims of giving employees some financial participation and a real sense of ownership. The distinctive feature of an ESOP (Employee Share Ownership Plan) is that a trust is used to acquire and hold equity and to distribute it to employees. Pendleton argues that ESOPs have their most profound effect, in participation terms, where setting up the ESOP has been accompanied by innovative governance structures with well-developed systems for representative participation and close links between the system for participation in management and that for participation in governance. Examples of innovative governance structures include providing for worker-directors and the establishment of employee-shareholder committees. In these cases, employee ownership was found to have a significant intrinsic impact on employees' psychological commitment.[71]

It seems that the new governance institutions in employee-owned firms do make a difference; there are greater flows of information from management to representatives, especially on financial matters, worker-directors are involved in all types of board-level decisions and do seem to have some influence. They do not lead to worker-control though. The new governance structures can be thought of as being akin to German-style co-determination:

> Property rights give workers and their representatives legitimate access to information and decision-making that is rare in the UK. Whilst formal veto powers are given to worker directors in the Articles of many of these companies, these are rarely exercised. Instead, the primary importance of board or trust membership is that it provides a mechanism for the expression of employee interests at the highest level of management, and for the transmission of company information to employee representatives. These institutions create the potential for top managers to incorporate employee and employee-owner interests and concerns into top-level decisions but they do not lead to top managers making decisions at the behest of employees and their representatives. Boards of directors in these companies are best seen as coalitions of interests rather than as vehicles for translating employee-owner interests into corporate policy.[72]

---

dealt with. See G. Dow, *Governing the firm: Workers' control in theory and practice*, (Cambridge: Cambridge University Press, 2003), pp. 260–289 for some suggestions on achieving greater employee ownership and control.

[71] A. Pendleton, *Employee ownership, participation and governance – a study of ESOPs in the UK*, (London and New York: Routledge, 2000).

[72] Pendleton, *Employee ownership, participation and governance – a study of ESOPs in the UK*, pp. 187–188.

Blasi *et al.* contrast the US and EU experience of employee share ownership. They point out that employee shares and options should be distributed in addition to, not as a partial replacement for, the employee's salary. Otherwise, employees would be poorly diversified, having both their human and financial capital in the same boat. Second, they report that in the US (where employee ownership is more widespread) the availability of a large established market for corporate shares creates an infrastructure for corporations seeking to promote employee share ownership. Thus, contrary to what one might have thought, active stock markets favour employee ownership (at least to some extent). Finally, they note that advocates of employee share ownership are subjected to an unreasonably high burden of proof; their opponents insist on evidence that employee ownership leads to superior performance. Amongst other deficiencies, this approach ignores the fact that there are grounds other than performance on which to base the call for measures to promote employee ownership.[73]

Michie and Oughton argue that employee participation can be a way of ensuring that employee interests are reflected in corporate decision-making. They suggest that employee participation and ownership can align the interests of owners with those of employees and that institutional shareholders lose value by not actively engaging with employees. Ownership matters, they contend, because it is associated with control rights and financial incentives.

The problem for corporations and for employees is that financial shareholders may have shorter time horizons than employees and management. In addition, corporate governance needs to address the conflict of interests between owners and employees and between managers and non-managerial employees. Change is needed to overcome short-termism. Employee participation can engender loyalty and commitment and so reduce the need for supervision costs. Incentives for individual effort do not reward contributions to a team effort but employee commitment to the firm is especially important in sectors that rely on innovation. Michie and Oughton advocate an integrated approach to corporate governance that includes ownership, employee participation and high performance work systems and shareholder activism. When it comes to devising governance structures that might facilitate employee voice, Michie and

---

[73] J. Blasi, D. Kruse, J. Sesil and M. Kroumova, 'An assessment of employee ownership in the United States with implications for the EU', *The International Journal of Human Resource Management* 14 (2003), pp. 893–919.

Oughton point out that employee ownership both allows employees to benefit from the success of the company and (because of the resulting employee voice) can help to ensure the prevalence of participatory HR management practices.

To maximise shareholder voice, it makes sense for employees to find ways of pooling their voting rights; trade unions could play an important part in helping to ensure that the voice of employee/shareholders is heard. The problem with current board structures lies in the importance given to the views of the Finance Director and of others with a focus on the bottom line; their perspective might discourage the adoption of progressive human resource practices. Michie and Oughton argue that reform of corporate governance/company law is needed so that the importance of stakeholders other than shareholders can be recognised. There should be experimentation with new corporate forms and employee share trusts should play a more active role in corporate governance.[74]

It would clearly be undesirable if employee share ownership became a source of division within the company. The aim to be achieved is for share ownership to become a means of fostering a partnership approach within the company. This is achievable given management skill and the right investors. It is a mistake to believe that financiers are a homogeneous group even within a system. Different investors have their own preferences concerning time frames, respect for other stakeholders and so on; it would be mistaken to see them all as being driven by a simple desire for profit.[75]

Pension funds and other institutional investors have become major players in corporate governance. Ghilarducci *et al.* have looked at whether pension funds, given their links with employee interests, might play a part in using their ownership rights to raise labour standards. They are sceptical about this as the US experience shows that pension funds have had to balance the need to maximise long-term shareholder wealth and their desire to protect employee interests. They argue that:

> Labour's new project should be to recast arguments about time horizons and ownership rights so that pension funds in the global economy can work with skilled management, political democratic parties, central banks, world trade organisations, and traditional investors to link tech-

---

[74] J. Michie and C. Oughton, 'Employee participation and ownership rights', *Journal of Corporate Law Studies* 2 (2002), pp. 139–154.
[75] Gospel and Pendleton, 'Finance, governance and the management of labour: a conceptual and comparative analysis', p. 557.

nology and funds to forms of capitalist production which economically more stable and sustainable.[76]

This is an interesting vision of the sort of sophisticated alliances that governance of the global economy demands.

Shareholders should be responsible citizens of the corporate community by contributing to governance. This is especially true of institutional investors given that they have greater power in individual companies and in the economy as a whole and that they have the resources to play an informed role in corporate governance[77]. Corporate governance policy should aim to encourage individual shareholders, especially institutional shareholders, to accept the responsibility that comes with their extensive control rights. This responsibility obviously includes a responsibility to assess whether or not the corporation's assets are being put to productive and profitable use. It goes wider than this, however. Part of this responsibility is that shareholders should seek to cultivate a spirit of partnership with employees. Shareholders should give life to the idea that property ownership is at the service of human needs and human work. Share ownership has ethical and cultural dimensions that need to be emphasised to a far greater extent than has been true in the past.

The John Lewis Partnership

The John Lewis Partnership (owning the John Lewis and Waitrose chains) is an employee-owned business that competes successfully with aggressive businesses with more conventional governance structures. Commercially, it is no pushover and yet its central philosophy is that it exists for the sake of the all-round well-being of its employees. The commercial success of the John Lewis Partnership gives the lie to those who argue that firms that put employees at the heart of their ownership and governance are doomed to failure.

Its Constitution is a remarkably sophisticated document and it deserves careful attention as a possible working model for a business that aspires to be run in accordance with CST's insights.[78] It declares that the

---

[76] T. Ghilarducci, J. Hawley and A. Williams, 'Labour's paradoxical interests and the evolution of corporate governance', *Journal of Law and Society* 24 (1997), pp. 40–41.

[77] J. Hawley and A. Williams, *Fiduciary capitalism. How institutional investors can make corporate America more democratic*, (Philadelphia, University of Pennsylvania Press, 2000).

[78] *The Consitution of the John Lewis Partnership* ('the John Lewis Constitution' is available at www.johnlewispartnership.co.uk/Display.aspx?MasterId=9d2aa2cb-e971–4782-b6c1–028cc8374ae4&NavigationId=586 (last accessed on 28th July 2009).

Partnership's ultimate purpose is the happiness of all its members through their worthwhile and satisfying employment in a successful business.[79] It aims to make sufficient profit to sustain its commercial vitality, to finance its continued development, to distribute a share of profits to members and to enable it to undertake other activities consistent with its ultimate purpose.[80]

The Constitution creates three governing authorities, the Partnership Council, the Partnership Board and the Chairman.[81] The Chairman appoints a Management Committee comprising the top layer of management but this is not a governing authority. The power of the governing authorities depends on the consent of the Partners (employees).[82] The shared aim of the governing authorities is to safeguard the partnership's future and to enhance its prosperity. They should encourage creativity and an entrepreneurial spirit without risking any loss of financial independence.[83]

The Partnership Council is predominantly composed of employee representatives as they are to outnumber any of the Chairman's appointees by at least four to one.[84] Its role is to hold principal management to account by discussing, asking questions about and making recommendations on any subject it wishes. The Partnership Council is intended to act as a channel of communication between management and employees (Partners). The Partnership Council can ask the Partnership Board (the board of directors of John Lewis Partnership plc) and the Chairman any question it wishes and they must answer unless doing so would, in their opinion, damage the Partnership's interests.[85] The Chairman has to appear half yearly before the Partnership Council to review the Partnership's trading position and general progress and to answer questions.[86] If the Council judges that the Chairman has failed to fulfil his responsibilities or is no longer a suitable person to do so than it may pass a resolution to dismiss him.[87] Thus, the most powerful figure in the whole system is ultimately answerable to employee representatives. The Partnership Council has counterparts at Division and Local levels with broadly the same responsibilities as

---

[79] The John Lewis Constitution, Principle 1.
[80] The John Lewis Constitution, Principle 3.
[81] The John Lewis Constitution, Principle 2.
[82] The John Lewis Constitution, rule 2.
[83] The John Lewis Constitution, rule 4.
[84] The John Lewis Constitution, rule 12.
[85] The John Lewis Constitution, rule 7.
[86] The John Lewis Constitution, rule 9.
[87] The John Lewis Constitution, rule 10.

those of the Partnership Council in respect of their Division, branch or unit (as the case may be).[88] The Chairman can make appointments to the Partnership Council, principally to ensure that its work benefits from the full participation of senior management and has immediate access to specialist knowledge.[89]

The Partnership Board is the board of directors of John Lewis Partnership plc and it exercises the traditional corporate governance functions.[90] The Partnership Council elects five Partners to the Partnership Board[91] (there are currently twelve members of the Board[92]). So there is strong employee representation in corporate governance. There is also a Chairman's Management Committee the members of which are appointed by the Chairman. The Management Committee coordinates executive responsibility in the partnership and the views of principal management.[93]

The Chairman is absolutely central to the working of the Constitution. As already seen, he can make appointments to the Partnership Council and appoints the Chairman's Management Committee. He is the senior executive in the partnership.[94] He has the duty to ensure that the partnership retains its distinctive character and its democratic vitality[95]. On taking office, he makes a written undertaking that, among other things, he will uphold the Constitution and work to the utmost of his energy and ability for the fulfilment of the partnership's principles.[96] The Partnership Council, as we have seen, can hold the Chairman to account and even resolve to dismiss him.[97]

A commitment to subsidiarity is one of the most striking features of the John Lewis Partnership Constitution. It emphasises that every partner has a responsibility to promote the well-being of the business. It encourages the exercise of initiative and tries to devolve decision-making power to as local a level as possible. It seeks to create as many opportunities as possible for partners to voice their opinion on partnership matters. The Introduction to the Constitution states that the

---

[88] The John Lewis Constitution, rules 25 – 37.
[89] The John Lewis Constitution, rule 12.
[90] The John Lewis Constitution, rules 38–40.
[91] The John Lewis Constitution, rule 18(iii).
[92] John Lewis Partnership annual report and accounts 2008, p. 1.
[93] The John Lewis Constitution, rule 42.
[94] The John Lewis Constitution, rule 42.
[95] The John Lewis Constitution, rule 41.
[96] The John Lewis Constitution, rule 43(i).
[97] The John Lewis Constitution, rules 9 and 10.

partnership is the general body of partners, working together for the success of the business.[98] The partners 'share the responsibility for ownership as well as its rewards – profit, knowledge and power'.[99] The partnership operates on democratic principles and seeks as much sharing of power among its members as is consistent with efficiency.[100] The partnership's management should devolve as much power to its representative bodies as is commercially prudent.[101] In carrying out his duties, the Chairman is actively to seek to share power with his subordinates, delegating as much responsibility and encouraging as much initiative as possible.[102] The partnership encourages partners to fulfil their potential and increase their career satisfaction in a number of ways.[103] The Chairman is to maintain open communication with partners at all levels and partners have a duty to inform the Chairman of anything he reasonably should know.[104] The partnership's in-house journals rely upon intelligent co-operation from partners and a determination on the part of management to share as much information with partners as possible.[105] All of this comes on top of the ability to participate in governance that has already been discussed.

The Constitution emphasises the duties and responsibilities of individual partners; this clearly goes hand in hand with the benefits of membership. The partnership aims to employ and retain as its members people of ability and integrity who are committed to working together and supporting its principles.[106] It seeks to recruit only those who share its values and will contribute to its success.[107] The partnership will not retain any partner who cannot contribute satisfactorily, nor will it retain Partners in positions that are no longer required.[108] The whole of Section 2 of the Constitution's Rules section is devoted to the partners' rights and responsibilities.

As for job security, the Constitution's rules contain a section dealing with security of employment. The partnership aims to offer secure

[98] The John Lewis Constitution, Introduction, para. 4.
[99] The John Lewis Constitution, Principle 1.
[100] The John Lewis Constitution, rule 1.
[101] The John Lewis Constitution, rule 4.
[102] The John Lewis Constitution, rule 45(i).
[103] The John Lewis Constitution, rule 56.
[104] The John Lewis Constitution, rule 45(iii).
[105] The John Lewis Constitution, rule 77.
[106] The John Lewis Constitution, Principle 4.
[107] The John Lewis Constitution, rule 53.
[108] The John Lewis Constitution, rule 68

employment[109] though the commitment is not absolute since partners can be dismissed if they cannot contribute satisfactorily[110] and partners will not be retained in a position that is no longer required.[111] The partnership commits itself to give all the help it reasonably can to any partner who has difficulties at work.[112] Partners with more than five years' membership are to be encouraged to develop their skills so that they can continue in the partnership for the rest of their working lives.[113] When a position becomes redundant, the partnership will seek to provide alternative employment if possible.[114]

The principles section of the John Lewis Partnership Constitution set out the partnership's aims and ultimate purpose. Three (out of seven) principles concern the partnership's relationships with principal stakeholders (although that term is not used by the Constitution; these set out the partnership's approach to dealing with customers,[115] its business relationships[116] and the community.[117] These principles are elaborated upon in a section of the rules in the Constitution entitled 'responsibilities to others'.[118] The 'others' in question are customers,[119] suppliers,[120] and competitors.[121] The rules also encourage the partners to get involved in public service[122] and require them to comply with all legal requirements.[123] The partnership commits itself to taking all reasonable steps to minimise any detrimental effect its operations may have on the environment and to promote good environmental practice.[124]

The Constitution of the John Lewis Partnership has been described in some detail because it fits so admirably with CST principles. It makes employee well-being (defined in terms of financial returns and satisfying careers) the firm's ultimate purpose. Its sophisticated governance

---

[109] The John Lewis Constitution, rule 65.
[110] The John Lewis Constitution, rule 67.
[111] The John Lewis Constitution, rule 68.
[112] The John Lewis Constitution, rule 65.
[113] The John Lewis Constitution, rule 68.
[114] The John Lewis Constitution, rule 68.
[115] The John Lewis Constitution, principle 5.
[116] The John Lewis Constitution, principle 6.
[117] The John Lewis Constitution, principle 7.
[118] The John Lewis Constitution, rules 92–108.
[119] The John Lewis Constitution, rules 92–94.
[120] The John Lewis Constitution, rules 95–103.
[121] The John Lewis Constitution, rule 104.
[122] The John Lewis Constitution, rule 105.
[123] The John Lewis Constitution, rule 106.
[124] The John Lewis Constitution, 108.

structure allows for dialogue between employee representatives and management and generally encourages all employees to voice their opinion on matters related to the partnership. Crucially, it requires partners to take responsibility for the business and encourages the delegation of power. All of this contributes to a general sense that the firm belongs to the partners. The partnership sets itself high standards in its dealings with stakeholders but makes it clear that they are 'others', not partners in the firm. Clearly, the constitution is worthless without an effective commitment to put it into effect. The partnership seeks to recruit only those who share its values and will contribute to its success.[125]

Mandatory co-determination?

Should the state intervene and impose some form of employee participation as a matter of law? The principle of subsidiarity suggests that the state should be reluctant to intervene in the internal affairs of its intermediate associations. Promoting research into the issue, discovering and disseminating best practice are better approaches.

Nevertheless, the state may sometimes legitimately feel that it has to intervene; indeed, Bellace suggests that it is crucially important for the state to devise mechanisms that will 'serve as bulwarks for independent employee voice'.[126] Legally mandated systems might be better able than systems relying on 'soft' power to stand up to the spread of an aggressive shareholder value mentality and legal intervention might allow capital and labour to overcome mutual distrust to reach a solution that each group would find preferable and that enhances total firm value.[127] Management and capital might systematically oppose any form of participation in ways that threaten to leave workers as permanent outsiders. Legislation might be needed to overcome this. The state might feel that important political values affecting the state as a whole are at stake and that this justifies intervention.[128]

The fact that employees at a given time voiced opposition to a move to participation should be investigated and considered carefully. It may be

---

[125] The John Lewis Constitution, rule 53.
[126] J. Bellace, 'The role of the law in supporting employee representation systems', *Comparative Labour Law Journal* 15 (1994), p. 460.
[127] D. Charny, 'Workers and corporate governance: The role of political culture', in Blair and Roe (eds.), *Employees and corporate governance*.
[128] M. Roe, *Political determinants of corporate governance*, (New York: Oxford University Press, 2003),

that employees do not understand what the change might mean for them and fear that it is a ruse to impose extra work for the same or less pay. They may have concerns, perhaps well-grounded, that the seemingly benign proposal will be abused by management. There could be genuine employee fears about management's agenda or its willingness or ability to improve the content of employees' jobs and the causes of those fears would need to be addressed. That aside, in the last analysis the fact that some employees express reluctance about a move to employee participation is not a reason in principle to abandon a commitment to a participatory workplace.[129] The firm is a community with interests that are directed towards, but that are larger than, the fulfilment of the needs of a given individual or group of individuals (such as those of employees at a given moment in time). The firm has to be structured in such a way as to serve all employees, shareholders and customers over its lifespan. Further, the firm forms part of a broader social fabric and its ability to engage and develop its employees has broader social implications.

Johnston argues the case for legally-imposed or facilitated co-determination. There are a number of reasons why efficient co-determination would not be generated by purely market processes. There are problems of bounded rationality and opportunism to contend with and these may prevent parties from seeing the benefits of shared governance or, if they do, on being able to devise adequate structures. There could also be an adverse selection problem: if co-determination were not mandatory the least able employees would go to the co-determination firms where they are more secure. Further, managers may resist co-determination because they do not want to share power with employees or to be monitored by them. He also points out that where co-determination is not the norm, sheer unfamiliarity with this governance structure is an obstacle to its emergence.[130]

Singer argues that governmental intervention, in corporate governance and more generally, to promote fundamental employee rights (including rights to participate in the formulation of corporate policy) is both necessary and morally justifiable. He rejects the argument that this is an

---

[129] Despite the arguments of some in the law and economics camp that the expressed preferences of current employees should be taken at face value and should be determinative of the question as to whether employee participation should be introduced. See, for an example of this view, S. Bainbridge, 'Corporate decision making and the moral rights of employees', 43 (1998) *Villanova Law Review*, pp. 769–771.

[130] A. Johnston, 'EC freedom of establishment, employee participation in corporate governance and the limits of regulatory competition', *Journal of Corporate Law Studies* 6 (2006), pp. 71–112.

intervention in private contracting that would necessarily harm everyone by imposing higher terms than employers would be prepared to offer or employees would be prepared to accept (the unintended consequences type of argument). He argues that this logic does not apply when there is a radical inequality of bargaining power. More fundamentally, there are some things that are due as a matter of common decency. Consistently with a natural law approach, Singer's starting point is to say that employment (by which he seems to mean stable and well-paid employment) is a prerequisite for participation in the economic system and is necessary for human flourishing. Thus, a just economic system will have to provide: access to well-paid employment (providing a wage that will support a family at least above subsistence level); some reasonable guarantees of job security; retraining and job placement when employees are in transition; and a right to participate in formulating corporate policy in a democratic manner. He suggests that this outcome is most likely to be achieved by some form of co-determination or by giving employees ownership of voting shares or by a combination of the two. Worker participation is justified, he believes, by analogy with democracy in the political system.[131]

Dundon *et al.* point out, however, that the state of legislation or regulation is only one factor in determining whether or not employees will be given a voice in the organisation. In the last analysis, it is the attitude of management that will be crucial in this regard. The outcome for any given firm will result from a dialectic between regulation and management choice.[132]

Conclusion

Corporate governance is the system within the corporation for setting corporate strategy and ensuring effective use of corporate assets. It allocates power and responsibility, typically between senior management, shareholders and employees. The way that corporate governance is organised can have a very significant impact on employees.

CST has stressed and explained the ethical importance of employee participation in corporate governance and of giving employees some form of ownership of the firm that they work for and a share of its profits.

---

[131] J. Singer, 'Jobs and justice: rethinking the stakeholder debate', *University of Toronto Law Journal* 43 (1993), pp. 473–510.

[132] T. Dundon, A. Wilkinson, M. Marchington and P. Ackers, 'The meanings of employee voice', *International Journal of Human Resource Management* 15 (2004), pp. 1149–1170.

As this chapter` has shown, there are real and significant difficulties in the way of workable employee participation in governance and share ownership. It is argued, however, that they can be overcome with skilful design and a resolve on the part of senior management.

British companies are almost always under the control of shareholders and senior management. The shareholder value system means that management is under a duty to promote the best interests of shareholders. Even then, management can do much to promote a partnership between shareholders and employees. This calls for skill on its part in choosing the right investors and in creating the space for a partnership approach to work. The human resources director has a very important role to play in this regard.

The most obvious way of achieving employee ownership and financial participation is for employees to buy or be given shares in the company that employs them. ESOPs are an established tool for achieving this. In the right circumstances, ESOPs can lead to innovative governance structures that give employees a greater say in corporate governance.

Co-determination can do much to improve corporate governance and to improve the flow of information between management and employees. There is, however, virtually no prospect of co-determination being introduced on a widespread scale in the United Kingdom. Even in Germany, where it is well-established, it has been subjected to criticism. It is also under pressure from the spread of the shareholder value system. Nevertheless, it seems certain to survive though possibly in a modified way that is more accommodating of shareholder value practices.

The principle of subsidiarity suggests that states should be very slow to impose governance structures on corporations. It is unlikely that market forces would lead to co-determination being introduced where it is not already present. This suggests to some that they are inefficient but it may also be that serious market failures play a part in obstructing the spread of co-determination. In any event, there are important moral and political issues at stake that markets are not capable of addressing.

8

Corporate Governance in the United Kingdom

Introduction

This chapter describes the British system of corporate governance and appraises it from a CST-inspired ethical perspective. It would not be possible, or helpful, to describe British company law and corporate governance in detail. The aim, instead, is to point out the features of British corporate governance that many perceive to be its salient characteristics. The chapter looks at the sources of British corporate governance norms and the principal actors in it. In particular, of course, the focus is on whether it offers, or at least allows space for, employee participation and employee ownership.

The UK's shareholder value ideology is reinforced by (and is probably partly the result of) the dominance of institutional investors as the most important and influential group of investors in UK shares. The ideology has support amongst economists and may also reflect an intuition that the public company has strong structural similarities to the trust. Shareholder value is reflected in a number of important features of corporate governance law and practice and this chapter will describe these. The sophistication of the mechanisms that make it likely that the firm will be well-governed and that ensure that shareholders' expectations are met are, of course, no bad thing in themselves.

From the ethical perspective developed in earlier chapters, it is important to ask whether the British approach helps companies to meet the needs of customers or clients, whether it helps employees and shareholders to achieve the goals that brought them to the corporation and whether it encourages businesses to recognize their responsibility to the broader communities of which they form part.

Catholic Social Thought's prescriptions for an ethically sound approach to corporate governance

It is possible to set out a series of guidelines for an ethically sound approach to corporate governance based on CST. This chapter looks at

British corporate governance and evaluates it with these principles in mind.

First, the firm exists to allow employees and shareholders to combine in such a way as to meet the needs of consumers or clients more fully (in terms of what is offered and in terms of quality and price and so on). The firm's role is to meet some need or range of needs of customers or clients. At the same time, the modern firm often plays a part in shaping consumers' perceptions of their own needs. In this respect, the firm has a duty to avoid creating false needs.[1]

Profitability is essential since without it the firm can neither be kept in existence nor meet the needs of its employees and shareholders. Profitability provides a way of ensuring that the firm's resources are being put to good and socially valuable use. In the last analysis, however, profit is a means and not an end. The goals of the firm centre on the needs of its customers or clients, its employees and its shareholders. On occasions, its social responsibility may lead or require it to focus, in addition, on the needs of other people or groups. These goals provide a specific and tangible focus for management. It goes without saying that the pursuit of profit does not legitimize immoral decisions; those who take decisions on behalf of the corporation have to accept personal moral responsibility for them.

Employees find in the firm an outlet for their ability and desire to work. The sophistication of the modern organisation and the resources of all types at its command mean that it provides working opportunities that could not be conceived of in pre-modern economies. The organisation and the technology and other resources at its disposal mean that the modern worker can achieve much more within the organisation than he could when acting alone. They add immeasurably to what those employees can achieve but they are at the service of employees; employees are not mere fodder for the organisation. Management is at the service of employees.

Contemporary discussion of corporate governance tends to think in terms of a tension between the interests of capital and those of labour. And it is clear that a business can in fact tend to prioritise the interests of shareholders over those of employees. CST suggests, however, that this mental construct is the unhelpful product of a rather mechanistic way of thinking about human affairs. An ethically correct approach to corporate governance would look for ways of highlighting the synergies between

---

[1] John Paul II, *Centesimus annus*, para. 36.

capital and labour. It would look for ways of aligning the interests of labour and capital and seek to promote a spirit of partnership.

CST calls for employees to be given a stake in the ownership and profits of the businesses that they work for. This is one way of giving effect to, and reinforcing, the concepts of the complementarity of capital and labour, of labour's ethical priority over capital and of the biblical call for the human person to exercise dominion and stewardship over creation. Employee ownership and sharing in profits goes together with employee participation in governance and in relevant aspects of management. Employee participation in corporate governance could help employees to become full citizens of the corporate community and allow them (through their representatives) to exercise initiative and to take responsibility for the affairs of the firm. Employee participation in governance becomes especially important when the firm is passing through a crisis that could put the interests of employees in jeopardy and where management might be exposed to the temptation to subordinate the interests of employees to their own personal interests or those of shareholders.

Employee participation in management (direct participation in decisions affecting one's own daily work) is the liveliest form of participation so far as the individual employee is concerned. In general, the firm's employment practices should avoid anything that would have the practical effect of turning employees into cogs in a machine or of turning labour into a mere commodity.

The natural law concept of a community provides a way of understanding why employees are members of the firm and are not mere 'stakeholders'. Employees and shareholders have a prior claim on management's attention. The firm does, of course, have a responsibility to deal justly with other stakeholders. It also has a more general social responsibility since the firm is part of other communities (of a broader social fabric) which, in principle, could be global in scope.

Ownership of shares in UK listed companies

Some of the principal characteristics of British corporate governance are related to the pattern of corporate finance and the fact that institutional shareholders have been able to shape a governance environment that meets their needs. Deakin points out that:

> Company law, in particular in its Anglo-American form, is essentially concerned with a set of financial claims on the assets and income stream of the firm. It is not directly interested in the relations of production, and

employees only feature either as marginal subjects … or in so far as they happen to be creditors or shareholders.[2]

In other words, company law, despite its name, does not deal with all of the relations within the corporation. It concentrates on the interests of shareholders and, for practical purposes, treats them as being owners not just of their shares but, through them, of the corporation itself.

The ownership of shares in the UK's listed companies is dominated by institutional investors such as pension funds, insurance companies and investment companies. As at 31 December 2004, insurance companies owned 17.2% of UK equities and pension funds a further 15.7%. When one takes into account holdings by overseas institutions and other collective investment vehicles, the proportion of shares held by institutions makes them collectively much more important than individuals (holding just 14.1% of UK shares).[3]

Corporate governance for UK listed companies has been profoundly influenced by this institution-dominated ownership structure. In the second half of the twentieth century, financial institutions (pension funds, insurance companies and the like) replaced families as the dominant shareholder group[4] and they shape the corporate governance environment for listed companies. Franks, Mayer and Rossi carried out a survey of the evolution of UK corporate ownership over the course of the twentieth century and the impact that this evolution had on corporate governance institutions[5]. The emergence of the hostile takeover in the 1950s was the catalyst for a significant realignment of British corporate governance. Recognising the threat that the hostile takeover posed to their position, directors began to erect defences. These took the form of dual class voting shares and the sale of majority stakes to friendly parent companies (such as Whitbread). In these respects, the UK came to resemble continental Europe. But institutional shareholders, who were becoming a dominant force in UK listed companies, persuaded stock markets to deny access

---

[2] S. Deakin, ' "Enterprise-Risk": The juridical nature of the firm revisited', *Industrial Law Journal* 32 (2003), p. 98.

[3] *Share ownership: A report on ownership of shares as at December 31, 2004*, Office of National Statistics.

[4] M. Goergen and L. Renneboog, 'Strong managers and passive institutional investors in the UK', in F. Barca and M. Brecht (eds), *The Control of Corporate Europe*, (Oxford: Oxford University Press, 2001).

[5] J. Franks, C. Mayer and S. Rossi, 'Spending less time with the family: The decline of family ownership in the United Kingdom', in R. Morck (ed.), *A history of corporate governance around the world*, (Chicago, The University of Chicago Press, 2005).

to companies that employed these measures which were dismantled as a result.

> By the beginning of the 1970s the key factors of current UK corporate ownership and control were in place: substantial institutional share-holdings, a hostile takeover market and extensive minority shareholder protection. Together they had the effect of establishing active markets in corporate control.[6]

Institutions and the London Stock Exchange opposed takeover defenses because they were concerned about the interference with the takeover process, management entrenchment and the withdrawal of voting rights. Franks *et al.* comment:

> The distinct nature of the UK corporate sector is therefore in part a consequence of the dominance of equity institutions that placed shareholder returns above the private interests of either corporate shareholders or management.[7]

Institutional investors have both formal and informal means to act collectively thus maximising their influence on corporate governance; the formal means of collective action derives from their membership of representative bodies such as the Association of British Insurers ('ABI') or the National Association of Pension Funds ('NAPF'). These bodies in turn are members of the Institutional Shareholders' Committee ('ISC'). Both the ABI and the NAPF have issued best practice guidelines on corporate governance and the ISC has issued a statement on the responsibilities of institutional investors. There is increasing emphasis on the need for institutional shareholders to engage actively with management with a view to improving corporate governance.[8]

The Combined Code encourages boards to engage in a constructive dialogue with institutional investors[9] and has a separate section outlining the responsibilities of institutional shareholders to reciprocate.[10] The ISC has promulgated a statement of principles on the responsibilities of institutional shareholders and agents to engage with the companies that they invest in.[11] There are also long established practices of road shows and

---

[6] Franks *et al.*, 'Spending less time with the family', p. 585.
[7] Franks *et al.*, 'Spending less time with the family', p. 605.
[8] *Myners Report on Institutional Investment*, HM Treasury, London (2001).
[9] *The Combined Code on Corporate Governance*, section 1D.
[10] *The Combined Code on Corporate Governance*, section 2.
[11] Available at http://institutionalshareholderscommittee.org.uk/sitebuildercontent/site-builderfiles/ISCStatementofPrinciplesJun07.pdf (last accessed on 18th June 2008)

briefings by boards to their most important investors. The Companies Act 2006 has tried to encourage boards to intensify their communications with shareholders generally.[12] It has also tried to encourage major companies, through the medium of the Business Review to report on employee and social and environmental issues as they affect the company.

Shareholder value

The shareholder value approach to corporate governance requires directors to focus on maximising returns to shareholders. As the next section will show, UK corporate governance has been shaped by the shareholder value concept. Those who support the shareholder value approach often do so because they believe that it not only benefits shareholders but also advances aggregate social welfare.[13]

Alford and Naughton criticise the shareholder value approach. They argue that it gives profit (an instrumental good) priority over human development. They call for a re-ordering of corporate governance so as to give priority to the 'organisational common good', which is the promotion of all the goods necessary for integral human development in the organisation. They argue that the shareholder value model creates a culture in which every action focuses on financial gain and thus inverts the order of instrumental goods and what they term inherent or excellent goods (those open to all-round human development).[14]

Shareholder value and British corporate governance

Company law (the Companies Act 2006 and judicial decisions) forms the bedrock for corporate governance in the United Kingdom. It creates the framework for establishing companies and deals with a range of central governance questions. The Companies Act 2006 received the Royal Assent on 8th November 2006 and has been implemented in stages.

---

[12] See, for example the enhanced ability of shareholders to propose resolutions for discussion at general meetings in Companies Act 2006, section 338.

[13] H. Hansmann and R. Kraakman, 'What is corporate law', in *The anatomy of corporate law, A comparative and functional approach*, (Oxford: Oxford University Press, 2004), p. 18.

[14] H. Alford and M. Naughton, 'Beyond the shareholder model of the firm: Working towards the common good of a business', in S. Cortright and M. Naughton (eds), *Rethinking the purpose of business. Interdisciplinary essays from the Catholic Social Tradition*, (Notre Dame, Indiana, University of Notre Dame Press, 2002), p. 27.

Listed companies are also bound to comply with the Combined Code on Corporate Governance promulgated by the Financial Reporting Council. Section 1273 of the Companies Act 2006 amends the Financial Services and Markets Act 2000 and makes the Financial Services Authority ('the FSA') the 'competent authority' to make 'corporate governance rules'. The FSA makes and enforces the rules governing admission to listing. Issuers have to comply with all Listing Rules applicable to them[15]. The Combined Code is annexed to the Listing Rules. Listed companies have to include in their annual reports and accounts a statement as to how they apply the principles set out in section 1 of the Combined Code in a manner that would enable shareholders to evaluate how the principles have been applied. Reports and accounts also have to include a statement as to whether the company has complied with all of the provisions set out in section 1 of the Combined Code. Listed companies have to identify any failures to comply with section 1 of the Code and to give reasons for non-compliance[16]. Nominated advisers to companies applying for a listing on the Alternative Investment Market of the London Stock Exchange are required to consider with the directors of the applicant the adoption of appropriate governance measures[17]. Smerdon comments that in practice AIM companies hoping to attract institutional investors will have to show that their governance procedures match those of smaller listed companies.[18]

The code, like many other corporate governance codes, is principally concerned to improve investor confidence and to address the agency problems facing shareholders where there is a separation of ownership and control.[19] The Listing Rules require listed companies to issue a statement either confirming that they complied with the Combined Code or specifying how they failed to do so and giving an explanation of their reasons. The Combined Code is concerned with issues related to the appointment, remuneration and monitoring of the directors. In general, it seeks constructive engagement between the board and shareholders, especially institutional shareholders.

The shareholder value approach characterises British company law. It can be seen, for example, in the Companies Act provisions concerning

---

[15] Listing Rules, rule 1.1.   [16] Listing Rules, rule 9.8.6.
[17] London Stock Exchange, AIM rules for nominated advisers, Sch. 3 (Nominated Adviser Responsibilities), Rule AR2.
[18] R. Smerdon, *A practical guide to corporate governance*, (3rd edn), (London: Sweet & Maxwell, 2007), p. 45.
[19] C. Mallin, *Corporate Governance* (2nd edn), (Oxford: Oxford University Press, 2007) p. 22.

the appointment and removal of board members, the duties of directors and the disclosure and accountability mechanisms provided for. In each of these respects, it is clear that the Companies Act 2006 focuses on the needs of shareholders.

British company law and corporate governance practice provide for shareholder control over management. This is one of the most important practical manifestations of the shareholder value methodology. This control is manifested through a variety of mechanisms. First, it is the shareholders who appoint board members and they always have the right to remove them. The directors' fiduciary duties focus their attention predominantly on the interests of shareholders. Finally, the board is accountable to shareholders. Indeed, the trend is towards engaging shareholders in a conversation with management.

The directors are appointed by shareholders and can be removed by them. The procedure for appointing directors is to be found in the company's articles of association. The current Table A specifies that directors are appointed by the general meeting.[20] The board can make appointments on an interim basis but these have to be ratified later by the general meeting.[21] Equally, the general meeting always has the power to remove directors[22] and the default position established by Table A is that each director should stand for re-election at least once in every three years.[23]

British company law imposes a number of fiduciary duties on directors. These duties are now set out in sections 170 to 177 (inclusive) of the Companies Act 2006. These duties attach to every aspect of the board's activity. Section 172, the duty of loyalty, makes it clear that the directors' role is to promote the interests of shareholders. Section 172 begins:

> A director of a company must act in the way he considers, in good faith, would be most likely to promote the success of the company for the benefit of its members as a whole.[24]

---

[20] Companies (Tables A to F) Regulations 1985, Table A, regulation 78. See also article 20 in Schedule 3 to the Companies (Model Articles) Regulations 2008/3229. Article 20 allows members or the board to appoint but if directors are appointed by the board then article 21 requires them to stand for re-election at the next general meeting.
[21] Companies (Tables A to F) Regulations 1985, Table A, regulation 79. See also article 21 in Schedule 3 to the Companies (Model Articles) Regulations 2008 / 3229.
[22] Companies Act 2006, s. 168. See the discussion in P. Davies, *Gower and Davies' Principles of Modern Company Law*, (London: Thomson/Sweet & Maxwell, 2008), pp. 389–391.
[23] Companies (Tables A to F) Regulations 1985, regulation 73. See also article 21 in Schedule 3 to the Companies (Model Articles) Regulations 2008/3229.
[24] Companies Act 2006,

Thus, directors' duties are based on the principle of shareholder value according to which the litmus test is whether or not any given decision is good for shareholders.

Section 172 continues with some guidance for directors that is intended to cast further light on what they should consider as they pursue shareholder value. It requires directors to have regard to:

(a) the likely consequences of any decision in the long term,
(b) the interests of the company's employees,
(c) the need to foster the company's business relationships with suppliers, customers and others,
(d) the impact of the company's business operations on the community and the environment,
(e) the desirability of the company's maintaining a reputation for high standards of business conduct, and
(f) the need to act fairly as between members of the company.

These factors are clearly subject to the paramount duty to promote the success of the company for the benefit of its members; employees' interests, along with the other factors mentioned in (a) – (f) are means to an end, not ends in themselves. They are intended to reflect the concept of 'enlightened shareholder value'. The White Paper that preceded the Companies Act 2006 explained:

> The CLR proposed that the basic goal for directors should be the success of the company for the benefit of its members as a whole but that, to reach this goal, directors would need to take a properly balanced view of the implications of decisions over time and foster effective relationships with employees, customers and suppliers, and in the community more widely.[25]

Section 172 primarily requires directors to further the interests of shareholders. Indeed, it can be argued that the place of employees has gone backwards since they now vie with other stakeholders for the regard of directors. This formulation of the duty of good faith makes it clearer than before that, so far as company law is concerned, employees are not part of the company but are regarded as external to the company; employees are seen as standing in the same relation to the company as do long-term suppliers. The statute that the Companies Act 2006 replaced, the Companies Act 1985, gave explicit recognition to employee interests. Section 309 required directors to have regard to the interests of employees. Although

---

[25] DTI White Paper, *Company Law Reform*, (2005), Cm 6456, para. 3.3.

this was a duty owed to the company, it at least had the effect of requiring employee interests to be considered.[26] Implicitly, section 309 made the point that the company was not simply the sum of its shareholders.[27]

Lord Wedderburn suggests that the approach taken by the Companies Act 'hark[s] back to nineteenth century concepts as interpreted by the needs of modern capital'.[28] Burbidge remarks that this dilution of the protection for employee interests does not tally with the heightened duty to inform and consult employees imposed by the EU directives.[29] Certainly, if one is persuaded that employees are as much part of the enterprise as shareholders are then our company law seems curiously lop-sided. The Companies Act enshrines the idea that shareholders are the patrons of the board and from this follows an expectation that the board will act as agents or stewards of the shareholders.

Some argue that the duty of loyalty should be altered to require directors to promote the interests of employees as well as those of shareholders. This could be seen as a useful complement to the inclusion of employee representatives on the corporate board; it would give employee representatives useful leverage in boardroom discussions as they act to promote employee welfare. It would be a further expression of the centrality of employees within the corporation.

Davies looks at employee participation in UK corporate governance.[30] He concedes that shareholder primacy is not an inevitable feature of UK company law but, rather, is the product of corporations' reliance on equity finance. At the same time, he argues that modifying the fiduciary duty of directors will do nothing to further the employee cause. He suggests that one way forward for employees is to develop new information and consultation institutions to represent workers and to bargain more effectively on their behalf. Further, he suggests that greater disclosure can be of help. Even if the disclosure is primarily addressed to shareholders, there is nothing to stop employees from making use of it. Disclosure (and

---

[26] See the judgment of Vinelott J. in *Re Saul D Harrison & Sons plc* [1994] BCC 475 at 484.
[27] See the *obiter dictum* of Neill LJ in *Fulham Football Club Ltd v Cabra Estates plc* (1993) 65 P & C.R. 284 at 299.
[28] Lord Wedderburn of Charlton, 'Employees, partnership and Company Law', *Industrial Law Journal* 31 (2002), p. 99.
[29] P. Burbidge, 'Creating high performance boardrooms and workplaces – European corporate governance in the twenty first century', *European Law Review* 28 (2003), p. 663.
[30] P. Davies, 'Employee representation and Corporate Law reform: A comment from the United Kingdom', *Comparative Labour Law and Policy Journal* 22 (2000 – 2001), pp. 135–147.

preparation for it) may sensitise managements to the interests of non-shareholder constituents.

The board's reporting obligations and the mechanisms for holding them to account are all directed at shareholders. Directors are under a duty to prepare a directors' report for each financial year of the company.[31] This report is to contain the names of the directors during the relevant financial year and is to state the principal activities of the company during the course of the financial year.[32] Except in the case of companies subject to the small companies' regime, the directors' report must include a business review,[33] the aim of which is to make directors accountable to shareholders.[34] The directors' report is to be a balanced and comprehensive analysis of the development and performance of the company's business and of its position at the end of the relevant financial year.[35]

So far as necessary for this purpose, the business review of a quoted company is to include the main trends and factors likely to affect the future development, performance and position of the company's business.[36] It is also to provide:

information about –

(i) environmental matters (including the impact of the company's business on the environment),
(ii) the company's employees, and
(iii) social and community issues,

including information about any policies of the company in relation to those matters and the effectiveness of those policies.[37]

For all companies, quoted or not, (save for those subject to the small companies' regime) the business review must contain an analysis using key financial performance indicators and key performance indicators concerning other issues such as environmental matters and employee matters.[38] Medium-sized companies are not subject to the requirement to provide analysis using non-financial key performance indicators.[39]

[31] Companies Act 2006, s. 415.
[32] Companies Act 2006, s. 416.
[33] Companies Act 2006, s. 417(1).
[34] Companies Act 2006, s. 417(2).
[35] Companies Act 2006, s. 417 (4).
[36] Companies Act 2006, s. 417(5)(a).
[37] Companies Act 2006, s. 417(5)(b).
[38] Companies Act 2006, s. 417(6).
[39] Companies Act 2006, s. 417 (7).

One would expect that directors would be concerned about the image that they portray through the business review and that they will be concerned to live up to the standards implied by the key performance indicators. They complement the enlightened shareholder value approach embodied in section 172 in that, indirectly, they suggest (without expressly imposing) a sort of obligation to stakeholders such as employees.

Some commentators have high hopes for the business review; they believe that it can play a significant part in shaping UK corporate governance. It does not seem, however, that the Business Review is likely to do much to promote the view that employees are the central concern of directors or of UK company law in general. The problem with the Business Review, as with the duty of loyalty, is that employees are seen as just one more stakeholder. In effect, employees are seen as a resource or asset and directors are reporting to shareholders on how effectively the asset has been deployed.

There were hopes in some quarters that the Company Law Review would lead to a fundamental realignment of corporate law resulting in a shift to a stakeholder view of the corporation that would be reflected in the duty of loyalty. Clearly, these hopes were not realised. In truth, there was probably never any prospect of changes to our system of company law that disrupted its almost exclusive concern with shareholder issues. The reform process was guided by a concern with technical and procedural issues and there seems to have been no appetite for a debate on fundamental questions such as the social purpose of the corporation and the role of the employee within it.[40] The assumption is that company law is a system that allows shareholders to engage with the corporation, to ensure that directors are responsible to them and to act collectively. The best that can be said is that it is agnostic on the question of whether the corporation has any social significance or purpose other than to promote shareholder value. Paradoxically, the enlightened shareholder value concept (and its reflection in the Business Review provisions) actually weaken the hints in the pre-Companies Act 2006 law that employees might have some special status in the company.

---

[40] The White Paper, *Company Law Reform*, DTI, March 2005, Cm 6456 highlighted issues such as enhancing shareholder dialogue, ensuring better regulation and making it easier to set up a company.

Takeovers

Armour, Deakin and Konzelmann challenge the idea that the share-holder value ideology is in any way hard-wired into the UK's system of corporate governance. They argue that the current preoccupation with shareholder value does not date back beyond the 1980s and 1990s. Although takeovers are often said to be a means of disciplining poorly performing management, they may also be driven by the possibility of expropriating employees. The result is that takeovers may make it difficult to make credible *ex ante* commitments to employees; and so it becomes correspondingly more difficult to persuade employees to invest in firm-specific skills.[41] Deakin argues that the current pre-occupation with shareholder value began with the arrival of the hostile takeover in Britain and contests the view that hostile takeovers improve corporate performance and enhance overall social welfare. Further, the ensuing downsizing may be no more than a rent-shifting exercise that creates value for shareholders by reneging on implicit promises made to employees.[42]

Poor management leads to a reduction in a company's share price and, in the right conditions, this reduction in share price increases the prospects of a hostile takeover. The result of the takeover, according to this theory, is that the new owners will replace the under-performing management. The buyers' return on the risk and expense of the takeover comes in the form of the premium that they earn when the appointment of a competent management team increases the share price. According to this theory, the threat of takeover in a listed company provides strong incentives for management to promote shareholder welfare as measured by the share price.[43] Thus, takeovers (or the credible threat of them) can make a positive contribution to corporate governance. This positive view of the social value of takeovers has not, however, gone unchallenged. Some believe, however, that at least part of the premium earned by acquirers results from a reneging on implicit promises given to employees. Shleifer and Summers have argued that, in fact, takeovers do not necessarily create extra value but rather

[41] J. Armour, S. Deakin and S. Konzelmann, 'Shareholder primacy and the trajectory of UK corporate governance', *British Journal of Industrial Relations* 41 (2003), p. 531.

[42] S. Deakin, 'The coming transformation of shareholder value', *Corporate Governance: An International Review*, 13 (2005), p. 11.

[43] H. Manne, 'Mergers and the market for corporate control', *The Journal of Political Economy* 73 (1965), p. 110.

that they act as a mechanism that transfers wealth from employees to shareholders.[44]

Howse and Trebilcock look at how employee participation could provide reasonable protection for employees. They point out that workers invest human capital in their employers and that there is a need for mechanisms to protect these stakes in the firm. Accepting the nexus of contracts approach, they note that (despite Williamson's analysis) it is difficult to craft *ex ante* contractual commitments that adequately protect employees. Earnings are often set below an employee's contribution to productivity in the early years but rise with seniority. Shareholders can engage in rent-shifting by reneging on the implicit agreement about employee entitlements.

Employee participation could give employee representatives a right to constrain certain types of management decisions (such as plant closures). Even if employee representatives are in a minority, they would gain valuable information about the economic condition and strategy of the firm. The employee representatives could also act as whistle-blowers and raise an early warning about management proposals that have the potential to harm employee interests. Employee representatives would also be able to add a new dimension to boardroom discussions by pointing out difficulties or strategies that management had simply not considered. Howse and Trebilcock make the point that it is possible to design arrangements for useful employee participation at board level that would not involve employees in the governance structure for worker-management relations.[45]

The legal rules governing UK takeovers are now to be found in the Companies Act 2006. In general, directors are under a duty to act in the company's best interests and this primarily means that they are to act in the best interests of employees although they are also to take into account the effect of the takeover on other stakeholders such as employees.[46] The Companies Act 2006 also includes a code dealing specifically with the conduct of takeovers. This code puts British takeover regulation on a statutory footing after four decades during which the Takeover Panel and the City Code operated as a self-regulatory system. The Companies Act

---

[44] A. Shleifer and L. Summers, 'Breaches of Trust in Hostile Takeovers'. (Cambridge, Mass., National Bureau of Economic Research, 1987).

[45] R. Howse and M. Trebilcock, 'Protecting the Employment Bargain', *University of Toronto Law Journal* 43 (1993), p. 751.

[46] Companies Act 2006, s. 172.

provisions have to reflect the provisions of the EC Takeover Directive[47] that seeks to create a harmonised set of rules governing the conduct of takeover bids for listed companies in the European Community. The Companies Act 2006 makes the Panel on Takeovers and Mergers the body responsible for implementing the Takeover Directive in the United Kingdom.[48] The Panel had previously operated on a self-regulatory basis. The Panel has created, and now amends, interprets and enforces, the Takeover Code.[49]

The Code articulates its general aims as follows:

> The Code is designed principally to ensure that shareholders are treated fairly and are not denied an opportunity to decide on the merits of a take-over and that shareholders of the same class are afforded equivalent treatment by an offeror. The Code also provides an orderly framework within which takeovers are conducted. In addition, it is designed to promote, in conjunction with other regulatory regimes, the integrity of the financial markets.[50]

The Code makes only the briefest of mentions of employees and their interests. General Principle 2, amongst other things, requires the target company's board to give its views on the effect of the implementation of the bid on employment, conditions of employment and the location of the company's places of business. This is reflected in rules 24.1 and 25.1(b). Rule 24.1 requires offerors to explain in their offer documents (among other things): their intentions regarding the future business of the company; their strategic plans for the target and their likely implications on employment and places of business; and their intentions with regard to continued employment of the target's employees and management. The target's board has to give its opinion on the offer and this opinion must include its views on all the company's interests including, specifically, employment and its views on the offeror's strategic plans for the company and on their likely repercussions on employment and the locations of the target company's places of business.[51] Both the offer document and the target board's opinion are to be made available to employee representatives or, where there are no such representatives, to employees themselves.[52]

---

[47] Directive 2004/25/EC of the European Parliament and of the Council on of 21 April 2004 on Takeover Bids.

[48] Companies Act 2006, s. 942.

[49] The latest edition (9th edn, 2009) is available at www.thetakeoverpanel.org.uk/wp-content/uploads/2008/11/code.pdf, (last accessed on 28th July 2009).

[50] Code, *Introduction*, 2(a).   [51] Code, Rule 25.1(b).

[52] Code, Rules 30.1 and 30.2.

Where does this leave employee participation?

Davies points out that British company law views shareholders as the members of the company to the exclusion of all other groupings and this leads naturally to the adoption of the view that shareholders' interests predominate in company law.[53] Shareholders control the corporation through their control over the company's constitution, management and economic surplus.[54]

It is clear, even from this sketchiest of introductions to UK corporate governance, that shareholders (either directly or through institutions or organisations that represent their interests) are actively engaged in framing the corporate governance process. Naturally, then, the process tends to focus on their needs and to see employee interests as relevant only to the extent that those interests further shareholder interests. In theory, company law could seek to build employees into corporate governance. While some systems around the world have taken this opportunity, UK company law has not done so. The UK's corporate governance norms have become more sophisticated and try to secure a positive role for shareholders, especially institutional shareholders, in evaluating the activity of corporate boards. This is to be welcomed and it seems that at least some institutional shareholders use their influence to help add value to the company in the longer term.[55] The development of better channels for engagement by shareholders in corporate governance, however, throws into even sharper relief the lack of mechanisms to engage employees in corporate governance. The emergence of bodies representing the interests of shareholders suggests the need for trade unions (or other bodies representing the interests of employees) to engage in dialogue with them to see how they can make common cause.

British company law gives shareholders access to a bundle of control rights in respect of the corporation that is so extensive as to amount almost to ownership of the corporation. The image that is suggested is that of the board as trustees for their shareholder/beneficiaries. This image is reinforced by the fiduciary duties that directors owe to the company. Indeed, British company law and corporate governance

---

[53] P. Davies, *Introduction to Company Law*, (Oxford, Oxford University Press, 2002), p. 2.
[54] Davies, *Introduction to Company Law*, pp. 15–16.
[55] P. Lee, 'Institutional shareholder activism – part 2', in R. Smerdon, *A practical guide to corporate governance*, 3rd edn, (London: Sweet & Maxwell, 2007),

actively seek to encourage shareholders to view themselves as responsible owners of the corporation. If one sees shareholders as being the rightful owners of the corporation, uniquely possessing the incentives to act as responsible stewards of it, then employee participation is problematical; making employees share their control rights might make it more difficult for them to exercise an appropriate level of control over senior management.[56]

The Companies Act 2006 was preceded by a lengthy consultation process during which a steering group produced eight detailed consultation documents. These were followed by two White Papers and then by the parliamentary procedure culminating in the eventual birth of the Act. Employee participation was never on the agenda and it can be argued that the Act actually downgraded the status of employees within the corporate governance framework. That employee participation did not even feature in the principal policy documents is eloquent testimony to the depth of the conviction in the UK that this is not an issue that falls within the range of proper topics for company law and corporate governance.

It was not always so. In the late 1970s, the UK flirted with some form of mandatory co-determination. The 1977 Bullock Report proposed that there should be a system of employee participation on the boards of companies with more than 2,000 employees. There were to be equal numbers of shareholder and employee representatives and a third group selected by the first two groups. The third group would both provide expertise and act as a tie-breaker in the event of deadlock. A committee of shop-stewards was to decide on the mechanism for appointing the employee representatives. The system would only apply to businesses once employees had voted in favour of its introduction. Bullock recommended that certain functions (appointment of senior management, changes in capital structure and major disposals) would be reserved to the board regardless of the wishes of shareholders. The report recommended that there should be a statutory statement of directors' duties and that one of these should require directors to take employee interests into account. As is well-known, however, the change of government in the late 1970s meant that any momentum that there might have been behind the idea of employee participation was completely lost.[57]

---

[56] See, for example, M. Roe, 'Codetermination and German securities markets', in M. Blair and M. Roe (eds.), *Employees and corporate governance*.

[57] For a discussion of the Bullock Report see P. Davies, 'The Bullock Report and employee participation in corporate planning in the UK', *Journal of Comparative Corporate Law and Securities Regulation* 1 (1978), pp. 245–272.

Later attempts to re-introduce the idea through the European Company Law Harmonisation Programme met with stiff, and successful, resistance. The United Kingdom (amongst other EU member states) fought hard, and largely successfully, to keep mandatory employee participation measures out of EU corporate governance initiatives. It has been left to legislation under other policy banners to deal with the void where employee participation might have been expected to be found. Against this background, there would have been little point in revisiting issues such as co-determination in the lead up to the Companies Act 2006.

Can institutional shareholders help?

Clearly, one would expect institutional investors to be primarily concerned with extracting financial value from their shareholdings; after all, they owe a fiduciary duty to their beneficiaries to do exactly that. Some have argued that, in the last analysis, achieving this aim will necessarily require them to look beyond short-term financial considerations. Institutional investors are fiduciary investors (subject to a fiduciary duty to foster the interests of their beneficiaries). They are also universal investors: they are so diversified that they must take an interest in the entire economy and not just in a particular group of firms. Exit is no longer a strategy that they can rely on. So they must find ways to exercise voice if they are dissatisfied with the performance of the companies that they have invested in. Because they are interested in the entire economy, they internalise concerns which could be seen as externalities from the perspective of the individual firm. Thus, they maximise returns to beneficiaries by taking account of environmental concerns, education and training, research and development and so on. Universal owners have both stockholder and stakeholder perspectives.[58] It is doubtful, however, whether institutional investors will play a very significant role in advancing the employee participation cause. Davies points to the US where even trade unions acting as institutional investors have pursued a traditional corporate governance agenda; they have not used their rights as shareholders to further employee interests.[59] That said, the ability and willingness of institutional shareholders to play a positive role in corporate governance is something

---

[58] J. Hawley and A. Williams, *The rise of fiduciary capitalism. How institutional investors can make corporate America more democratic*, (Philadelphia: University of Pennsylvania Press, 2000).
[59] Davies, 'Employee representation and corporate law reform', p. 135.

to be welcomed. As Donald points out, it is important that the law should facilitate their active engagement.[60]

Conclusion

The shareholder value ideology is deeply entrenched in British corporate governance. It is manifested in the directors' duty of loyalty, in their reporting obligations and, pre-eminently, in the market for corporate control. Institutional investors now own a very significant proportion of UK equities. Working through their representative bodies they have been able to create an environment that is very receptive to their interests and concerns. Employee interests, by contrast, have never occupied centre-stage in British corporate governance and they have lost ground as a result of the Companies Act 2006.

UK corporate governance is now shareholder-centred. Company law requires directors to give priority to the interests of shareholders. An active market for corporate control reinforces the priority given to share-holder interests. The Combined Code and the processes and incentive structures associated with it also seek to concentrate the minds of dir-ectors on the needs of shareholders. This shareholder-centred approach could have a number of positive effects. In principle, it creates a system of accountability and sets appropriate incentives for a specialised, unified managerial class to work for the benefit of the company and its sharehold-ers. It gives a relatively small group of institutional shareholders the task of monitoring management on behalf of shareholders as a whole. It cre-ates formal mechanisms for dialogue between management and institu-tional investors. When the system works well, then, it can provide strong professional leadership and offer reasonable guarantees that shareholder needs will be addressed.

The system does not always work well, however. The managerial class can manipulate the system so as to further its own interests at the expense of shareholders; the control mechanisms might fail to some sig-nificant extent. Non-executive directors and other key players within the institutional investor sector may lack the courage, the will or the incentives to play the part expected of them. In these circumstances, corporate governance might to some degree provide a fig-leaf for an

[60] D. Donald, 'Shareholder voice and its opponents', *Journal of Corporate Law Studies* 5 (2005), pp. 305–361.

inappropriate transfer of wealth and power from shareholders to senior management.

From this book's perspective, the shortcomings of UK corporate governance are obvious. The duty of loyalty ranks employees alongside other stakeholders and far behind shareholders. There is no mechanism that makes management accountable to employees nor any channel for employees to make their contribution to corporate governance. On the positive side, within certain limits, management is free to provide whatever financial rewards it sees fit to its employees.

The provisional conclusion must be that British corporate governance is seriously defective in that it gives no place to employee representatives and fails to acknowledge its duty to promote the interests of employees. British corporate governance has developed extremely sophisticated mechanisms to ensure that shareholders are represented in governance. There is, however, a total vacuum when it comes to corresponding forms of employee participation. In other words, parts of the design of British corporate governance are very well-developed but other essential aspects are untouched. The conclusion can, however, only be provisional. The next chapter will look at whether labour law has satisfactorily remedied the deficiency.

9

Labour law and employee participation

Introduction

In the previous chapter we saw that British company law and corporate governance are inspired by the shareholder value principle. The corporation, technically distinct from its shareholders, is seen as existing principally to promote their interests. The board is required to take the advancement of shareholder interests as its principal decision-making criterion and is accountable to shareholders. Greater dialogue between the board and shareholders, especially institutional shareholders, is a major policy goal.

The increasing sophistication of corporate governance mechanisms is clearly welcome to the extent that it truly leads to well-run businesses that meet the needs of their customers or clients at the same time as they promote the relevant interests of shareholders and employees. But where are the mechanisms that would allow employees both to play their part in promoting the well-being of the business and to protect their own reasonable interests?

Serious engagement with the possibility of mandatory employee participation on the corporate board came to an end by the late 1970s. From then on, it has been taken for granted in the UK that company law and corporate governance belong to the shareholder. Employees, their interests and mechanisms for participation have been hived off into a separate labour law compartment. This chapter looks at the contributions made by labour law to the search for institutions that facilitate employee participation in governance. It considers whether or not they give adequate expression to employees' status as members of the corporate community and asks whether they give sufficient protection to employees' interests in the firm. It also considers whether the current boundaries between company law and labour law in the United Kingdom are desirable.

Deakin and Morris define labour law as the rules that govern the employment relationship. More broadly, they see it as providing the normative framework for the existence and operation of all the institutions of the labour market. In this latter sense, it has to do with the business enterprise, trade unions, employers' associations and the state.[1] This chapter is concerned with labour law in Deakin and Morris' broader sense. It is concerned especially with the labour law institutions that give employee representatives some ability to be informed about the company they work for and a voice in at least some aspects of corporate governance. The chapter also looks at the mechanisms to facilitate dialogue between the representatives of capital and labour at sectoral level and at the level of the economy as a whole.

The opening section of the chapter looks at collective bargaining. It will then be seen that the UK system has been supplemented by two imports from the European Union, the European Works Council and the information and consultation mechanisms introduced by the Information and Consultation Directive.[2] These each amount to clear steps in the right direction. It can be argued, however, that they tacitly accept that employees are not full citizens of the corporate community.

CST has repeatedly argued for dialogue between capital and labour to occur not only at the enterprise level but also at the level of the broader economy. The economy can be seen as a group, community or society in its own right. It can be seen as a co-operative endeavour by economic actors to meet the need for goods and services of the communities it serves. Free, fair and vigorous competition is an important characteristic of the economy but this fact should not be allowed to detract from the fact that, when all is said and done, economic actors are engaged in a joint effort to help meet society's needs and to make best use of finite resources. Human weakness, aided and abetted by economistic modes of thinking, can obscure the sense of striving together for a common purpose. When this gets out of hand, the state may need to step in. CST's principle of subsidiarity suggests that so far as possible, however, governance of the economy, as a distinct society, should be left in the hands of economic actors. CST suggests that dialogue between representatives of labour and capital, in the economy as a whole, or in particular sectors of it, is an important element of economic governance. One purpose of this chapter is to look at whether the UK has mechanisms in place to encourage this dialogue.

[1] S. Deakin and G. Morris, *Labour Law*, (4th edn), (Oxford: Hart Publishing, 2005), p. 1.
[2] Information and Consultation Directive, article 3(1). 'Undertaking' and 'establishment' are defined in article 2.

Trade unions

Work plays a central part in our well-being as individuals. The organisation of work in such a way as to promote the well-being of labour is one of the primary responsibilities of those in charge of the governance of the firm, the economy and the state. Labour should play an active part in decision-making that vitally concerns its interests. At the level of the economy, of the state and internationally, this participation will necessarily be through representative institutions such as trade unions.

CST speaks of trade unions as being an indispensable element of social life. They are an expression of the freedom of association and their central mission is to defend the vital interests of workers. Although they may have to engage in a struggle to perform this role, this struggle is to be seen as an element of a duty to contribute positively to the well-being of the economy's institutions. Unions should not see themselves as being combatants in a class struggle. Thus, unions are under a duty to collaborate with other social institutions (including, presumably, representatives of management and capital); they have responsibilities concerning the production, and not only the distribution, of wealth. The *Compendium of the Social Doctrine of the Church* puts it this way:

> Beyond their functions of defending and vindicating, unions have the duty of acting as representatives working for 'the proper arrangement of economic life' and of educating the social consciences of workers so that they will feel that they have an active role, according to their proper capacities and aptitudes, in the whole task of economic and social development and in the attainment of the universal common good.[3]

One of the challenges facing unions is to bring labour issues into the political arena without being political parties themselves. In the political arena, unions should try to help create conditions that will allow the right to work to be exercised by all who are able and willing. Changing patterns of work mean that trade unions will need to represent those on non-standard or fixed-term contracts, the unemployed, immigrants and seasonal workers.

CST has repeatedly spoken out in favour of trade unions.[4] John Paul II summed up this previous teaching in *Laborem exercens*:

---

[3] *Compendium*, para. 307.
[4] Leo XIII, *Rerum novarum*, 50, John XXIII, *Mater et magistra*, 22, Second Vatican Council, *Gaudium et spes*, 68 and Paul VI, *Octogesima adveniens*, 14.

[Unions'] task is to defend the existential interests of workers in all sectors in which their rights are concerned. The experience of history teaches that organisations of this type are an *indispensable element of social life*, especially in modern industrialised societies.[5]

In the same passage, he stresses that unions should see themselves as having an essentially positive role and take responsibility for the economic common good; their role includes, but transcends, getting a good deal for their members. John Paul II warns unions against the temptation of becoming instruments of group or class egoism.[6] The same encyclical speaks of the need for 'ever new movements of solidarity of the workers'; they are especially needed to protect workers from exploitation, poverty and hunger.[7]

Collective bargaining

British employment law is derived from a number of sources including common law, statute and a number of Codes of Practice such as those issued by the Secretary of State for Employment and ACAS.[8] The Trade Union and Labour Relations (Consolidation) Act 1992 ('TULR(C)A') incorporates provisions designed to promote the practice of a form of voluntary joint regulation of some aspects of the employment relationship by management and employee representatives.[9] In principle, it is a way for employees (acting through their representatives) to play a part in the regulation of a limited range of employment issues.

Section 178 of TULR(C)A defines 'collective agreement' to mean an agreement or arrangement made by or on behalf of one or more trade unions and one or more employers or employers' associations relating to one or more of the following matters:

(a) terms and conditions of employment, or the physical conditions in which any workers are required to work;

(b) engagement or non-engagement, or termination or suspension of employment or the duties of employment, of one or more workers;

(c) allocation of work or the duties of employment between workers or groups of workers;

[5] John Paul II, *Laborem exercens*, 20.
[6] John Paul II, *Laborem exercens*, 20.   [7] John Paul II, *Laborem exercens*, 8.
[8] Deakin and Morris, *Labour Law*, pp. 53–59.
[9] See S. Honeyball, *Honeyball & Bowers' textbook on Employment Law*, (10th edn), (Oxford: Oxford University Press, 2008), pp. 364–387 for an introduction to the domestic and European legal issues dealt with in this chapter, including the British law on collective bargaining.

(d) matters of discipline;
(e) a workers' membership or non-membership of a trade union;
(f) facilities for officials of trade unions; and
(g) machinery for negotiation or consultation, and other procedures, relating to any of the above matters, including the recognition by employers or by employers' associations of the right of a trade union to represent workers.

'Collective bargaining' means negotiations relating to or connected with one or more of the above matters. Recognised trade unions have a right to information for collective bargaining purposes. TULR(C)A establishes a mechanism for identifying employee representatives.[10] It requires employers to disclose to the representatives of recognised trade unions all of the information in their possession (or in that of an 'associated employer') relating to the employer's undertaking:

(a) without which the trade union representatives would be to a material extent impeded in carrying on collective bargaining, and
(b) which it would be in accordance with good industrial relations practice to disclose for the purposes of collective bargaining.[11]

The trade union representative triggers the disclosure obligation by making a written request.[12] If the employer fails to make adequate disclosure, the trade union can invoke TULR(C)A's dispute resolution mechanism. This can result in an order by the Central Arbitration Committee as to the information to be disclosed or confirmed; it can even lead to the insertion of terms and conditions into the employment contracts of some or all employees.[13]

The TULR(C)A disclosure provisions are obviously subject to a number of significant weaknesses and, in practice, are little-used.[14] One of the weaknesses of the British collective bargaining system is that employers are only obliged to respond to union proposals; they are under no compulsion actually to reach an agreement. Gospel, Lockwood and Willman point to a number of problems with the traditional British approach to disclosure. The first is that disclosure is limited to the matters in respect of which the union is recognised; so access to information as to costs or potential restructuring may be denied to unions if this has not previously

[10] TURL(C)A, Sch. A1.   [11] TULR(C)A 1992, s. 181(2).
[12] TULRCA 1992, ss. 181(1) and (3).   [13] TULR(C)A 1992, ss. 183–185.
[14] Deakin and Morris, *Labour Law*, pp. 849–854.

been a subject for bargaining.[15] Then there are problems as to timing: unions may need urgent access to information and be unable to spare the time to exhaust the CAC procedure.[16] Finally, the mechanisms for enforcing disclosure obligations in collective bargaining agreements are weak since the CAC can neither force disclosure nor include a punitive element in any award made against the employer.[17]

Deakin and Morris make the point that the scope for redistribution through collective bargaining has been limited by the law but also, and to a much greater extent by increased product market competition and growing financial pressure on corporate management. These factors make it difficult for unions to promote a partnership agenda.[18]

Gospel *et al.* are adamant that trade unions must have a role in the information and disclosure process if it is to be meaningful:

> [T]hey have the organisational capability to use information in that they are continuous associations with a real independence of the employer and with expertise and resources beyond the workplace.[19]

They have several suggestions for reform of the disclosure requirements associated with UK collective bargaining law; the areas to be covered should be made more extensive (to include non-labour costs, financial matters, the state of the organisation and corporate strategy); the statutory restrictions on disclosure could be more narrowly defined; and there should be more stringent penalties for failure to disclose.[20]

Deakin and Morris argue that the common law's sceptical attitude towards collectivism is deeply-rooted and that economic liberalism has long been one of its consistent themes.[21] They make the comment that:

> In its present form it perpetuates a view of workers as 'on the outside' of the enterprise.[22]

Collins argues that British employment law has witnessed a struggle between a 'liberal' approach, on the one hand, and an 'industrial pluralist'

---

[15] H. Gospel, G. Lockwood and P. Willman, 'A British dilemma: Disclosure of information for collective bargaining and joint vonsultation, *Comparative Labour Law & Policy Journal* 22 (2000–2001), p. 338.

[16] Gospel, Lockwood and Willman, 'A British dilemma', p. 339.

[17] Gospel, Lockwood and Willman, 'A British dilemma', pp. 339–340.

[18] Deakin and Morris, *Labour Law*, p. 44.

[19] Gospel, Lockwood and Willman, 'A British dilemma', p. 346.

[20] Gospel, Lockwood and Willman, "A British dilemma', p. 347.

[21] Deakin and Morris, *Labour Law*, p. 12.

[22] Deakin and Morris, *Labour Law*, p. 854

model, on the other. The former is rooted in *laissez faire* notions of free-dom of contract while the latter looks for ways of mitigating the conflict between capital and labour. Acceptance of the pluralist approach has fostered a search for mechanisms that allow power to be shared between employers and employees; collective bargaining arrangements are one product of this approach.[23] The British approach to collective bargaining seeks to support workplace partnership.[24]

European Works Councils

The information and consultation measures outlined in the European Works Council Directive[25] and the Information and Consultation Directive[26] offer some hope for advocates of employee participation. They build on foundations laid by the Acquired Rights Directive,[27] the Collective Redundancies Directive[28] and the Insolvency Directive.[29] The purpose of these latter directives was to try to protect jobs in the case of restructuring and at times of financial crisis. Important as they are, they do not meet the need for employee participation mechanisms of more general application. It can be argued that the European Works Council Directive and the Information and Consultation Directive go some way towards remedying this deficiency. As Deakin and Morris point out, how-ever, the EC directives require employers to consult employee representa-tives in certain circumstances but do ultimately leave decision-making in the hands of the employer.[30]

Over the years, several EC Directives have imposed an obligation on employers to inform and consult their employees.[31] The most thorough-going information and consultation mechanisms, however, are those

[23] Hugh Collins, *Employment Law*, (Oxford, Oxford University Press, 2003), pp. 17–20.
[24] Collins, *Employment Law*, p. 121.
[25] Council Directive 94/45/EC of 22 September 1994 on the establishment of a European Works Council or a procedure in Community-scale undertakings and Community-scale groups of undertakings for the purposes of informing and consulting employees and Council Directive 97/74/EC of 15 December 1997 extending, to the United Kingdom of Great Britain and Northern Ireland, Directive 94/45/EC on the establishment of a European Works Council or a procedure in Community-scale undertakings and Community-scale groups of undertakings for the purposes of informing and consulting employees.
[26] Directive 2002/14/EC.   [27] Directive 2001/23/EC.
[28] Council Directive 75/129/EEC.   [29] Directive 80/987/EEC.
[30] Deakin and Morris, *Labour Law*, p. 860.
[31] Directives 98/59/EC, 2001/23/EC and 89/391/EC.

created by the European Works Council Directive[32] and the Information and Consultation Directive.[33] Originally, the Treaty of Rome paid little attention to labour issues, devoting only three articles to them. The Treaty on European Union, however, included a Protocol on Social Policy. The EU Charter of Fundamental Rights states that:

> Workers or their representatives must, at the appropriate levels, be guaranteed information and consultation in good time in the cases and under the conditions provided for by Community law and national laws and practices.[34]

The European Works Council Directive is one of the principal measures giving effect to this proclamation. Its most basic function is to act as a conduit for information and consultation between employers and employees.

The European Works Council Directive requires every 'Community-scale undertaking' (one with 1000 employees in Member States and at least 150 employees in each of at least two Member States) and every 'Community-scale group of undertakings' to negotiate with a Special Negotiating Body representing employees. The negotiations are to result in an agreement for the creation either of a European Works Council ('EWC') or of an information and consultation procedure. Member States are to prepare a statutory default agreement that will apply if, for example, the parties fail to conclude their negotiations within three years of a request from employees to do so. The annex to the Directive specifies the essential items that are to appear in Member States' schemes. Since negotiations will take place against this template, the annex might be regarded as establishing the core elements of the agreement. Amongst other things, the annex stipulates that the EWC's competence is limited to issues that concern the Community-scale undertaking or group of undertakings as a whole.

---

[32] Council Directive 94/45/EC of 22 September 1994 on the establishment of a European Works Council or a procedure in Community-scale undertakings and Community-scale groups of undertakings for the purposes of informing and consulting employees and Council Directive 97/74/EC of 15 December 1997 extending, to the United Kingdom of Great Britain and Northern Ireland, Directive 94/45/EC on the establishment of a European Works Council or a procedure in Community-scale undertakings and Community-scale groups of undertakings for the purposes of informing and consulting employees.

[33] Directive 2002/14/EC establishing a general framework for informing and consulting employees in the European Community (OJ L 80, 23/3/2002 p. 29).

[34] The EU Charter of Fundamental Rights, article 27.

Paragraph 2 of the Annex lists the matters on which employees are to be consulted:

> The European Works Council shall have the right to meet with the central management once a year, to be informed and consulted, on the basis of a report drawn up by the central management, on the progress of the business of the Community-scale undertaking or Community-scale group of undertakings and its prospects. The local managements shall be informed accordingly. The meeting shall relate in particular to the structure, economic and financial situation, the probable development of the business and of production and sales, the situation and probable trend of employment, investments, and substantial changes concerning organisation, introduction of new working methods or production processes, transfers of production, mergers, cut-backs or closures of undertakings, establishments or important parts thereof, and collective redundancies.

The succeeding paragraph discusses what is to happen where there are exceptional circumstances affecting the employees' interests to a considerable extent (particularly relocations, the closure of establishments or undertakings or collective redundancies). The EWC, or a select committee of it, shall have the right to be informed. It shall have the right to meet, at its request, the central management, or any other more appropriate level of management within the Community-scale undertaking or group of undertakings having its own powers of decision, so as to be informed and consulted on measures significantly affecting employees' interests. These rights to be consulted and informed are, however, without prejudice to the prerogatives of the central management. Thus, managements in shareholder-centred systems need not be diverted from shareholder value as their guiding principle.

The European Works Council Directive is an improvement on the earlier directives mentioned above. The European Works Council is to be informed and consulted every year and not simply at times of restructuring or financial crisis. The reference to consultation implies some form of dialogue and this too is a positive feature. The disclosure required covers matters relating to the business in general as well as more specifically employee-focused issues. The directive could be seen as an employee-focused version of the Companies Act's Business Review. On a speculative note, the mere fact that top management has to report to employees might have interesting long-term consequences; it might build a more employee-centred view of the firm into the management psyche. Further, on the basis that what gets measured gets done, the work required to prepare the required disclosure might well, over time, give management a greater focus on employee issues. This is especially so given that it will be possible to compare each year's disclosure with its predecessors, with the reports of similar companies and with the historical reality. Governments and agencies representing employees should be particularly concerned to carry out this comparison.

On the negative side, the European Works Council Directive only applies to businesses that have the necessary numbers of employees and transnational dimension. This raises the question as to what is to be done to procure the directive's benefits for other businesses. Further, the directive requires information and consultation to deal only with those issues that concern the whole Community-scale undertaking or group of undertakings. There could be issues that are extremely important to employees in a particular location but that appear trivial from the broader perspective that the directive requires. Again, this suggests the need for a complementary mechanism to focus on issues at a more local level. It is hard to believe that this would impose significant extra cost since, presumably, the necessary data have to be gathered locally before being aggregated to meet the needs of the directive.

Waddington's review of the experience of the first few years of the operation of EWCs suggests that the practical benefits of EWCs are often far short of what the 'Euro-optimists' had hoped.[35] He concludes:

> While the institution of EWCs may thus be in place in many MNCs, the practices conducted therein require much development if they are to move beyond the partial provision of information and become a meaningful component of a European system of industrial relations. Currently, most EWCs do not meet the initial expectations of the European Commission regarding information and consultation. They represent a case of structure before action.[36]

He advocates wide-ranging reforms of the Directive's provisions concerning the coverage and scope of agreements and the meaning of 'information' and 'consultation'. Reforms should also seek to improve the quality and timeliness of information and consultation.[37]

Lorber offers a more optimistic view. He argues that practical experience of the operation of European Works Councils shows that they have acted as a catalyst to improve communication between management and

---

[35] J. Waddington, 'What do representatives think of the practices of European Works Councils? Views from six countries', *European Journal of Industrial Relations* 9 (2003), pp. 303–325.
[36] Waddington, 'What do representatives think?', p. 321.
[37] Waddington, 'What do representatives think?', pp. 321–322.

employees. This has allowed employees to achieve a better understanding of managerial decisions. In some cases, the Councils have gone beyond being a conduit for information and consultation and have become joint negotiating partners with management on issues such as corporate social responsibility. On the downside, he concedes, it seems that they have had little practical impact on decision-making. Further, managements have been reluctant to consult the Councils in advance of sensitive decisions.[38]

The Information and Consultation Directive

The Information and Consultation Directive seeks to create a framework for informing and consulting employees; it provides for a dialogue between management and employee representatives. It applies to either undertakings with 50 or more employees in one Member State or to establishments having 20 or more employees in one Member State.[39]

'Information' is defined to mean, 'transmission by the employer to the employees' representatives of data in order to enable them to acquaint themselves with the subject matter and to examine it'.[40] 'Consultation' is 'the exchange of views and establishment of dialogue between the employees' representatives and the employer'. 'Information and Consultation' is to cover:

(a) information on the recent and probable development of the undertaking's or the establishment's activities and economic situation;
(b) information and consultation on the situation, structure and probable development of employment within the undertaking or establishment and on any anticipatory measures envisaged, in particular where there is a threat to employment;
(c) information and consultation on decisions likely to lead to substantial changes in work organisation or in contractual relations, including those covered by the Community provisions referred to in Article 9(1).[41]

Article 4(3) sets out principles governing the giving of information to employee representatives; it is to be given at such time, in such fashion and with such content as are appropriate to enable, in particular, employees'

---

[38] P. Lorber, 'Reviewing the European Works Council Directive: European progress and United Kingdom perspective', *Industrial Law Journal* 33 (2004), pp. 191–199.

[39] Information and Consultation Directive, article 3(1). 'undertaking' and 'establishment' are defined in article 2.

[40] Information and Consultation Directive, article 2(f).

[41] Information and Consultation Directive, article 4(2).

representatives to conduct an adequate study and, where necessary, prepare for consultation. Consultation is to take place:

(a) while ensuring that the timing, method and content thereof are appropriate;
(b) at the relevant level of management and representation, depending on the subject under discussion;
(c) on the basis of information supplied by the employer in accordance with Article 2(f) and of the opinion which the employees' representatives are entitled to formulate;
(d) in such a way as to enable employees' representatives to meet the employer and obtain a response, and the reasons for that response, to any opinion they might formulate;
(e) with a view to reaching an agreement on decisions within the scope of the employer's powers referred to in paragraph 2(c).

The Information and Consultation Directive leaves it to Member States to determine the practical arrangements for exercising the right to information and consultation at the appropriate level.[42] The Directive stipulates that information and consultation arrangements can be produced by agreement between management and labour 'at the appropriate level, including at undertaking or establishment level'.[43] Negotiated agreements can differ from the provisions in article 4 (which includes the provisions setting out the principles governing the giving of Information and the process of Information and Consultation) but have to respect the principles set out in Article 1. Articles 1(2) and (3) read:

2. The practical arrangements for information and consultation shall be defined and implemented in accordance with national law and industrial relations practices in individual Member States in such a way as to ensure their effectiveness.
3. When defining or implementing practical arrangements for information and consultation, the employer and the employees' representatives shall work in a spirit of co-operation and with due regard for their reciprocal rights and obligations, taking into account the interests both of the undertaking or establishment and of the employees.

Article 6 requires Member States to establish the rules governing the confidentiality obligations of employee representatives.[44] Member States are also to establish the conditions that would excuse employers from their obligations to inform and consult on the grounds that this would

---

[42] Information and Consultation Directive, article 4(1).
[43] Information and Consultation Directive, article 5.
[44] Information and Consultation Directive, article 6(1).

seriously harm or be prejudicial to the undertaking or establishment. Member States are to set up administrative or judicial review procedures to deal with disputes in cases where employers seek to invoke the confidentiality rules. Further, Member States are to create measures concerning non-compliance[45] and are to provide for adequate sanctions to be applicable in the event of infringement by either employers or employee representatives.[46]

Some Member States may confer rights on employees or their representatives which exceed those of the Directive; the Directive does not justify any regression compared with the *status quo ante* or in relation to the general level of protection of workers in the area to which it applies.[47] Other Member States may previously have lacked any general, permanent and statutory information and consultation system. The Directive contains transitional provisions setting higher employee number thresholds than those in article 3. By 23 March 2008, however, all Member States were to apply the Information and Consultation Directives whenever either of the thresholds in article 3 is reached.

The UK promulgated the Transnational Information and Consultation Regulations 1999[48] ('TICER') to implement the European Works Council Directive. TICER came into force on 15th July 2000,[49] the UK having at first opted out of the Directive. Even before then, however, many UK companies complied voluntarily with the provisions of the Directive which had already come into force in the other EU member states. Having voluntary agreements allowed central managements to take the initiative on issues such as the number and place of meetings.[50]

The Information and Consultation Directive continues the work begun by the European Works Council Directive. It extends the obligation to inform and consult so that it applies to smaller businesses and to businesses with most of their employees in a single EU member state. Also to be welcomed is the possibility of disclosure and consultation taking place at multiple levels within the organisation (since article 4(3) requires it to take place at the relevant level of management and representation, depending on the subject under discussion). The range of issues to be

---

[45] Information and Consultation Directive, article 7(1).
[46] Information and Consultation Directive, article 7(2).
[47] Information and Consultation Directive, article 9(4).
[48] SI 1999 No. 3323.   [49] TICER, reg. 1(1).
[50] J. Bellace, 'The European Works Council Directive: Transnational information and consultation in the European Union', *Comparative Labour Law Journal* 15 (1996–1997), p. 353.

covered is broadly similar to those specified in the European Works Council Directive. Carley and Hall comment on the significant changes that TICER has brought to UK labour law; they extend the range of issues on which employees have to be consulted and, for the first time ever, create a statutory works council body to represent UK employees. Whether they are the basis for a general move towards the introduction into the UK of works-council-type employee representation bodies is, they suggest, still unclear.[51]

Bercusson argues that the European Works Council should be seen as part of a general development of EU policy concerning labour in the enterprise.[52] He argues that the Information and Consultation Directive can be seen as a further step down this line:

> EU law is shaping an economic model incorporating mandatory information and consultation of employees and their representatives as it develops its particular concept of the single European market. This economic model is embedded in what has been called the 'European social model', which includes information and consultation of employees in undertakings.[53]

According to Bercusson, the engagement of organisations of workers and employees is one of the defining features of the European Social Model.[54]

Gospel et al. suggest that the Information and Consultation Directive could be seen as a move away from disclosure for specified purposes towards a more generalised disclosure obligation.[55] They argue that EWCs should have access to less aggregated information and that employers should face tougher sanctions for failure to comply with their obligations.[56] Gospel et al. conclude:

> Improvements to disclosure of information for collective bargaining and joint consultation could have significant benefits for employee relations. Trade unions and worker representatives would be in a better position to assess the employment requirements of firms and their ability to afford pay increases. In addition, they would be better placed to assess

[51] M. Carley and M. Hall, 'The implementation of the European Works Councils Directive', *Industrial Law Journal* 29 (2000), pp. 123–124.
[52] B. Bercusson, *European Labour Law*, (London: Butterworths, 1996), p. 221.
[53] B. Bercusson, 'The European social model comes to Britain', *Industrial Law Journal* 31 (2002), at p. 213.
[54] Bercusson, 'The European social model', at p. 215.
[55] Gospel, Lockwood and Willman, 'A British dilemma', p. 334.
[56] Gospel, Lockwood and Willman, 'A British dilemma', p. 348.

development plans, to monitor efficiency, and to ensure that management is best exploiting business opportunities.[57]

Collins argues that the default rules contained in the European Works Council and Information and Consultation Directives serve two useful purposes. First, they provide the parties with a 'framework of normative expectations' and, second, they steer the parties towards a particular style of 'partnership'. He suggests that it would be useful to bring all of the information and consultation rules together into a single framework.[58] He offers the following suggestion and prediction:

> It seems likely that a more comprehensive institution like a works council will have to be invented, in order to consolidate and facilitate these diverse obligations for consultation. Elements of such an institution will have to include provisions regarding the integrity of the election of worker representatives, the protection of the freedom of representatives to speak their mind without retaliation by an employer, the extent to which agreements with a works council bind both parties, and how the institution can be protected against abuse by both sides. But what is clear is that partly through legal requirements and partly through employer initiatives, these consultation mechanisms will become an increasingly significant part of the experience of workers.[59]

Corporate governance and labour law as complementary governance mechanisms

UK corporate governance in its narrower sense focuses the board's attention on the needs of shareholders and provides a range of legal and market-based mechanisms allowing for the exercise of shareholder voice. It does not provide any employee participation mechanisms. The most that can be said for it is that it does not actively prevent management from engaging with employees in a spirit of partnership or from involving workers in some aspects of management or decision-making. Labour law has begun the task of establishing formal employee participation mechanisms. They are currently relatively weak when compared with their corporate governance counterparts but could conceivably become more important and come to exercise greater influence within the corporation.

---

[57] Gospel, Lockwood and Willman, "A British dilemma', p. 348.
[58] Collins, *Employment Law*, pp. 128–129.
[59] Collins, *Employment Law*, pp. 128–129.

If that were to happen, it would become necessary to consider the desirability of continuing to have two separate governance mechanisms within one and the same corporation. On the positive side, it would avoid the need to raise once more the idea of co-determination when the UK has shown itself to be so resistant to the idea. It would also be consistent with Rock and Wachter's suggestion that shareholders and employees have distinctive areas of concern and of expertise. Corporate governance could provide the mechanism that deals with shareholder issues while the labour law mechanisms could concentrate on the issues that are the province of employees. On the other hand, the division would probably reinforce the sense that employees are outside the corporation. And, in the last analysis, there is only one corporation and it needs a governance mechanism that is equally concerned with concerns of both shareholders and employees. Having parallel corporate and employee governance institutions would, in practice, tend to subordinate the claims of employees to those of shareholders. Zumbansen points out that corporate governance and labour law tend to be seen as two parallel worlds. 'Corporate governance' is interpreted in terms of investor protection and the well-being of employees is seen as a matter of 'corporate social responsibility'. Employees lose out as a result and the greater use of 'soft law' in transnational governance has, he argues, the effect of weakening the position of labour *vis-à-vis* capital.[60]

Catholic Social Thought and employee involvement in economy-wide dialogue

From *Rerum novarum* onwards, CST has pointed out the community of interests shared by capital and labour[61]; shareholders and employees each benefit from the contribution that the other makes to the smooth running of business and of society as a whole. In *Quadragesimo anno*, Pius XI called for the re-establishment of 'Industries and Professions', groupings organised at sectoral level[62] and at the level of the wider economy[63] and these groupings are expressly stated to be the most likely way of putting an end to hostile relations between capital and labour.[64] These groupings would be independent of the state and membership would always be voluntary.[65] They can be seen as an expression of the principle

---

[60] P. Zumbansen, 'The parallel worlds of corporate governance and labour law', *Indiana Journal of Global Legal Studies* 13 (2005), pp. 261–312.
[61] Leo XIII, *Rerum novarum*, 19.   [62] Pius XI, *Quadragesimo anno, 83.*
[63] Pius XI, *Quadragesimo anno, 84.*   [64] Pius XI, *Quadragesimo anno,* 81.
[65] Pius XI, *Quadragesimo anno,* 87.

of subsidiarity, pursuing 'decentralised freedom'[66] articulated earlier in the encyclical.[67]

Laborem exercens recalls CST's effort 'to strive always to ensure the priority of work and, thereby, man's character as a subject in social life and, especially, in the dynamic structure of the whole economic process.'[68] A little later, it calls for:

> a wide range of intermediate bodies with, economic, social and cultural purposes. They would be bodies enjoying real autonomy with regard to the public powers, pursuing their specific aims in honest collaboration with each other and in subordination to the demands of the common good, and they would be living communities both in form and in substance, in the sense that the members of each body would be looked upon and treated as persons and encouraged to take an active part in the life of the body.[69]

The aim of these communities would be to ensure that 'each person is fully entitled to consider himself a part-owner of the work-bench at which he is working with everyone else.'[70] It is assumed that this passage is a continuation of Pius XI's reference to bodies in which representatives of labour, capital and management would take responsibility for aspects of economic life. The benefit of this would be to make it easier for employees, for example, to be more active participants in the organisation of the economy or part of it. This is in line with the principle of subsidiarity and the effort to ensure the subject character of society. In other words, it calls for dialogue and for the exercise of personal responsibility and initiative. It is a call for these 'private' (for want of a better word to designate bodies that are not appendages of the state) institutions to take on real governance functions. The encyclical appears to be deliberately unspecific about the composition that these bodies might have and their responsibilities. One might imagine, for example, representatives of labour and capital in general forming such a body. Or it might be composed of representatives of labour and capital engaged in a particular line of commerce or industry. Employee representatives would, no doubt, want the body to deal with the terms of employment and with working conditions. They would also be expected to think more generally about the common good.

---

[66] P. Chmielewski, 'Workers' participation in the United States; Catholic Social Teaching and democratic theory', *Review of Social Economy* LV (1997), p. 498.

[67] Pius XI, *Quadragesimo anno*, 79 – 80.

[68] John Paul II, *Laborem exercens*, para. 14.

[69] John Paul II, *Laborem exercens*, para. 14.

[70] John Paul II, *Laborem exercens*, para. 14.

Laborem exercens states that:

> Social and socioeconomic life is certainly like a system of 'connected vessels', and every social activity directed towards safeguarding the rights of particular groups should adapt itself to the system.[71]

CST presents a hierarchical model of society, with the political authority (typically the nation state but the concept is more fluid than that) at the apex overseeing the activity of a huge range and number of groupings. Structures facilitating dialogue between employers and employees at national and sectoral level should, CST repeatedly insists, be part of this institutional fabric. They would take their place alongside, for example, the corporation and the trade union, as institutions that stand between the family and the individual, on the one hand, and the political authority on the other.

Mater et magistra also called for employee representatives to have a say in decision-making at the political level.[72] The encyclical points out that this is reasonable since many of the decisions that most affect employees are not taken at firm level but 'by public authorities and by institutions which tackle the various economic problems on a national or international basis'. If the political authorities consult management representatives on economic issues, the reasoning goes, the opinion of employee representatives ought also to be taken into account.[73]

CST calls for representatives of capital and labour to get involved in the running of the economy. Indeed, the principle of subsidiarity requires that economic governance should, at least to some significant extent, be left in the hands of intermediate associations comprising representatives of capital and labour. The political authority's role is to co-ordinate and monitor but not to intervene directly unless necessary. If these bodies are to play the role envisaged for them in humanising governance of the economic arena, then they will need to find ways of engaging the energies of those that they represent. Far from being an extra layer of bureaucracy, these bodies should reduce the distance between themselves and the individual. As *Laborem exercens* explains, they are to be 'living communities'.

The EU has developed institutions and mechanisms capable of being developed so as to meet CST's requirements. Article 257 of the EC Treaty creates the European Economic and Social Committee ('ECOSOC'). The members are 'representatives of the various economic and social components of organised civil society, and in particular representatives

---

[71] John Paul II, *Laborem exercens*, para. 20.
[72] John XXIII, *Mater et magistra*, paras. 97–99.
[73] John XXIII, *Mater et magistra*, para. 99.

of producers, farmers, carriers, workers, dealers, craftsmen, professional occupations and the general interest'.[74] Article 262 requires the
Commission and the Council to consult ECOSOC when the treaty itself
so provides and allows them to do so whenever they consider it appropriate. The EC Treaty also requires the Commission to promote 'social
dialogue' between 'management and labour'. The Commission is to consult management and labour before submitting proposals in the social
policy field. It is also to consult on the content of any envisaged proposal.[75]
Blainpain comments that social dialogue has historically been conducted
with the sword of Damocles hanging over the heads of employers' representatives: they bargained in the shadow of an implicit threat to impose
a legislative solution if dialogue failed. In this way, he suggests, the
European institutions used their political power to compensate for the
relatively weak bargaining position of employee representatives.[76]

Article 139(1) EC provides:

> Should management and labour so desire, the dialogue between them
> at Community level may lead to contractual relations, including
> agreements.

Article 139 envisages that social dialogue might lead to contractual relations between management and labour; any such agreement may, if the
parties so desire, take the form of a Council decision. Schiek points to
the agreement made under article 139 on 'Telework' as a path-breaking
development for the social partners decided to implement the agreement
autonomously and without seeking the blessing of a Council decision. She
argues that European social partner agreements made under article 139
amount to law-making by private parties. They are an example of the sort
of arrangements that will be necessary given that it is impossible for the
political authority to regulate every aspect of social and economic life. She
argues that article 139 acknowledges that publicly generated law is not
the only possible source of social regulation. It absorbs social conventions
and gives them legal relevance.[77] Kohler argues that social dialogue can
be seen as an example of the principle of subsidiarity in action.[78]

---

[74] EC Treaty, article 257.   [75] EC Treaty, article 138.
[76] R. Blanpain, *European Labour Law*, (11th revised edn), (The Hague: Kluwer Law
International, 2008), p. 699.
[77] D. Schiek, 'Autonomous collective agreements as a regulatory device in European Labour
Law: How to read article 139 EC', *Industrial Law Journal* 34 (2005), pp. 23–56.
[78] T. Kohler, 'Lessons from the Social Charter: State, corporation and the meaning of subsidiarity', *University of Toronto Law Journal* 43 (1993), p. 626.

Conclusion

British company law and corporate governance focus attention on whether the corporation promotes shareholder value. To that end, both company law and corporate governance try to engage shareholders, especially institutional shareholders, in a dialogue with the board. They also look for ways of enhancing the shareholders' ability to monitor the board and hold it to account. So far, so good! The problem is that this leaves virtually no space for a consideration of the legitimate interests of employees. Further, company law and corporate governance lack any mechanisms that would allow employee representatives to contribute to corporate governance. On the face of it, these are very serious shortcomings.

This chapter considered whether labour law satisfactorily fills the employee participation void. Collective bargaining involves joint regulation of some aspects of the employment relationship. It falls a long way short of involvement in the full range of corporate governance; although it involves employees in the issues that are of central concern to them it is open to the criticism that it perpetuates the image of employees as being outside the corporation. The EC has arguably gone some way towards creating the missing employee participation mechanisms at enterprise level in the form of European Works Councils and the rights contained in the Information and Consultation Directive. No doubt there are gaps to be filled in but at least there is something to work with.

It is doubtful, however, whether these mechanisms can fully protect employees. In the last analysis, employee representatives do not enjoy parity of status with shareholder representatives. Indeed, as things stand, the entire board sees itself as representing shareholders; they are bound to do so because of the formulation of the duty of care. Further, company law and corporate governance have found a number of ways of forcing the board to engage with the interests of shareholders. These include: the formulation of the duty of loyalty that equates the interests of the company primarily with the interests of shareholders; the duty to report to shareholders; the presence of non-executive directors on the board and the effort to engage institutional shareholders in corporate governance. The derivative action makes it possible for individual shareholders, or groups of shareholders, to enforce directors' duties. The mechanisms for employee representatives to get involved are meagre in comparison.

This is regrettable since it beggars belief to suggest that employee representatives could not play a useful role in corporate governance. Carefully designed mechanisms could surely be created to bring employee representatives onto the board while threatening neither management's right to manage nor the legitimate interests of shareholders. The presence of an employee representative, or of employee representatives, on the board could help to create the sense that the corporation is a genuine partnership between capital and labour. Clearly, employee representatives would have to be well-trained and be supported by institutions that enabled them to be aware of employee concerns and insights so that these could be channelled into board discussion.

In an ideal world, there would be no need for legislation to bring about employee participation. The problem is, however, that such a move represents a radical change to the *status quo*. It flies in the face of the perceived self-interest of both management and capital. Management might fear that its authority to manage would be compromised. Shareholders would undoubtedly be reluctant to share the benefits of corporate governance with employees. Employee participation in corporate governance is very unlikely to become a widespread reality without state intervention.

CST is interested in employee participation in all of its meanings. At the level of the enterprise (and below) it seeks to ensure that the individual is the active subject of the production process. This explains CST's calls for employees to share in management, ownership and profit. CST is also keen to humanise the governance of the economy and each of its sectors. Joint governance by representatives of capital and labour is its proposal for improving the social ecology of the economy. Again, the EU has taken some of the necessary steps.

10

Employee participation and EU corporate governance

Introduction

It is no longer reasonable to think of national corporate governance systems as if they existed in splendid isolation from each other. Businesses and investors have become more willing to shop around the world for opportunities. No doubt the features of national corporate governance systems are one factor that they take into account when deciding where to invest. This fact alone means that each country has to make sure that it does not fall behind in meeting best practice requirements of investors. Failure to do so could make it more difficult for its businesses to raise the capital they need and for their stock exchanges to attract listings. It has been pointed out that for this and other reasons there is a strong tendency for corporate governance systems to copy each other.

This has knock-on effects since national corporate governance arrangements are intimately connected with labour/management outcomes for employees. The UK system's refinement in catering for investor needs has left little room for employee participation in corporate governance. To the extent that the UK system becomes the international norm is there not a serious danger that other national systems, such as that in Germany, will be put under pressure to emulate it to the detriment of employee participation institutions? In other words, efforts to promote employees' reasonable demands will be undermined by a combination of market forces and the spread of an ideology.

These considerations prompt the reflection that the common good can no longer be adequately conceived of as if it existed within the confines of national boundaries. It now has a transnational dimension and there is a need for new supranational political authorities. This raises questions that CST can help with. First, can the international economy (or any other human community) be adequately conceived of as a giant market? Is there a giant invisible hand that will lead to benign (optimal) outcomes provided only that governments across the globe try not to interfere? If so, political intervention to secure employee participation would be misplaced. It would simply be to introduce a source of inefficiency and friction into the smooth running of the international economic machine. Second, assuming that there is a case to be made for political co-ordination of the globalisation of business, who is to carry it out? CST's principle of subsidiarity suggests that as much as possible should be left to national governments. In their turn, as we have seen, they ought to rely on joint bodies comprised of representatives of capital and labour. It would be consistent with CST's general approach if these bodies were replicated at international level. And it would plainly be sensible, and consistent with the principle of subsidiarity, for multinational enterprises themselves to be given responsibility for the international common good.

The European experience of dealing with employee participation in corporate governance offers an interesting case study. It shows that national corporate governance systems can differ radically from each other in terms of the way that they deal with the relationships between capital, labour and management in the enterprise. The contrast between British and German experience is well-known but bears repetition for our purposes. The European experience also illustrates the need for supranational political institutions when important relationships spill over national boundaries. It shows how deeply entrenched is the divide between corporate governance systems that embrace employee participation and those that do not. Employee participation appears to be a kind of governance fault-line.

Divergence of approach to employee participation across the EU

Countries differ very significantly from each other in their approaches to corporate governance. It is common, for example, to contrast the United Kingdom and Germany. The basis for the distinction, it is said, lies in the relationship between capital and management. British businesses rely on the capital markets while their German counter-parts rely more heavily on bank finance; the former is impatient and insists on short-term performance while the latter is patient and has longer-term horizons. Thus, one can speak of British businesses as belonging to a market / outsider system while the German system is a relational / insider system. The varieties of capitalism literature, similarly, contrasts liberal market economies (like the United Kingdom) with co-ordinated market economies (of which Germany is an example). Gospel and Pendleton argue that these typologies (though they are open to the charge of a simplistic appeal to pure national types) have useful descriptive and explanatory properties. They also argue that countries have distinctive approaches to labour management. Some approaches are more market-oriented (with a greater tendency to hire or fire in response to economic fluctuations and to rely on external labour markets for the skills they need). Others are less market-oriented and place greater emphasis on internal labour markets. It also appears that there is a linkage between a country's corporate governance style and its approach to labour management; it is no accident that the UK belongs both to the market oriented corporate governance and labour management camps since there is a causal relationship between corporate governance and labour management. If, as current orthodoxy has it, there will be global convergence on the UK's corporate governance style then it is possible that it will also bring with it convergence of approaches to labour management. This is relevant to a discussion of employee participation since, as Gospel and Pendleton point out, market-oriented labour management systems rely on arrangements based on direct employee involvement and on profit-sharing or share ownership to secure employee commitment. This contrasts with other systems (such as Germany) that rely instead on formal employee involvement in corporate governance and on notions of social partnership.[1]

Germany has mandatory employee participation rules, both at enterprise and works level; its system of company law specifies the size of the supervisory board of any *Aktiengesellschaft* ('AG') and of a *Gesellschaft mit beschraenkter Haftung* ('GmbH') with more than 2,000 employees. An AG established after 1994 with fewer than 500 employees is exempt from the co-determination rules.[2] Above these thresholds, German law requires minimum levels of employee representation on the supervisory board[3] although, ultimately, shareholder representatives have a majority of the voting rights. In addition, Germany has a system of National Works Councils and these may apply even to quite small businesses.[4]

---

[1] H. Gospel and A. Pendleton, 'Corporate governance and labour management: An international comparison', in *Corporate governance and labour management: An international comparison*, H. Gospel and A. Pendleton (eds.), (Oxford: Oxford University Press, 2005).

[2] *Gesetz für Kleine Aktiengesellschaften und zur Derelegierung des Aktienrechts* ('Law for Small Stock Companies and to Deregulate Stock Law').

[3] *Bertriebsverfassungsgesetz* ("Industrial Constitution Act").

[4] See D. Sadowski, J. Junkes and S. Lindenthal, 'Employees and corporate governance: Germany: The German model of corporate and labour governance', *Comparative Labor Law & Policy Journal* 22 (2000), p. 33 for an explanation of the German system,

Whether, the German system delivers better corporate performance than its rivals appears to be a very difficult question to answer.[5] It is clear, however, that the German view is that employees are members of the corporation and this is a positive factor. It may well be that the German system ensures a more equitable distribution of corporate wealth as between employees and shareholders. Convergence on market-oriented corporate governance and labour management systems would raise important questions of public policy since it would imply that German corporate governance would be radically reshaped. The question then is how these issues are to be settled. One could simply let the market settle the matter. This is the approach favoured by those who believe in the benefits of regulatory competition. The likely result is that employees would lose out. The alternative is to envisage some kind of political intervention with a view to mitigating the impact of convergence on employees.

Regulatory competition

This section looks at the theory of regulatory competition, especially as it is applied to employee participation rights, in general and in the EC in particular. It considers whether supranational institutions can take a *laissez-faire* approach to legal differences between states (on legislating for employee co-determination rights, for example). The theory of regulatory competition implies that shareholders will seek out the jurisdictions that offer the most congenial regulatory environment. Regulation (such as corporate governance rules) then becomes a product that is purchased when a firm moves to or from a particular state. The behaviour of businesses in this market discloses important information about business preferences to regulators. Within limits, this may well be useful with regard to the regulatory preferences of capital. But the theory of regulatory competition relies on mobility of the consumer of the regulatory product. Capital is far more mobile than labour so that the regulatory preferences of employees will count for less than those of investors. Further, not all types of capital are completely mobile (or responsive purely to regulatory factors). Issues such as the quality of the workforce, the general infrastructure and so on also come into play.

an evaluation of the economic efficiency of the German insistence on compulsory rather than voluntary co-determination.

5 See B. Frick and E. Lehmann, 'Corporate governance in Germany: ownership, codetermination and firm performance in a stakeholder economy', in Gospel and Pendleton (eds), *Corporate governance and labour management: An international comparison*.

Tiebout was the first to propose the idea of competition between regulators. His seminal article, 'A pure theory of local expenditures', departs from the observation that most expenditure in the US on public goods was incurred at the local rather than the federal level. He asked whether there was any mechanism to ensure that local expenditure on public goods would approximate the proper level. His analysis centres on the hypothetical voter-consumer intending to move from the city centre to a suburban district. When deciding where to live, the voter-consumer will look for the community which best satisfies his preference pattern for public goods. The voter-consumer's chances of finding a community that suits his preferences increase with the number of communities and the variance in approaches to spending on public goods. Ideally, the voter-consumer will be confronted with a market in which communities compete with different public good offerings. The consumer-voter's demand preferences are revealed by his decision to move, or fail to move, to a given community. Costs of moving from one community to another are a source of friction in the market that could impede its operation; thus, the theory suggests, policies that promote residential mobility and increase the knowledge of the consumer-voter will improve the allocation of government expenditures.[6]

Charny argues that there are several different types of labour regulation and that regulatory competition threatens redistributive rules (such as employee participation/co-determination measures) but not efficient rules (such as minimum wage rules that lead to a better-educated workforce).[7] Charny believes that redistributive measures favouring employees might be justified on the grounds of democratic theory since they are often core social values.[8] Regulatory competition could not be relied on to protect redistributive rules and some form of political intervention would be needed. He suggests that strategies to protect such standards would probably have to proceed on an *ad hoc* basis and may involve a network of actors such as unions, businesses, NGOs, governments and regional and international associations[9]. To avoid public choice problems (such as the risk of regulatory capture by powerful players), it may be better for any agreement upon standards to take the form of benchmarking criteria:

[6] C. Tiebout, 'A pure theory of local expenditures', *The Journal of Political Economy* 64 (1956), p. 416.
[7] D. Charny, 'Regulatory competition and the global co-ordination of labour standards', *Journal of International Economic Law* 3 (2000), p. 294.
[8] Charny, 'Regulatory competition', p. 297.
[9] Charny, 'Regulatory competition', pp. 297– 01.

The point would be to facilitate transnational coordination without intruding upon a core set of national prerogatives in labour policy-making.[10]

It is easy to appreciate that Charny's recommendations tie in neatly with an approach that might be inspired by CST. Employee participation can fittingly be described as a core social value; it respects the dignity of the worker, helps to establish an ethically adequate relationship between the employee and the tools of his or her trade and by engaging the active participation of the worker helps to humanize the workplace. Charny's suggested strategy of leaving detailed governance to a network of actors working within the framework established by benchmarking criteria respects the principle of subsidiarity.

Once a political framework that can exercise oversight in the name of the common good has been established, regulatory competition could play a useful part. The EC experience shows that regulatory competition can yield benefits in the form of greater choice of regulatory systems, by exercising a disciplining effect on national regulators and by allowing space for local discovery, experimentation and innovation. But there are also costs and problems. First, firms may fail to move in response to differences in regulatory regime: whilst portfolio capital is mobile, direct investment is less mobile since it responds to a variety of factors (such as the quality of the local workforce) and not only to regulation. Regulatory competition may also cause regulatory drift when regulators indulge in a series of rule changes as they discover more about business preferences. Regulatory drift undermines legal certainty and thus imposes a cost on business. Arguably, the EC approach to harmonization now embodies this modified type of regulatory competition; the former emphasis on detailed and rigid norms has given way to the use of more flexible, framework directives which concentrate on essentials. This shift can be seen by comparing the employee protection provisions of the draft fifth directive with those contained in the directive accompanying the European Company statute. Sun and Pelkmans conclude that the optimal regulatory solution combines minimum harmonization of essential requirements and regulatory competition beyond this level.[11] This is a conclusion that is compatible with Charny's. Charny, of course, would engage non-state actors in the creation of the detailed rules.

[10] Charny, 'Regulatory competition', p. 302.
[11] J.-M. Sun and J. Pelkmans, 'Regulatory competition in the single market', *Journal of Common Market Studies* 33 (1995), p. 68.

The threats to the German co-determination system: the danger of regulatory competition

The creation of the European Community threatened the German system: there was a danger of a flight from jurisdictions like Germany that built co-determination into corporate governance if businesses and capital could move freely throughout the Community. The fear is that management and shareholders might seek to reincorporate in jurisdictions such as the UK (or, in the early days of the EC, the Netherlands) so as to take advantage of their capital-centred systems and escape from the German labour-centred system. This is precisely the type of outcome that Charny predicts.

Freedom of establishment is an important aspect of the EC Treaty that is likely to lead to a situation where businesses can migrate from one jurisdiction to another. Migration will result in a change in the system of company law applicable to their internal affairs. If migration becomes a real possibility then the way will be open for a process of regulatory competition to establish itself; states would vie with each other to attract corporations by offering terms that are attractive to management and shareholders. Labour is less mobile than capital and so its interests are less likely to be taken into account by governments that engage in regulatory competition for capital. Indeed, capital-centred corporate governance systems are hostile to employee participation and so states might have a positive incentive not to create employee participation rights (or to abolish them).

It must be acknowledged, however, that there is currently no simple procedure for migration. A German company that wanted to be governed by UK company law would have to establish a new UK company incorporated under UK company law and transfer its assets to that company. The administrative and taxation consequences would, no doubt, be enormous. But the EC is clearly disposed to remove this obstacle. The Commission has proposed that there should be a mechanism for the migration of companies. This clearly favours the interests of capital and puts pressure on labour-centred corporate governance systems and on employees and trade unions. As explained above, mobility is an essential precondition for the emergence of regulatory competition.

Member States have used their private international law systems to defend mandatory company law rules. The conflict of laws rules that Germany applies to company law uses the real seat theory to deal with the question of corporate recognition and to determine which system of corporate law applies to the internal affairs of the corporation. According to this theory, the law prevailing in the jurisdiction in which the company has its real seat, where its head office or central management and control are actually located, is the law most fitted to govern the affairs of that company.[12] The beauty of this arrangement, in the eyes of the Member States that adopt it, is that it prevents businesses from incorporating in the UK, for example, when their central administration is in Germany.[13]

In real seat systems, companies which are incorporated in one Member State but which have their real seat in another run the risk that they will not be recognised as corporate entities. This could mean, for example, that the shareholders face unlimited liability for the company's debts. Thus, along with the lack of a mechanism for migration, the real seat system prevented the emergence of a European Delaware.

Unfortunately for Germany, the decisions of the European Court of Justice in *Centros Ltd v Erhverus-og Selkabsstyrelsen*[14] and in *Uberseering BV v Nordic Construction Baumanagement GmbH (NCC)*[15] have cast considerable doubt on the effectiveness of the real seat doctrine as a means of preventing incorporation of German companies in other Member States. The EC Treaty rules on freedom of establishment guarantee the right of companies established under the company law of one Member State to set up a subsidiary, branch or place of business in another. These decisions clearly increase corporate mobility (and hence the scope for regulatory competition) within the European Community.

The need for rules that would at the very least protect employee participation measures that already exist becomes more urgent as corporate migration within the European Community becomes more of a reality. The EC initially essayed the rather heavy-handed solution of attempting to use the company law harmonisation programme to impose German style co-determination across Europe. This was bitterly opposed by a number of Member States including the United Kingdom. Whether the opposition can be justified in objective ethical or economic terms is open to doubt. Certainly, however, this approach can be accused of failing to respect the principle of subsidiarity. It left no room for the details of employee participation to be hammered out by the relevant actors at

---

[12] For an explanation, see R. Drury, 'Migrating Companies', *European Law Review* 24 (1999), p. 354.

[13] For an explanation of this and the whole question of the migration of companies from one member state to another see P. Davies, *Gower and Davies' Principles of Modern Company Law*, (8th ed.), (London: Thomson/Sweet & Maxwell, 2008), pp. 138–148.

[14] (C 212 / 97) [1999] ECR I–1459 (ECJ).   [15] (C 208 / 00) [2002] ECR I–9919 (ECJ).

national or community level. The following sections of this chapter briefy explain the evolution of the EC's approach to employee participation in corporate governance and its abandonment of a one-size fits all approach in favour of one which is considerably more flexible.

The European Community's Company Law harmonisation programme

The Member States had foreseen the opportunities for regulatory arbitrage offered by the Community's rules on freedom of establishment. The European Community sought to counter the threat by developing a programme of Company Law harmonisation. Wouters' review of the history of the harmonisation programme shows that it has had multiple aims. These have included: facilitating freedom of establishment; preventing the emergence of a European Delaware; the industrial policy goal of making European companies more competitive than their non-European competitors and sheer pragmatism.[16] Insofar as the aim of this programme was to harmonise important aspects of company law (such as co-determination) and so protect mandatory company law rules, harmonisation has failed. Thus, the draft Fifth Directive[17] sought to impose a German style dual board as well as co-determination. But it was impossible to secure agreement in the face of UK opposition. In the light of the now-lengthy history of the harmonisation programme, it seems that attempts to agree on a mandatory pan-European code of company law are only of limited usefulness. This is pre-eminently true when it comes to the question of employee participation in corporate governance. Wouters notes that further company law harmonisation will be difficult because of:

> deeply-rooted national traditions which are closely linked to the organisation of the national economy and ... of their collective labour relations.[18]

Deep divisions over the question of employee participation made progress on the draft Fifth directive impossible and caused considerable delay in the creation of a European Company. In the end, however, the European Company legislation was sufficiently altered to allow the project to proceed. Interestingly, the approach finally taken involves the use of local

---

[16] J. Wouters, 'European Company Law: Quo Vadis?', *Common Market Law Review* 37 (2000), pp. 269–271.
[17] [1972] O.J. C 13/49.   [18] Wouters, 'European Company Law', p. 280.

actors to implement broad criteria established in the legislation. That is to say that it follows the approach suggested by Charny.

The Societas Europeae and employee participation

The *Societas Europeae* ('SE' or 'European Company') is interesting since it combines a form of corporate migration with employee involvement provisions.[19] The relevant legislation takes the form of a Regulation ('the SE regulation') providing for the existence of the SE as a new form of business organisation[20] and an accompanying directive dealing with employee involvement[21]. The SE Regulation came into force on 8 October 2004.[22] The Regulation allows for the creation, in four circumstances, of a European Company. Existing public companies incorporated under the laws of a Member State can become European Companies provided that they had a subsidiary in at least one other Member State. European Companies can also be the result of a merger between public companies incorporated under the laws of at least two member states; they can also be the holding or subsidiary company of two or more companies incorporated under the laws of two or more Member States.[23] They are governed by the company law system of the Member State in which the SE has its registered office.[24] The head office and the registered office must be in the same Member State[25] (a clear concession to the real seat theory) but this requirement was to be reviewed by October 8 2009.[26] The registered office (and hence the applicable system of company law) can be changed provided that the the registered office and the head office are in the same Member State; that is, if the SE changes the Member State in which it is registered, it must also change the situation of its head office.

The SE legislation has had a difficult history. Earlier, unsuccessful, proposals sought to create a self-contained system of law for the European Company. This meant that a choice would have to be made as to which elements of the conflicting European systems would be adopted. As with the doomed draft Fifth Directive, this raised the difficult question

---

[19] See P. Davies, 'Employee involvement in the European Company' in J. Rickford (ed.), *The European Company. Developing a Community Law of Corporations*, (Antwerp/Oxford/ New York: Intersentia, 2003).

[20] Council Regulation (EC) No. 2157/2001 on the Statute for a European Company.

[21] Council Directive 2001/86/EC supplementing the Statute for a European Company with regard to the involvement of employees ('the employee involvement directive').

[22] The SE Regulation, article 70.   [23] The SE Regulation, article 2.

[24] The SE Regulation, article 9.   [25] The SE Regulation, article 7.

[26] The SE Regulation, article 69.

of whether or not a system of employee involvement should be mandatory for the European Company. The problem was overcome by abandoning the attempt to create a European system of company law and relying instead on the domestic company law system of the SE's registered office. This clearly opens the door for companies to register in the Member State with the company law system most acceptable to shareholders and managers. Thus, the European Company could facilitate regulatory competition between Member States (and forum shopping on the part of capital) with resulting pressure on employee involvement in governance.

This fear held up agreement on the European Company. A group of experts was commissioned to consider whether employee co-determination should be a mandatory feature of the European Company. The Final Report ('*the Davignon Report*') appeared in 1997. It ruled out the possibility of a general harmonisation of Member States' approach to employee participation because of the scale of the divergence between the existing national systems. It proposed an approach which would seem to be very much in line with the principle of subsidiarity: employees and management were to negotiate whatever approach they thought best for their European Company.[27] The negotiating parties, it was proposed, would have complete freedom concerning the terms of the agreement; there would be no minimum requirements.[28] There would be a timetable for reaching agreement on employee participation and a set of default rules that would apply if agreement had not been reached within the time frame stipulated. In effect, of course, these default requirements would be likely to act as a set of minimum requirements since employee representatives could refuse to agree on terms that they saw as being less advantageous than the default terms. The default rules gave employee representatives rights of information and consultation.[29] Employee representatives were to be members of the board (of either of the two organs in the case of a company with a two-tier board),[30] there were to be at least two employee representatives on the board representing not less than one fifth of the membership.[31] The default rules, it was proposed, would give employee representatives full voting rights.[32]

This approach is reflected in the terms of the Directive accompanying the SE Regulation.[33] Once the intention to create an SE has been

[27] *The Davignon Report*, para. 40.   [28] *The Davignon Report*, para. 56.
[29] *The Davignon Report*, para. 78.   [30] *The Davignon Report*, para. 80.
[31] The Davignon Report, 83.   [32] *The Davignon Report*, 88.
[33] The employee involvement directive.

announced, a special negotiating body comprised of employee representatives is to be set up to negotiate the terms of employee involvement in the
governance of the SE.[34] Article 4(2) specifies the matters to be covered in
any agreement. Member States are required, by article 7, to lay down rules
on employee involvement that conform with the standards specified in
the annex to the directive. The annex deals with the composition of the
body that is, under the terms of the agreement, to represent employees.
It also deals with information and consultation. Finally, the annex deals
with employee participation rights but article 7(2) explains that the rules
in this part of the annex only apply where specified percentages of the
employees of the SE had already enjoyed such rights. The standard rules
established by a Member State will apply to SEs that have their registered
office there unless agreement has been reached within the six month time
period (extendable to a year by agreement between the parties) stipulated
by article 5. They will also apply where the parties agree that they should.[35]
Member States' standard rules must satisfy the provisions of the annex to
the directive.

The special negotiating body charged with agreeing the terms of the
employee involvement agreement may decide not to open negotiations or,
having begun them to discontinue them. Two-thirds of the special negotiating body, representing two-thirds of employees must give its approval
before this step can be taken. In this event, the provisions of the European
Works Council directive would apply to the European Company and
would amount to a decision to rely on the rules on information and consultation of employees in force in the Member States where the SE has
employees.[36]

The tenth recital to the directive refers to a fundamental principle that
employees' acquired rights are to be secured as regards involvement in
employee decisions. This fundamental principle is reflected in a number
of the provisions of the directive. Article 3(4), for example, requires
approval by two-thirds majority of the special negotiating body (rather
than a simple majority) for an agreement that would reduce the existing participation rights of specified percentages of employees. Article
4(4) provides that where an SE is to be established by transformation of
an existing public company, the agreement is to provide for at least the
same level of all elements of employee involvement as existed prior to

[34] The employee involvement directive, article 3(1).
[35] The employee involvement directive, article 7(1).
[36] The employee involvement directive, article 3(6).

transformation. As already mentioned, article 7(2) requires the standard rules to apply in default of agreement of other terms to include employee participation rules where specified percentages of employees already enjoyed such rights.

Arrangements that would lead to a reduction in existing levels of employee participation for percentages of the workforce specified in the Directive need the approval of special majorities of the special negotiating body. The arrangements are to result in the creation either of a representative body or of an information and consultation procedure; they may, and in certain circumstances must, result in rules for board level participation. Failure to agree on the arrangements for employee participation within the time period specified by the Directive results in the application of a set of standard rules established by Member States in accordance with guidelines contained in the Directive.

Appraisal

When it comes to corporate governance (including employee participation) there is much to be said for leaving as much as possible to be settled by the market (that is, by the agreement of the parties or their representatives and the institutions that seek to protect their interests). Management, employees and investors are the best judges of their own self-interest and of how the corporation can best achieve its goals. This is expressed in CST's principle of subsidiarity.

Pacem In Terris argues that legal protection for human rights is itself a demand of human dignity.[37] Primary responsibility rests, however, with individuals (alone and in collaboration with others in intermediate associations) rather than the State since freedom to choose one's own path towards the good is a core requirement for human self-realisation.[38] This allows for the exercise of initiative and for solutions to be developed by those whose interests are most affected (who are therefore likely to put most energy into devising appropriate solutions). It is likely too that, the shareholders and employees in a given company, sector of the economy or country will have more detailed knowledge of their own respective needs and of the terms on which they can most effectively collaborate. Thus, respect for freedom, as well as operational efficiency, demand self-restraint

---

[37] John XXIII, *Pacem in terris*, para. 27.
[38] John XXIII, *Pacem in terris*, para. 34.

on the part of the state. All of this is captured by the well-known state-ment of the principle of subsidiarity in *Quadragasimo anno*.[39]

When it comes to employee participation in governance, the principle of subsidiarity suggests that it would be appropriate for matters to be dealt with by negotiations between employee representatives and the individ-ual firm or with institutions that represent shareholder interests such as institutional investors, stock exchanges and so on. The state would be pre-sent in the background to promote these negotiations, monitor their out-comes and, if necessary, to give statutory force to them. Such an approach would be consistent with the approach suggested in *Centesimus annus*:

> what is being proposed as an alternative is not the socialist system, which in fact turns out to be State capitalism, but rather *a society of free work, of enterprise and of participation*. Such a society is not directed against the market, but demands that the market be appropriately controlled by the forces of society and by the State, so as to guarantee that the basic needs of the whole of society are satisfied.[40]

These words raise another aspect of subsidiarity according to which the market enjoys a relative autonomy *vis-à-vis* the state. The corporation and its relationships with shareholders and employees are all, in large meas-ure, contractual in nature. Institutions such as stock exchanges, corporate governance bodies, institutional investors, trade unions and so on have grown up to support these relationships. Their specialised knowledge and ability shape the relationships of shareholders and employees within the firm and help ensure that the needs of capital and labour are harmonised and attained in a reasonably effective way. If the market (the relevant con-tracts buttressed by the supporting institutions) effectively guarantees the relevant rights of shareholders and employees then there is no warrant for regulatory intervention.

Clearly, however, the state might have to intervene to protect employee rights because, for example, of the inequalities of bargaining power as between shareholders and senior management, on the one hand, and employees on the other or because employees find it difficult to organ-ise themselves in such a way as to be capable of protecting their own interests.

Ogletree remarks that free markets are effective but have harmful social tendencies;[41] regulation is necessary even though it often inhibits market

---

[39] Pius XI, *Quadragesimo anno*, para. 79.   [40] John Paul II, *Centesimus annus*, para. 35.
[41] T. Ogletree, 'Corporate capitalism and the common good', *Journal of Religious Ethics* 30 (2002), p. 98.

processes.[42] Corporations themselves will benefit from high levels of cultural and social stability but the effort to achieve these goals transcends immediate corporate horizons and so corporate resistance to regulation is to be expected. Indeed, this resistance is healthy since it puts the onus on government to justify its intervention.[43]

He goes on to argue that capitalism requires limited government:

> Limited government opens social spaces for individuals to pursue their visions of truly good and fulfilling human lives, so long as these visions do not violate or jeopardise the rights of others.[44]

And when the state does intervene, it should do so in ways that are broadly compatible with market operations.[45] Some types of intervention (such as anti-trust law) facilitate market transactions (go with the grain, as it were) whilst others (labour or environmental legislation) do not facilitate markets and might even disturb them (whilst being necessary and, in the longer term, market-friendly). Given the fact that regulatory intervention often has undesirable side-effects, Ogletree agrees with Sunstein that command and control interventions should be replaced by policies focusing on disclosure, education, financial incentives and decentralisation. And public policies should be subjected to continuous review.[46]

CST sees the state and intermediate communities (such as the corporation and even labour and capital) as being part of an ordered whole. There is room for dispute as to how relations between them should be structured, but the underlying theme is that of co-operation for the sake of integral self-realisation rather than tension.

Then there is the question of the relationship between the state, on the one hand, and other states and supranational institutions, on the other. Capital mobility means that individual states can no longer necessarily impose terms on business, for businesses might respond by moving elsewhere. Thus, a form of bargaining takes place between the state and its major businesses and the state has to frame its regulatory system with an eye to what is acceptable to those businesses. Other states may offer corporate/workplace governance packages that are more attractive to shareholders and they may be tempted to engage in regulatory competition of this type so as to attract employment, taxes and so on.

[42] Ogletree, 'Corporate capitalism', pp. 98–99.
[43] Ogletree, 'Corporate capitalism', p. 99.
[44] Ogletree, 'Corporate capitalism', p. 92.
[45] Ogletree, 'Corporate capitalism', pp. 92–93.
[46] Ogletree, 'Corporate capitalism', p. 99.

Benedict XVI acknowledged the potential harm to human dignity that a race to the bottom would bring with it and suggested that:

> The repeated calls issued within the Church's social doctrine, beginning with *Rerum Novarum*, for the promotion of workers' associations that can defend their rights must therefore be honoured today even more than in the past, as a prompt and far-sighted response to the urgent need for new forms of co-operation at the international level, as well as the local level.[47]

Clearly, globalisation undermines the state's capacity to take effective action in favour of the common good.[48] The result, as Finnis points out, is that:

> If it now appears that the good of individuals can only be fully secured and realised in the context of international community, we must conclude that the claim of the nation state to be a complete community is unwarranted and the postulate of the national legal order, that it is supreme and comprehensive and an exclusive source of legal obligation, is increasingly what lawyers would call 'a legal fiction'.[49]

Pacem in Terris addresses this point when it discusses the idea of a common good between states. It insists that powerful states should not improve their position 'by the use of methods which involve other nations in injury and unjust oppression'.[50] Solidarity demands that states should pool their material and spiritual resources; the common good of the state cannot be divorced from the common good of the entire human family.[51] States should cooperate to achieve the common good.[52]

The theme of globalisation is dealt with in *Pacem in Terris* (though the word is not mentioned). Section IV of the encyclical deals with the relationship of men and political communities with the world community. It begins by noting that material resources travel from one country to another. This has resulted in a phenomenal growth in relationships across national boundaries and between states. Thus:

---

[47] Benedict XVI, *Caritas in veritate*, para. 25.
[48] This point has been made very frequently. See, for example, L. Tavis, 'Corporate governance and the global social void', *Vanderbilt Journal of Transnational Law* 35 (2002), p. 487.
[49] J. Finnis, *Natural law and natural rights*, (Oxford: Oxford University Press, 2003), p.150.
[50] John XXIII, *Pacem in terris*, para. 92.   [51] John XXIII, *Pacem in terris*, para. 98.
[52] John XXIII, *Pacem in terris*, para. 99.

> National economies are gradually becoming so interdependent that a
> kind of world economy is being born from the simultaneous integration
> of the economies of individual states.[53]

The universal common good is not a new concept.[54] But there is a need
for a radical overhaul of the institutional arrangements used to achieve
it. In the past, the universal common good could be secured by negotiations, treaties and so on.[55] This approach is no longer sufficient.[56] The
moral order demands that the public authority be effective in achieving
its end.[57] The moral order calls for the establishment of a global political
authority (not, it is made clear, a world state):

> Today the universal common good presents us with problems which are
> worldwide in their dimensions; problems, therefore, which cannot be
> solved except by a public authority with power, organisation and means
> co-extensive with these problems, and with a worldwide sphere of activ-
> ity. Consequently the moral order itself demands the establishment of
> some such general form of public authority.[58]

This global authority must be set up with the consent of all nations[59]
although its legitimacy rests on the moral need for such an authority. The
principal purpose of the global public authority would be 'to evaluate and
find a solution to the economic, social, political and cultural problems
which affect the universal common good'.[60] Clearly, this idea of a global political authority brings the principle of subsidiarity into play once
more. Thus:

> ... it is no part of the duty of universal authority to limit the sphere of
> action of the public authority of individual States, or to arrogate any of
> their functions to itself. On the contrary, its essential purpose is to cre-
> ate world conditions in which the public authorities of each nation, its
> citizens and intermediate groups, can carry out their tasks, fullfill their
> duties and claim their rights with greater security.[61]

Benedict XVI suggested that globalisation means that the role and powers
of public authorities need to be 'prudently reviewed and remodeled so as

---

[53] John XXIII, *Pacem in terris*, para.130.
[54] John XXIII, *Pacem in terris*, para.132.
[55] John XXIII, *Pacem in terris*, para.133.
[56] John XXIII, *Pacem in terris*, para.134–5.
[57] John XXIII, *Pacem in terris*, para.136.
[58] John XXIII, *Pacem in terris*, para.137.
[59] John XXIII, *Pacem in terris*, para.138.
[60] John XXIII, *Pacem in terris*, para.140.
[61] John XXIII, *Pacem in terris*, para.141.

to enable them, perhaps through new forms of engagement, to address the challenges of today's world.' There follows an intriguing passage:

> Once the role of public authorities has been more clearly defined, one could foresee an increase in the new forms of political participation, nationally and internationally, that have come about through the activity of organisations operating in civil society; in this way it is to be hoped that the citizens' interest and participation in the *res publica* will become more deeply rooted.[62]

This suggests that governance will increasingly involve the co-operation of a range of state and non-state actors and that involvement in the latter will represent a new way for people to re-engage with public life. This is a modern take on the principle of subsidiarity. It might be added that corporations could be among the non-state actors helping states to exercise public powers.

Conclusions

The foregoing sketch of European company law and corporate governance shows the need for supranational bodies in the era of globalisation. The EC has facilitated freedom of movement of capital. At the same time, it appreciated the need to reconcile this with a reasonable social policy. The EC's efforts in this area are still developing; it is too early to say how the clash of company law systems will be resolved. It is interesting to note that the battle has been fiercest when there has been a question of taking a decision for or against employee participation in governance or of giving employee interests parity with shareholder interests when the two are seriously at odds with each other. Wouters talks of an employee participation 'bug' that has plagued the EC's efforts in the company law arena.[63] It will be several years, at least, before we know whether the employee participation arrangments in the Directive accompanying the European Company Regulation are the way forward or merely an uneasy truce.

The European Company legislation can be seen as embodying respect for the principle of subsidiarity by imposing responsibility on local actors to thrash out the terms concerning employee participation. This solution, however, raises several important questions. How far should Member States, or the EC, involve themselves in settling the terms of workplace

---

[62] Benedict XVI, *Caritas in veritate*, para. 24.
[63] Wouters, 'European Company Law', p. 263.

governance? How much detail can be left for employee representatives to settle in negotiation with employers?

There is a role for the EC to intervene to protect national approaches to the employee question whilst encouraging corporate mobility. The EC has found it impossible to impose any Member State's view (its concrete determination of the employee right) on all of the others. It has, however, been able, in the European Company legislation, to devise a framework that seeks to encourage corporate mobility, protect existing employee participation rights and create a framework for negotiations between representatives of shareholders and employees. It may be possible to transfer this solution to other contexts such as a directive on corporate governance matters. It is true, of course, that businesses are free to adopt the European Company form or not. They, and Member States, may prove more resistant to the same approach if it is part of a mandatory system affecting all major European businesses.

Subsidiarity, as well as political reality, may require the EC to play a more subtle role in the future. If a system of regulatory competition does emerge, the EC could try to develop mechanisms to help Member States to copy the best practice of others, where this is politically possible for them. It might do this through networks made up of representatives of Member States as well as of capital and labour. One by-product of this might be the development of model codes of company law (or aspects of company law) or of corporate governance. An outcome such as this might be transferable to the global stage.

At another level, it is suggested that CST can make use of much of what law and economics scholarship has to say. The concept of regulatory competition, an economic concept, can be of genuine help to policy-makers and legislators. The European experience analysed in this paper shows that it may be possible to make room for this concept whilst leaving states and supranational institutions with the ability to intervene for the sake of employees' human rights. The market-like approach of regulatory competition is highly consistent with the sort of decentralisation that subsidiarity demands. In *Centesimus annus*, John Paul II has pointed out the usefulness of markets. Not only are they incredibly useful mechanisms to guide the allocation of resources, they are also consistent with the notion of human freedom and with the principle of subsidiarity: they give effect to the decisions of the individual or of the business. Provided that these decisions are based on a proper notion of human goods and provided they satisfy genuine human needs then the market performs a very important function. And if this logic is harnessed, it can improve the quality of regulation at the same time as the mobility it implies imposes a discipline on state intervention.

CST has, however, always insisted that the state must ensure that markets serve the common good. In an ideal world, this may mean keeping a watchful eye on markets without intervening. Where, however, markets fail (in the economic sense), or where there are other social policy issues at stake, then explicit intervention is called for. Legal systems are not markets and laws are not mere prices. It is especially inappropriate to think of them as prices when core human rights are at stake. On the other hand, the idea of a market for incorporations can play a useful role. It serves to convey the impression that corporate law is a service to businesses and their shareholders (whatever else it is). It emphasises that jurisdictions can learn valuable lessons by evaluating the experience of their neighbours. And, no doubt, some ability to shop around for a business-friendly corporate law system can help to bring about limited government thus leaving space for other communities to play their part. But the metaphor can be taken too far. It can tend to suggest that the common good (of a nation or of a broader community) can be left to the tender mercies of an invisible hand. The truth is that there is a role, within the framework suggested by the principle of subsidiarity for the state and, increasingly, for supranational institutions.

11

Conclusion

Integral self-realisation is the point of it all

CST is a branch of moral theology. It looks at social phenomena from the perspective of integral self-realisation, the all-round human development of each person. To apply CST's perspective to thinking about corporate governance is to ask about how corporate governance arrangements can promote human well-being. In the first place, it is to ask about what life in the corporation means for the moral well-being of its employees and shareholders.

Chapter one sought to explain the concept of integral self-realisation. Christian anthropology sees the human person as having an innate disposition to self-realisation. Reflection on one's own tendencies, and experience in general, suggest that there are certain goods that can be pursued (such as the preservation of life, the pursuit of knowledge, friendship, play, aesthetic experience and religion). It is a characteristic of the natural law theory that is built into CST that it seeks to identify the goods that are, as it were, the building blocks to be used in the construction of the good life. The point of moral theology is to set out principles to guide the individual quest for self-realisation (the more or less successful effort to become the person that one can and ought to be given one's own aptitudes, circumstances and so on). Moral theology focuses on the development of the individual, each and every individual. It considers how the most fundamental, most characteristically human elements of one's personality can be developed.

CST has the same focus on the well-being of the individual but concentrates on the fact that we necessarily secure our needs and pursue our plans in a social setting. Indeed, life in society is itself one of the goods to be pursued. CST looks at the principles that make it more likely that a community will play its part in promoting the cause of self-realisation. Thus, there is a profound link between individual ethics and social ethics since each is concerned with the integral self-realisation of the individual.

One of CST's central themes is that societies should be personal. They are at the service of the human person. Moreover, a community should do what it can, consistent with operational effectiveness, to allow its members to shape the life of the community and to play their part in promoting the life of the community. Rigid bureaucratic structures that seek to impose solutions are alienating for those on the receiving end. CST's principles of participation and subsidiarity warn against the creation of stifling, hierarchical social arrangements. CST's calls for employee participation are largely rooted in this fear that employees will become mere cogs in an impersonal machine.

Work

Work is vital as a source of the material means to support oneself and one's family. Even this consideration provides a strong link between work and the goods that are constitutive or fulfilling for the human person. CST goes further, however, and speaks of work as being itself a human good. Through one's work, one develops one's personality and comes closer to being the person that one can be (in CST terms, one comes closer to living out one's God-given vocation). In *Laborem exercens*, John Paul II stressed that this subjective dimension of work is the aspect that is most important.

Laborem exercens also stresses that the economy is, in the last analysis, built on the personal contribution of the worker. It is not a machine or an abstract force or mechanism but a community that draws on and develops the collective effort of successive generations. It is helpful to keep this personal dimension in mind when thinking about the economy; the economy needs to draw on the committed effort of the individual and is at the service of the individual. *Laborem exercens* captures this idea by speaking of the priority of labour over capital.

The principle of subsidiarity is applicable to the economy just as it is to political society. So far as possible, the organisation of production should be personalised and pushed as close to the individual as possible. That is to say that the working environment should make it possible for the individual employee to make a meaningful contribution to work and to building up the productive capacity of the team or organisation. The state should be reluctant to interfere. Within organisations, meaningful control over productive effort should come as close to the individual worker as possible. This principle is quite compatible with a recognition of the need for strong and effective central leadership.

Private property

The defence of workers' rights has been one of the central themes of CST since *Rerum novarum*. CST has, at the same time, defended the right to ownership of private property. Having some capital to invest also serves the cause of self-realisation since it creates a certain freedom for manoeuvre. It gives one the space to plan for the future and to take active steps in pursuit of that plan. It allows one to provide for one's family and, again, to exercise a degree of creativity in that planning. It also gives one the resources out of which to make voluntary contributions to the individuals, organisations and causes of one's choice. Each of these facts represents enriched possibilities for the expression and development of one's character. The fact that one owns a certain amount of property gives added reasons for helping to build up the common good of one's community. For one thing, the more developed the community, the more valuable property that is located or rooted in it is likely to be.

Property ownership also has a vital part to play from the perspective of self-realisation. Property ownership is important from the perspective of work since work presupposes a stable link between the worker, on the one hand, and the tools used and the object worked upon on the other. At the deepest level, private property exists for the sake of work. Employee share ownership can be seen as an adaptation of that idea to modern circumstances. The employee's tools and the objects of his work and the customers or clients whom he serves all come to him through the firm that he works for.

Employee share ownership can help to forge the link between the worker and the things that he works on and the people whom he serves through his work. At the same time, employee share ownership (or some functional equivalent) can give the employee a sense of ownership of his work with the associated incentives to work well (assuming that the scheme is well-designed). Further, the votes that come with employee share ownership can be a tool for giving employees a greater say in corporate governance.

There are some important economic problems associated with employee share ownership and these have to be addressed. They include the fact that employees would be ill-served if they were put into a position where both their human capital and the best part of their financial capital were tied up in their employer; there would be the obvious problems associated with having too many of their eggs in one basket. Thus, employee shares should, arguably, be to a significant degree conferred in addition to a reasonable salary. Governments might help to bring this about by using tax incentives to subsidise employee share ownership.

CST thinks in terms of a profound complementarity between labour and capital with the latter being dependent on, and at the service of, the former. This is not how we tend to think of capital – labour relations today. Rather, we tend to think of capital and labour as being at one another's throats (more or less overtly). For people of a certain age, this mental image has been reinforced by the memory of bitter industrial conflicts. In *Laborem exercens*, John Paul II argued that the modern intuition that labour and capital are opposing forces is rooted both in materialist theories and in industrial practices that tended to treat the worker as if his or her work were no more than a commodity used in the production process. It should by now go without saying that, so far as CST is concerned, this is a complete inversion of the proper order of things.

CST's defence of private property has to be understood in the context of its belief that the earth and its resources have been given to the whole human race. Private property ownership is important but has a social dimension; put another way private property rights are subject to a social mortgage. Thus, in appropriate cases, governments are justified in redistributing wealth if, for example, some live in opulence while people alongside them live in misery. This redistribution would be a work of justice. This consideration has implications for employee ownership and participation. It might be justifiable to redraw voting and control rights of shareholders in order to promote the cause of employee ownership and participation. Whether and how this should be done would be a matter for management and for governments. They would have the difficult task of achieving a balance between the private property rights of shareholders and the legitimate interests of employees. This task has both moral and economic elements.

CST tries to urge people within corporations to take responsibility for their own decisions. An executive has a duty to act for the good of the corporation and its participants. This does not, however, justify the taking of moral short-cuts. Similarly, shareholders, especially major shareholders, should take moral responsibility for corporate decisions insofar as they have the capacity to influence them one way or another. Indeed, there is an ethical dimension to the decision to invest in one company rather than another.

The corporation

The corporation is a community of persons. It has its own common good (arrangements that help its members to achieve the relevant aspects of their

own self-realisation). Corporate governance and managerial arrangements are central elements of the common good of the corporation. They
make it possible to co-ordinate the efforts of the firm's employees and to
deploy the firm's resources for the benefit of customers or clients, employees and shareholders.

While the firm exists to help its members to achieve the specialised
range of goods that brought them to it, it can also make demands on those
members. Employees can usually see the point of exerting themselves for
the sake of the organisations to which they belong and often feel some
kind of loyalty to it. Membership of an organisation, like any relationship,
has the potential (not always actualised) to induce a shared viewpoint and
members can come to see the firm's good as an element of their own well-
being. That is to say that the firm can draw upon the fact that the human
person is accustomed to pursuing his or her personal good through membership of various groups (starting with the family) and to seeing successful participation in such groups as a good thing in its own right.

There is a long-running debate as to whether the corporation is a reality or a fiction. This debate partly reflects the nominalist scepticism as to
the reality of universal or abstract objects. Our own experience (both of
external, observable reality and of our own intellectual processes) suggests that we think of organisations as having an existence and a capacity
to act that is independent of their individual members. Thus, it seems reasonable to grant that the corporation does have some being or existence
that is profoundly related to the being of the individuals who, over time,
form part of it but that is more than just the sum of those individuals and
the contracts between them.

It is possible to speak of some people as being inside the corporation and
of others as being outside its walls. A sense of shared purpose is decisive
here. Those who make a conscious decision to co-operate within the
framework of the firm and who see the promotion of its purpose as being
at the same time the furtherance of some goals of their own are members
of the firm. Employees are the people who usually fit this description most
fully. Shareholders do so as well but in the context of the modern corporation their participation and engagement with the purposes of the firm is
often less apparent than is the case with employees. In this respect, efforts
to engage shareholders in corporate governance are to be welcomed since
they help to draw shareholders more fully into the life of the corporation.
This movement can be seen as consistent with CST's desire to personalise
communities of all types.

The corporation is not a self-sufficient grouping but is part of a broader economy and political community. The political community has wider concerns than the corporation. It is responsible for providing the common good that can facilitate the pursuit of the full range of goods that are the building blocks of self-realisation. Thus it is responsible for creating the arrangements that will allow its citizens to be fed, educated, housed, employed, physically safe and so on. The firm, by contrast has a much more limited set of concerns.

The state can make demands on the individuals and groups that are subject to it. Its responsibility for the common good means that it can impose taxes and regulate the activities of the corporation (for example through environmental or product safety regulation). Individuals are capable of seeing the point of making efforts for the sake of the communities to which they belong and often do so. Similarly, when individuals combine in some group (such as the firm) they can see that the group has responsibilities to the broader community within which the firm is located.

The state, as the co-ordinating body within society, has a right and duty to make laws that will promote the common good and to expect them to be followed. It should also foster and be able to count on the active and creative participation of its citizens in promoting the common good. The same considerations apply to the corporation. Its board (acting in accordance with corporate law and the company's constitution) are responsible for deciding how the corporation can and should play its part as a responsible citizen. This might well involve a search for ways of helping out that are consistent with its particular goals.

There is a practical tension between the political community's range of concerns and its ability to play a direct role in meeting them. It necessarily relies on intermediate associations (such as the firm) to take direct responsibility for meeting the needs of the individuals for which it is responsible. The political authority's essential role is to co-ordinate the efforts of the individuals and groups that form part of the relevant society; ordinarily it should prefer to get others to act than to intervene directly itself. A whole-hearted acceptance of the principle of subsidiarity also helps to personalise society since it allows people to participate in decision-making and to connect with the political life of society in ways that are meaningful to them. Those in charge of the political community should be creative in the ways that they foster, support and co-operate with intermediate associations.

Employee participation

Employees are affected, by decisions taken at board level as well as by decisions taken at a range of levels (or by a range of functions) within the firm's hierarchy. Employee participation can refer to participation (through representatives) in board-level decision-making. CST suggests that this is desirable and argues for a spirit of partnership within the firm. It has never asserted that co-determination (or any other specific method of cultivating this partnership approach) should be adopted. This is a matter for those within the firm and, possibly, for governments to resolve. Participation at managerial levels closer to the worker's specific role can, of course, be more direct and more meaningful.

There seems to be no specific CST pronouncement on this type of participation. It is reasonable, however, to suppose that this type of participation should be encouraged. This is a more direct way of ensuring that the worker is actively engaged in the important decisions concerning his work. Representative participation at board level is important but rather remote from the practical, daily concerns of the employee. On its own, it could do little to avoid the creation of a bureaucratic system that alienates the employee from his or her work.

CST espouses the cause of employee participation in one sense because of work's role as a basic human good with a capacity to build up the humanity, the personality of the worker. Work can either be more or less of a humanising experience. Giving the employee the ability to exercise freedom, creativity and responsibility can play a major role in ensuring that the worker's humanity is respected and built up in the workplace. CST predicts that this will be good for the business of the firm. This is, of course, highly plausible, but not strictly speaking something that CST can pronounce upon. Nor can CST pronounce on how it is to be done. There is no doubt that designing the workplace and governance with these principles in mind calls for great intelligence and skill. When it comes to the promotion of employee participation in the British boardroom, there are few working models that can be followed.

Employee participation can also be seen as a response to CST's general drive towards encouraging more personalised communities. Those in charge of communities should see themselves as being responsible for helping the members of the community to achieve the aspects of their self-realisation that brought them to that community. In the case of the firm this means that those in charge of governance owe a duty to employees to ensure that their work is as remunerative and fulfilling as may be.

The ideal community will also try to ensure that its members can take an active part in its life. This may be irksome to those in charge who might prefer to be allowed to get on with things in their own way.

There are also potential economic benefits to employee participation though this is not CST's area of expertise. Employees are vulnerable to expropriation in the event of corporate restructurings and some minimum level of information-sharing and advance warning can help them to take steps either to prevent harmful restructurings or at least to take steps to minimize their personal loss. Employee participation can also be seen as a way of making some type of commitment to employees that their interests will be promoted through the firm's governance and management. This can be one element of a strategy to give employees incentives to acquire firm-specific skills. Employee participation can also be a way of allowing employees to contribute their knowledge of the firm and its activities to management and to corporate governance.

Employee interests are also affected by decision-making at levels higher than the firm. There have been calls in CST for employer and employee representatives to be involved in these decisions too. Employer representatives probably have no difficulty in getting access to the corridors of power and it is only reasonable that employee representatives are given a chance to be kept informed and to contribute to decision-making.

British corporate governance

British corporate governance is shaped by company law (the centre-piece of which is the Companies Act 2006), the Combined Code on Corporate Governance and the requirements of institutional investors. It seems to reflect a conceptual model of the corporation as a kind of trust with the board as trustees and the shareholders as its beneficiaries. Heavy emphasis is placed on the board's duty to promote the well-being of the corporation, principally for the benefit of its shareholders. The board is accountable to shareholders through the general meeting and the UK's financial reporting requirements. The Combined Code seeks to strengthen ties between institutional shareholders and the board.

There is no formal place for employee representatives in corporate governance. Proposals made in the 1970s to create a co-determination system came to nothing and the UK opposed efforts to build employee participation into the European Company legislation. The introduction of employee representatives onto the board would require some legal issues to be addressed. Employee representatives would need to be informed about and to observe their duty of confidentiality and their duty to act in the best interests of the corporation. There is, however, no legal barrier to the introduction of employee representatives onto the board. That is not to say, however, that the introduction of employee participation would be a simple matter. Regardless of the substantive merits of the case, share-holders and their representatives are certain to resist any major change to a system that gives them such a privileged position and their voice is a very powerful one when it comes to corporate governance. The lack of working models is a further barrier. The John Lewis example shows that it is possible to have a successful business that puts employees at the centre of corporate governance. It may not, however, be a model that can be cop-ied by businesses that have non-employee shareholders to answer to.

Labour law

The EC has supplemented the UK's collective bargaining systems with the European Works Council and Information and Consultation directives. These might be seen as partial responses to the need for mechanisms to keep employees informed of major events in the life of the company. They might develop, in time, into much more thorough-going mechanisms to involve employees in corporate governance. It is plausible to think that trade unions will have a major part to play. CST has called for this devel-opment but reminds unions that their role is to work in the interests of employees but with an understanding that they have a responsibility to work for the common good.

This would raise the question as to whether it is desirable to have such a high degree of separation between corporate governance as it is now understood and the mechanisms for dialogue with employees. Certainly this would be a pragmatic device for overcoming the severe barriers to acceptance of anything that resembles co-determination. It does, how-ever, raise the question as to how shareholder-centred corporate govern-ance will interact with the employee mechanisms.

European corporate governance

A comparison of the corporate governance systems of the member states of the European Union reveals, amongst other important differences, divergent approaches to the question of employee participation. The United Kingdom and Germany, for example, stand on opposite sides of this dividing line. The freedom of businesses to incorporate wherever they like in the European Union and the spread of the shareholder value ideology seem to threaten the survival of corporate governance systems that include employee participation. The European Union now pursues a strategy that makes freedom of incorporation easier at the same time as it has promoted the employee participation cause. It has reached this point by a tortuous route and it has been prodded this way and that by the member states and by interest groups within it. Be that as it may, its current approach seems to offer a sensible and coherent way of reconciling the seemingly irreconcilable demands of the advocates of shareholder value and employee participation.

The emergence of the European Union as a supra-national community with its own common good and political institutions is an illustration that nation states are not now (if they ever were) capable of operating as self-sufficient communities sealed off from each other. The European Union has been able to promote the economic benefits associated with freedom of movement (and freedom of incorporation as a special case of freedom of movement) and the social and economic benefits delivered by employee participation in ways that the member states would not otherwise have been able to achieve.

The European Union has also worked to give its own shape to the principle of subsidiarity. As a principle of social ethics, CST calls on 'the state' to refrain from interfering in the internal affairs of intermediate associations such as the corporation. Translated into the EU context, subsidiarity refers to the allocation of power and responsibility as between the legislative organs of the EU, on the one hand, and member states on the other. When it comes to employee participation in corporate governance, it will be important for the EU and member states to pursue the logic of subsidiarity still further. Employer and employee representative groups should be encouraged to work together on the issue both at European and national levels. Shareholders, management and employee representatives should be helped, and allowed, to tailor solutions for their corporation.

Faith and reason

One of the more important general themes of this book has been to show the relationship between CST as a branch of moral theology and the knowledge that can be attained by human reason. CST draws both on revelation and on philosophy. For example, much of what it says about work as a basic human good is accessible to unaided reason. The contribution made by revealed sources (the understanding of the role of work in the individual's relationship with God) builds on the philosopher's understanding but adds a dimension that the philosopher as such might suspect but could never demonstrate. Catholic theology presupposes that there is only one reality and that the intellect can make use both of data derived from revelation as well as data derived from sense experience and reflection on that experience to come to a deeper knowledge of that reality.

It is not necessary to be a Christian, nor to believe in God at all, to be able to engage to some extent with the theological aspects of CST. For example, anyone, having had the idea explained to them, can reflect on the idea of original sin. Any thinking person can reflect on whether the human person has an inner urge to pursue the good and has faculties of reason and will that are impaired and subject to difficulties and tensions but that still function reasonably well. Anyone can consider whether or not this is a better description of the human condition than one that gives excessive weight to social conditioning or that assumes that the human person is basically prone to evil and that the most that can be done is to mitigate the worst manifestations of this wickedness. A Christian (at least a Catholic) will frame his or her understanding of this positive view of human nature in terms of the doctrine of original sin. Others might be more or less open to the possibility that this is a true explanation. The same could be said of the Christian explanations of the place of work in a well-structured human life or of the social nature of the human person. These facts are accessible to unaided reason but have Christian dimensions which can also be understood to some extent by non-Christians and non-believers.

Catholic Social Thought and social sciences

CST argues that it can work with the human sciences to mutual benefit: it can learn from the detailed specialised knowledge of, say, the psychologist, at the same time contributing its own anthropology and knowledge of what makes for human self-realisation. The same can be said of the social sciences such as economics. Here, too, there is scope for fruitful collaboration. Any discipline that can make a contribution to human well-being deserves a welcome. CST has, however, made the point that the simplifying assumptions that the social sciences make can be a source of harm. Chapter five made this point when it explained the problems associated with theories of the firm that give excessive attention to the human propensity to behave selfishly and almost make the curbing of that behaviour the central point of corporate governance. The social sciences can offer partial-but-true insights into human realities. They can benefit from CST's explanation of the bigger picture. CST also roots its analysis in its all-round appreciation of human goods and of how integral self-realisation can be pursued effectively. A variety of disciplines make useful contributions to our understanding of the corporation. CST can draw on their insights in pursuit of its humanistic synthesis. It can take what is useful without fear of the reductionism that their methodologies can sometimes generate.

The impact of communities on the well-being of the individual

Catholic theology focuses on individual choices and asks whether they are or are not oriented towards integral self-realisation and whether or not they are consistent with an overall life plan that is so oriented. At the same time, however, it is alert to the fact that we are heavily shaped by our social *milieux*. We are heavily shaped by the communities to which we belong even though we are not usually so thoroughly conditioned by them as to rob us of free choice and personal moral responsibility.

Indeed, it is the appreciation that this is so that gives CST its urgency. Communities can either be more or less human. They can be said to be human if they are committed to the cause of integral self-realisation. This requires that those in charge be consciously committed to the service of the members of that community. Further, it implies that the common good of that community in all its dimensions is shaped by the individual personalities of its members. A well-functioning community offers its individual members the ability not only to pursue their own well-being but also the ability to contribute to building up the common good of that community. The opposite, harmful, approach is the creation of social structures where an elite seeks to impose its will on the others. Such a community is stifling, bureaucratic and alienating. Examples are only too abundant.

The firm is a community of persons. It is an important one because it organises human work. Work has a vital role to play in the development of the human personality and in meeting human needs. Because work is so central to human self-realisation the community which organises it should be truly committed to the well-being of its members.

BIBLIOGRAPHY

Alford, H. and Naughton, M., 'Beyond the shareholder model of the firm', in S. Cortright and M. Naughton (eds.), *Rethinking the purpose of business. Interdisciplinary essays from the Catholic Social Tradition*, (Notre Dame, Indiana: University of Notre Dame Press, 2002).

Annan, K., 'Two concepts of sovereignty', *The Economist* (September 18th, 1999)

Argandona, A., 'The stakeholder theory and the common good', *Journal of Business Ethics* **17** (1998), pp. 1093–1102.

Armour, J., Deakin, S. and Konzelmann, S., 'Shareholder primacy and the trajectory of UK corporate governance', *British Journal of Industrial Relations* **41** (2003), pp. 531–555.

Axworthy, C., 'Corporation law as if some people mattered', *University of Toronto Law Journal* **36** (1981), pp. 392–439.

Bainbridge, S., 'Corporate decision-making and the moral rights of employees', *Villanova Law Review* **43** (1998) pp. 780–828.

Barca, F. and Brecht, M. (eds.), *The control of corporate Europe*, (Oxford: Oxford University Press, 2001).

Bellace, J., 'The role of the law in supporting employee representation systems', *Comparative Labor Law Journal* **15** (1994), pp. 441–460.

'The European Works Council Directive: Transnational information and consultation in the European Union', *Comparative Labor Law Journal* **18** (1996–1997), pp. 325–361.

Benedict XVI, *Deus caritas est*, (2005) (available at www.vatican.va/holy_father/benedict_xvi/encyclicals/documents/hf_ben-xvi_enc_20051225_deus-caritas-est_en.html, last accessed on 13th July 2009).

Caritas in veritate, (2009) (available at www.vatican.va/holy_father/benedict_xvi/encyclicals/documents/hf_ben-xvi_enc_20090629_caritas-in-veritate_en.html, last accessed on 13th July 2009).

Bercusson, B., *European Labour Law*, (London: Butterworths, 1996).

'The European social model comes to Britain', *Industrial Law Journal* **31** (2002), pp. 209–244.

Blair. M., *Ownership and control. Rethinking corporate governance for the twenty-first century*, (Washington DC: The Brookings Institution Press, 1995).

'Firm-specific human capital and theories of the firm', in Roe, M. and Blair, M. (eds.), *Employees and corporate governance*, (Washington DC: Brookings Institution Press, 1999).

Blair, M. and Stout, L., 'A team production theory of corporate law', *Virginia Law Review* **85** (1999), pp. 247–328.

Blainpain, R., *European Labour Law*, (11th revised ed.), (The Hague: Kluwer Law International, 2008).

Blasi, J., Kruse, D., Sesil, J. and Kroumova, M., 'An assessment of employee ownership in the United States with implications for the EU', *The International Journal of Human Resource Management* **14** (2003), pp. 893–919.

The Bullock Report, Command Paper (Cmnd.) 6706, HMSO.

Burbidge, P., 'Creating high performance boardrooms and workplaces – European corporate governance in the twenty first century', *European Law Review* **28** (2003), pp. 642–663.

Calo, Z., ' "True economic liberalism" and the development of American Catholic Social Thought, 1920–1940', *Journal of Catholic Social Thought* **5** (2008), pp. 285–321.

Calvez, J.-Y. and Perrin, J., *The Church and social justice. The social teaching of the Popes from Leo XIII to Pius XII (1878–1958)*, (Chicago: Henry Regnery Company, 1961).

Calvez, J.-Y. and Naughton, M., 'Catholic Social Teaching and the purpose of a business organisation: A developing tradition', in Cortright, S. and Naughton, M. (eds.), *Rethinking the purpose of business. Interdisciplinary essays from the Catholic Social Tradition*, (Notre Dame, Indiana: University of Notre Dame Press, 2002).

Canavan, F., S. J., 'The popes and the economy', *Notre Dame Journal of Law, Ethics and Public Policy* **11** (1997), pp. 429–444.

Carley, M. and Hall, M., 'The implementation of the European Works Council Directive', *Industrial Law Journal* **29** (2000), pp. 103–124.

Carozza, P., 'Subsidiarity as a structural principle of international human rights law', *American Journal of International Law* **97** (2003), pp. 38–79.

Catechism of the Catholic Church, (available at www.vatican.va/archive/catechism/ccc_toc.htm, last accessed 13th July 2009).

The Catholic Bishops' Conference of England and Wales, *The common good and the Catholic Church's social teaching*, (1996), (available at www.catholic-ew.org.uk/ccb/catholic_church/publications, last accessed on 25th July 2009).

Charles, R., S.J., *Christian social witness and teaching. The Catholic tradition from Genesis to centessimus annus*, (**two** volumes), (Leominster: Gracewing, 1998).

An introduction to Catholic Social Teaching, (Oxford: Family Publications, 1999).

Cessario, R., O.P., *Introduction to moral theology*, (Washington DC: The Catholic University Press of America, 2001).

Charny, D., 'Workers and corporate governance: The role of political culture', in M. Roe and M. Blair (eds.), *Employees and corporate governance*, (Washington DC: Brookings Institution Press, 1999).

'Regulatory competition and the global co-ordination of labor standards', *Journal of International Economic Law* 3 (2000), pp. 281–302.

Chmielewski, P., 'Workers' participation in the United States; Catholic Social Teaching and democratic theory', *Review of Social Economy* LV (1997), pp. 487–508.

Collins, H., *Employment Law*, (Oxford: Oxford University Press, 2003).

The Constitution of the John Lewis Partnership (June 2008), (available at www.johnlewispartnership.co.uk/Display.aspx?MasterId=9d2aa2cb-e971-4782-b6c1-028cc8374ae4&NavigationId=586, last accessed on 18th July 2009).

Cortright, S. and Naughton, M. (eds.), *Rethinking the purpose of business. Interdisciplinary essays from the Catholic Social Tradition*, (Notre Dame, Indiana: University of Notre Dame Press, 2002).

Cooter. R., 'The best right values: value foundations of the economic analysis of law', *Notre Dame Law Review*, p. 817.

Cooter, R. and Ulen, T., *Law and economics*, (4th edn), (Boston: Pearson/Addison Wesley, 2004).

Copleston, F., *Medieval philosophy*, (New York: Harper Brothers, 1961).

Davies, P. ,'The Bullock Report and employee participation in corporate planning in the UK', *Journal of Comparative Corporate Law and Securities Regulation* 1 (1978), pp. 245–272.

'Employee representation and corporate law reform: A comment from the United Kingdom', *Comparative Labor Law and Policy Journal* 22 (2000–2001), pp. 135–147.

Introduction to Company Law, (Oxford: Oxford University Press, 2002).

'Employee involvement in the European Company', in J. Rickford (ed.). *The European Company. Developing a Community Law of Corporations*, (Antwerp/Oxford/New York: Intersentia, 2003).

Gower and Davies' Principles of Modern Company Law, (8th ed.), (London: Thomson/Sweet & Maxwell, 2008).

Davies, P. and Lord Wedderburn of Charlton, 'The land of industrial democracy', 6 (1977), pp. 197–211.

The Davignon Report, *'European systems of worker involvement' (with regard to the European Company Statute and the other pending proposals)*, (1997).

Deakin, S., The coming transformation of shareholder value', *Corporate Governance: An International Review* 41 (2003), pp. 11–18.

'"Enterprise-risk": The juridical nature of the firm revisited', *Industrial Law Journal* 32 (2003), pp. 97–113.

Deakin, S., Hobbs, R., Konzelmann, S. and Wilkinson, F., 'Partnership, ownership and control. The impact of corporate governance on employment relations, *Employee Relations* **24** (2002), pp. 335–352.

Deakin, S., Hobbs, R., Nash, D. and Slinger, G., *Implied contracts, takeovers and corporate governance: In the shadow of the City Code*, ESRC Centre for Business Research, University of Cambridge Working Paper 254.

Deakin, S. and Morris, G., *Labour Law*, (4th edn), (Oxford: Hart Publishing, 2005).

Department of Trade and Industry, *Company Law reform*, (2005), Cm. 6456.

Dinh, V., 'Codetermination and corporate governance in a multinational business enterprise', *Journal of Corporation Law* **24** (1999), pp. 975–999.

Donald, D., 'Shareholder voice and its opponents' *Journal of Corporate Law Studies* **5** (2005), pp. 305–361.

Donaldson, L., 'The ethereal hand: Organisational economics and management theory', *The Academy of Management Review* **15** (1990), pp. 369–381.

Dow, G., *Governing the firm: Workers' control in theory and practice*, (Cambridge: Cambridge University Press, 2003).

Dow, G. and Putterman, L., 'Why capital (usually) hires labour: An assessment of proposed explanations', in M. Roe and M. Blair (eds.), *Employees and corporate governance*, (Washington DC: Brookings Institution Press, 1999).

Du Plessis, J. and Sandrock, O., 'The rise and fall of supervisory codetermination in Germany', *International Company and Commercial Law Review* **16** (2005), pp. 67–79.

Dundon, T., Wilkinson, A., Marchington, M. and Ackers, P., 'The meanings of employee voice', *International Journal of Human Resource Management* **15** (2004), pp. 1149–1170.

Drucker, P., *Managing in turbulent times*, (London: William Heinemann Ltd, 1980).

Drury, R., 'Migrating companies', *European Law Review* **24** (1999), pp. 354–372.

Easterbrook, F. and Fischel, D., 'The corporate contract', *Columbia Law Review* **89** (1989), pp. 1416–1448.

The economic structure of corporate law, (Cambridge, Massachusetts: Harvard University Press, 1991).

Edwards, T., 'Corporate governance, industrial relations and trends in company-level restructuring in Europe: Convergence towards the Anglo-American model?', *Industrial Relations Journal* **35** (2004), pp. 518–535.

Finnis, J., *Aquinas. Moral, political and legal theory*, (Oxford: Oxford University Press, 1998).

Natural law and natural rights, (Oxford: Oxford University Press, 2003).

Fitzgibbon, S., ' "True human community": Catholic Social Thought, Aristotelean ethics, and the moral order of the business company', *Saint Louis University Law Journal* **45** (2001), pp. 1243–1279.

Fort, T., *Ethics and governance*, (Oxford: Oxford University Press, 2001).
'Business as a mediating institution', in S. Cortright and M. Naughton (eds.), *Rethinking the purpose of business. Interdisciplinary essays from the Catholic Social Tradition*, (Notre Dame, Indiana: University of Notre Dame Press, 2002).

Franks, J., Mayer, C. and Rossi, S., 'Spending less time with the family: The decline of family ownership in the United Kingdom', in R. Morck (ed.), *A history of corporate governance around the world*, (Chicago: The University of Chicago Press, 2005).

Frick, B. and Lehmann, E., 'Corporate governance in Germany: Ownership, code-termination and firm performance in a stakeholder economy', in H. Gospel and A. Pendleton (eds.), *Corporate governance and labour management: an international comparison*, (Oxford: Oxford University Press, 2005).

Friedman, M., 'The social responsibility of business is to make a profit', *The New York Times Magazine*, 13th September, 1970.

Gates, J., 'Reengineering ownership for the common good', in S. Cortright and M. Naughton (eds.), *Rethinking the purpose of business. Interdisciplinary essays from the Catholic Social Tradition*, (Notre Dame, Indiana: University of Notre Dame Press, 2002).

George, R., 'A defense of the new natural law theory', *American Journal of Jurisprudence*, **41** (1996), pp. 48–61.

Ghilarducci, T., Hawley, J. and Williams, A., 'Labour's paradoxical interests and the evolution of corporate governance', *Journal of Law and Society* **24** (1997), pp. 26–43.

Ghoshal, S. and Moran, P., 'Bad for practice: A critique of the transaction cost theory', *The Academy of Management Review* **21** (1996), pp. 13–47.

Goergen, M. and Renneboog, L., 'Strong managers and passive institutional investors in the UK', in F. Barca and M. Brecht (eds.), *The control of corporate Europe*, (Oxford: Oxford University Press, 2001).

Gomez, J., 'All you who labour: Towards a spirituality of work for the 21st century', *Notre Dame Journal of Law, Ethics & Public Policy*, pp. 791–814.

Goodijk, R., 'Corporate governance and workers' participation', *Corporate Governance* **8** (2000), pp. 303–310.

Gordon, J., 'Employee stock ownership in economic transitions: The case of United and the airline industry', in M. Roe and M. Blair (eds.), *Employees and corporate governance*, (Washington DC: Brookings Institution Press, 1999).

Gospel, H. and Pendleton, A., 'Finance, corporate governance and the management of labour', *British Journal of Industrial Relations* **41** (2003), p. 560.

Gospel, H. and Pendleton, A. (eds.), *Corporate governance and labour management: an international comparison*, (Oxford: Oxford University Press, 2005).

Gospel, H. and Pendleton, A., 'Corporate governance and labour management: an international comparison', in H. Gospel and A. Pendleton (eds.), *Corporate governance and labour management: an international comparison*, (Oxford: Oxford University Press, 2005).

Gospel, H., Lockwood, G. and Willman, P., 'A British dilemma: Disclosure of information for collective bargaining and joint consultation', *Comparative Labour Law & Policy Journal* **22** (2000–2001), pp. 327–349.

Green, S., *Serving God? Serving Mammon?*, (Grand Rapids, Michigan: Zondervan Publishing House, 1996).

Greenfield, K., 'The place of workers in corporate law' *Boston College Law Review* **39** (1998), p. 283.

Gregg, S., *Challenging the modern world. Karol Wojtyla/John Paul II and the development of Catholic Social Teaching*, (Lanham, Maryland: Lexington Books, 1999).

'Investing in morality', *Villanova Journal of Law and Investment Management* **4** (2002), pp. 57–66.

Grisez, G., *The way of the Lord Jesus. Christian moral principles*, (Quincy, Illinois: Franciscan Press, 1983).

The way of the Lord Jesus. Living a Christian life, (Quincy, Illinois: Franciscan Press, 1983).

Grisez, G., Boyle, J. and Finnis, J., 'Practical principles, moral truth and ultimate ends', *The American Journal of Jurisprudence* **32** (1987), pp. 99–151.

Gronbacher, G. and Sirico, R., 'Towards a personalist work ethic', in T. Machan (ed.), *Morality and work*, (Stanford: Hoover Institution Press, 2000).

Guest, D. and Peccei, R., 'Partnership at work: Mutuality and the balance of advantage', *British Journal of Industrial Relations* **39** (2001), pp. 207–236.

Halal, W., 'Corporate community: A theory of the firm uniting profitability and responsibility', *Strategy and Leadership*, February 28th, 2000, pp. 10–16.

Hansmann, H., 'When does worker ownership work? ESOPs, law firms, codetermination and economic democracy', *The Yale Law Journal* **99** (1989–1990), pp. 1749–1816.

'Worker participation and corporate governance', *University of Toronto Law Journal* **43** (1993), pp. 589–606.

Hansmann, H. and Kraakman, R., 'The end of history for corporate law', *Georgetown Law Journal* **89** (2001), pp. 439–468.

'What is corporate law?' in *The anatomy of corporate law. A comparative and functional approach*, (Oxford: Oxford University Press, 2004).

Harrington, L., 'Ethics and public policy analysis: Stakeholders' interests and regulatory policy', *Journal of Business Ethics* **15** (1996), pp. 373–382.

Hawley, J. and Williams, A., *Fiduciary capitalism. How institutional investors can make corporate America more democratic*, (Philadelphia: University of Pennsylvania Press, 2000).

Hervada, J., *The principles of the social doctrine of the Church*, (available at www. columbia.edu/cu/augustine/arch/social.html, last accessed on 25th July 2009).

Hollenbach, D., S.J., *The common good and Christian ethics*, (Cambridge, Cambridge University Press, 2002).

' "Economic justice for all" twenty years later', *Journal of Catholic Social Thought*, **5** (2008), pp. 315–321.

Honeyball, S., *Honeyball & Bower's textbook on Employment Law*, (10th edn), (Oxford: Oxford University Press, 2008).

Hopt, K., 'New ways in corporate governance: European experiments with labor representation on corporate boards', *Michigan Law Review* **82** (1983–1984), pp. 1338–1363.

Howse, R. and Trebilcock, M., 'Protecting the employment bargain', *University of Toronto Law Journal* **43** (1993), pp. 751–792.

Illanes, J.L., *The sanctification of work*, (New York: Scepter Publishers, 2003).

Institutional Shareholders' Committee, *The responsibilities of institutional shareholders and agents – a statement of principles (updated 2007)*, (available at institutionalshareholderscommittee.org.uk/sitebuildercontent/sitebuilderfiles/ISCStatementofPrinciplesJun07.pdf, last accessed on 18th July 2009).

Jacoby, S., *The embedded corporation*, (Princeton, NJ, Princeton University Press, 2004).

'Corporate governance and employees in the United States', in H. Gospel and A. Pendleton (eds.), *Corporate governance and labour management: an international comparison*, (Oxford: Oxford University Press, 2005).

Jackson, G., 'Towards a comparative perspective on corporate governance and labour management: Enterprise coalitions and national trajectories', in H. Gospel and A. Pendleton (eds.), *Corporate governance and labour management: an international comparison*, (Oxford: Oxford University Press, 2005).

Jackson, G., Hopner, M. and Kurdelbusch, A., 'Corporate governance and employees in Germany: Changing linkages, complementarities and tensions', in H. Gospel and A. Pendleton (eds.), *Corporate governance and labour management: an international comparison*, (Oxford: Oxford University Press, 2005).

Jensen, M. and Meckling, W., 'Theory of the firm: Managerial behaviour, agency costs and ownership structure', *Journal of Financial Economics* **3** (1976), pp. 305–360.

John XXIII *Mater et magistra* (1961) (available at www.vatican.va/holy_father/john_xxiii/encyclicals/documents/hf_j-xxiii_enc_15051961_mater_en.html, last accessed on 20th July 2009).

Pacem in terris, (1963) (available at www.vatican.va/holy_father/john_xxiii/ encyclicals/documents/hf_j-xxiii_enc_11041963_pacem_en.html, last accessed on 31st July 2009).

John Paul II, *Redemptor hominis* (1979), (available at www.vatican.va/holy_father/ john_paul_ii/encyclicals/documents/hf_jp-ii_enc_04031979_redemptor-hominis_en.html, last accessed on 13th July 2009).

Laborem exercens, (1981) (available at www.vatican.va/holy_father/john_ paul_ii/encyclicals/documents/hf_jp-ii_enc_14091981_laborem-exercens_ en.html, last accessed on 13th July 2009).

Sollicitudo rei socialis, (1987) (available at www.vatican.va/holy_father/john_ paul_ii/encyclicals/documents/hf_jp-ii_enc_30121987_sollicitudo-rei-socialis_en.html, last accessed on 11th July.

Centesimus annus, (1991) (available at www.vatican.va/holy_father/john_paul_ ii/encyclicals/documents/hf_jp-ii_enc_01051991_centesimus-annus_ en.html, last accessed on 11th July 2009).

Veritatis splendor, (1993) (available at www.vatican.va/holy_father/john_paul_ ii/encyclicals/documents/hf_jp-ii_enc_06081993_veritatis-splendor_ en.html, last accessed on 13th July 2009)

Evangelium vitae, (1995) (available at www.vatican.va/holy_father/john_paul_ ii/encyclicals/documents/hf_jp-ii_enc_25031995_evangelium-vitae_ en.html, last accessed on 13th July 2009).

Fides et ratio, (1998) (available at www.vatican.va/holy_father/john_paul_ii/ encyclicals/documents/hf_jp-ii_enc_15101998_fides-et-ratio_en.html, last accessed on 31st July 2009).

Johnston, A., 'EC freedom of establishment, employee participation in corporate governance and the limits of regulatory competition', *Journal of Corporate Law Studies* **6** (2006), pp. 71–112.

Kay, J. and Silberston, A., 'Corporate governance', in F. MacMillan Patfield (ed.), *Perspectives on Company Law: 2* (London: Kluwer Law International, 1997).

Keller, B., 'The European Company statute: Employee involvement and beyond', *Industrial Law Journal* **33** (2002), pp. 424–445.

Kennedy. R., 'The virtue of solidarity and the purpose of the firm', in S. Cortright and M. Naughton (eds.), *Rethinking the purpose of business. Interdisciplinary essays from the Catholic Social Tradition*, (Notre Dame, Indiana: University of Notre Dame Press, 2002).

'Business and the common good in the Catholic social tradition', *Villanova Journal of Law and Investment Management* **4** (2002), pp. 29–50.

Kershaw, D., 'No end in sight for the history of corporate law: The case of employee participation in corporate governance', *Journal of Corporate Law Studies* **34** (2002), pp. 34–81.

Klare, K., 'Workplace democracy and market reconstruction: An agenda for legal reform', *Catholic University Law Review*, pp. 1–68.

Kohler, T., 'Lessons from the Social Charter: State, corporation and the principle of subsidiarity', *University of Toronto Law Journal* **43** (1993), pp. 607–628.

Koslowski, P., 'The shareholder value principle and the purpose of the firm', in S. Cortright and M. Naughton (eds.), *Rethinking the purpose of business. Interdisciplinary essays from the Catholic Social Tradition*, (Notre Dame, Indiana: University of Notre Dame Press, 2002).

Kulik, B., 'Agency theory, reasoning and culture at Enron: In search of a solution', *Journal of Business Ethics* **59** (2005), pp. 347–360.

Learmount, S., *Corporate governance – what can be learned from Japan?*, (Oxford: Oxford University Press, 2004).

Lee, P., 'Institutional shareholder activism – part 2', in R. Smerdon, *A practical guide to corporate governance*, (3rd edn), (London: Sweet & Maxwell, 2007).

Leo XIII *Rerum novarum*, (1891) (available at www.vatican.va/holy_father/leo_xiii/encyclicals/documents/hf_l-xiii_enc_15051891_rerum-novarum_en.html, last accessed on 11th July 2009).

Lorber, P., 'Reviewing the European Works Council Directive: European Progress and United Kingdom Perspective', *Industrial Law Journal* **33** (2004), pp. 191–199.

Lower, M., 'Subsidiarity and the corporation', *Journal of Catholic Social Thought* **2** (2005), pp. 431–461.

'John Paul II and employee participation in corporate governance', *Notre Dame Journal of Law, Ethics & Public Policy* **21** (2007), pp. 111–158.

'Christian anthropology and the theory of the firm', *Journal of Catholic Social Thought* **5** (2008), pp. 413–435.

Lowisch, M., 'Job safeguarding as an object of the rights of information, consultation, and co-determintation in European and German law', *Comparative Labour Law & Policy Journal* **26** (2004–2005), pp. 371–379.

Lutz, D., 'Christian social thought and corporate governance', in R. Kennedy (ed.), *Religion and public life*, (Lanham, Md: University Press of America, 2001), pp. 121–140.

Lynch Fannon, I., *Working within two kinds of capitalism. Corporate governance and employee stakeholding. US and EC perspectives*, (Oxford: Hart Publishing, 2003).

Machan, T., *Morality and work. Philosophic reflections on a free society*, (Stanford: Hoover Institution Press, 2000).

Mallin, C., *Corporate governance*, (2nd edn), (Oxford: Oxford University Press, 2007).

Manne, H., 'Mergers and the market for corporate control', *The Journal of Political Economy* **73** (1965), pp. 110–120.

Maritain, J., 'The people and the state', reprinted in *Logos* 11 (2008).

Maxwell, J., 'Should Christians press for revision of Company law?', *University of Detroit Law Journal* **40** (1962), pp. 1–165.

May, W., *An introduction to moral theology*, (2nd edn), Huntington, Ind: Our Sunday Visitor Publishing Division, 2003).

McCall, J., 'Employee participation in corporate governance: A defense of strong participation rights', *Business Ethics Quarterly* **11** (2001), pp. 195–213.

McCann, D., 'Business corporations and the principle of subsidiarity', in S. Cortright and M. Naughton (eds.), *Rethinking the purpose of business. Interdisciplinary essays from the Catholic Social Tradition*, (Notre Dame, Indiana: University of Notre Dame Press, 2002).

Mele, D., *Cristianos en la sociedad. Introduccion a la doctrina social de la Iglesia*, (3rd edn), (Madrid: Ediciones Rialp, S.A., 2000).

'Not only stakeholder interests. The firm oriented towards the common good', in S. Cortright and M. Naughton (eds.), *Rethinking the purpose of business. Interdisciplinary essays from the Catholic Social Tradition*, (Notre Dame: Indiana, University of Notre Dame Press, 2002).

Michie, J. and Oughton, C., 'Employee participation and ownership rights', *Journal of Corporate Law Studies* **2** (2002), pp. 139–154.

Misner, P., *Social Catholicism in Europe. From the onset of industrialization to the First World War*, (New York: Dartford, Longman and Todd, 1991).

Messner, J., *Social ethics. Natural law in the western world*, (St Louis and London: B. Herder Book Co., 1965).

Monks, R. and Nell, M., *Corporate governance*, (Malden, Ma: Blackwell Publishing, 2004).

Morck, R. (ed.), *A history of corporate governance around the world*, (Chicago: The University of Chicago Press, 2005).

Murphy, J. and Pyke, D., 'Humane work and the challenges of job design', in S. Cortright and M. Naughton (eds.), *Rethinking the purpose of business. Interdisciplinary essays from the Catholic Social Tradition*, (Notre Dame, Indiana: University of Notre Dame Press, 2002).

Myners Report on corporate governance, HM Treasury, London, (2001).

Naughton, M., 'The corporation as a community of work: Understanding the firm within the Catholic social tradition', *Ave Maria Law Review* **4** (2006), pp. 33–75.

Newman, J., *Co responsibility in industry: Social justice in labour management relations*, (Cork: Cork University Press, 1954).

Njoya, W., 'Employee ownership and efficiency: An evolutionary perspective', *Industrial Law Journal* **33** (2004), pp. 211–241.

Property in work. The employment relationship in the Anglo-American firm, (Aldershot, Ashgate Publishing, 2007).

Novak, M., *The corporation: A theological inquiry*, (Washington: The American Enterprise Institute Press, 1981).

Toward a theology of the corporation, (Washington: The AEI Press, 1990).

O' Connor, J., 'Making a case for the common good in a global economy. The United Nations Human Development Reports (1990–2001)', *Journal of Religious Ethics* **30** (2002), pp. 157–173.

O' Connor, M., 'The human capital era: Re-conceptualising corporate law to facilitate labour management co-operation' *Cornell Law Review* **78** (1993), pp. 901–965.

'Global capitalism and the evolution of American corporate governance', in F. MacMillan Patfield (ed.), *Perspectives on Company Law: 2* (London: Kluwer Law International, 1997).

'Employees and corporate governance: United States: Labour's role in the American corporate governance structure', *Comparative Labour Law & Policy Journal* **22** (2000), pp. 97–133.

Oakeshott, R., *The case for workers' co-ops*, (Basingstoke: MacMillan Press Ltd, 1990).

Ogletree, T., 'Corporate capitalism and the common good. A framework for addressing the challenges of a global economy.' *Journal of Religious Ethics*, **30** (2002), pp. 79–106.

Parkinson, J., *Corporate power and responsibility. Issues in the theory of Company Law*, (Oxford: Clarendon Press, 1993).

'Models of the company and the employment relationship', *British Journal of Industrial Relations* **41** (2003), pp. 481–509.

Paul VI *Populorum progressio* (1967) (available at www.vatican.va/holy_father/paul_vi/encyclicals/documents/hf_p-vi_enc_26031967_populorum_en.html, last accessed 13th July 2009).

Octogesima adveniens (1971) (available at www.vatican.va/holy_father/paul_vi/apost_letters/documents/hf_p-vi_apl_19710514_octogesima-adveniens_en.html, last accessed on 20th July 2009).

Pecorella, R., 'Property rights, the common good and the state: The Catholic view of market economies', *Journal of Catholic Social Thought* **5** (2008), pp. 235–284.

Pendleton, A., *Employee ownership, participation and governance – a study of ESOPs in the UK*, (London and New York: Routledge, 2000).

Pendleton, A. and Gospel, H., 'Markets and relationships: Finance, governance and labour in the United Kingdom', in H. Gospel and A. Pendleton (eds.), *Corporate governance and labour management: an international comparison*, (Oxford: Oxford University Press, 2005).

Pesch, H., S.J., *Ethics and the national economy*, (translated by Dr Rupert Ederer), (Norfolk, VA: IHS Press, 2004).

Pinckaers, S., *The sources of Christian ethics*, (translated by M. Thomas Noble), (Washington DC: The Catholic University Press of America, 1995).

Morality. The Catholic view, (South Bend, Ind.: St. Augustine's Press, 2003).

Pistor, K., 'Codetermination: A socio-political model with governance externalities', in M. Roe and M. Blair (eds.), *Employees and corporate governance*, (Washington DC: Brookings Institution Press, 1999).

Pius XI *Quadragesimo anno*, (1931) (available at www.vatican.va/holy_father/pius_xi/encyclicals/documents/hf_p-xi_enc_19310515_quadragesimo-anno_en.html, last accessed on 15th July 2009).

Pontifical Academy of Social Sciences, *Work and human fulfillment*, (Ave Maria, Fl.: Sapientia Press, 2001).

Pontifical Council for Justice and Peace, *Compendium of the Social Doctrine of the Church*, (Vatican City: Libreria Editrice Vaticana, trans. 2004).

The report of the Committee on the Financial Aspects of Corporate Governance, ('the Cadbury Report') (1992).

Reberioux, A., 'European style of corporate governance at the crossroads: The role of worker involvement', *Journal of Common Market Studies* **40** (2002), pp. 111–134.

Rhodes, M. and van Appeldoorn, B., 'Capital unbound? The transformation of European corporate governance', *Journal of European Public Policy* **5** (1998), pp. 406–427.

Roberts, J., 'Trust and control in Anglo-American systems of corporate governance: the individualizing and socializing effects of processes of accountability', *Human Relations* **54** (2001), pp. 1547–1572.

'The manufacture of Corporate Social Responsibility', *Organisation* **10** (2003), pp. 249–265.

Rock, E. and Wachter, M., 'Tailored claims and governance: the fit between employees and shareholders', in M. Roe and M. Blair (eds.), *Employees and corporate governance*, (Washington DC: Brookings Institution Press, 1999).

Roe, M., 'Codetermination and German securities markets', in M. Roe and M. Blair (eds.), *Employees and corporate governance*, (Washington DC: Brookings Institution Press, 1999).

Political determinants of corporate governance, (New York: Oxford University Press, 2003).

Roe, M. and Blair, M. (eds.), *Employees and corporate governance*, (Washington DC: Brookings Institution Press, 1999).

Sadowski, D., Junkes, J. and Lindenthal, S., 'Employees and corporate governance: Germany: The German model of corporate and labor governance', *Comparative Labor Law & Policy Journal* **22** (2000), pp. 33–66.

Sargent, M., 'Utility, the good and civic happiness: a Catholic critique of law and economics', *Journal of Catholic Legal Studies* **44** (2005), p. 36.

Schall, J., S.J., 'Catholicism, business and priorities', in O. Williams and J. Houck (eds.), *The Judaeo-Christian vision and the modern corporation*, (Notre Dame, Ind.:University of Notre Dame Press, 1982).

Schiek, D., 'Autonomous collective agreements as a regulatory device in European Labour Law: How to read article 139 EC', *Industrial Law Journal* **34** (2005), pp. 23–56.

Schilling, F., 'Corporate governance in Germany: The move to shareholder value', *Corporate Governance* **9** (2001), pp. 148–151.

Schultze, G., S.J., 'Worker-ownership and Catholic Social Thought', *Social Policy* Winter 2001/2002, pp. 12–16.

'Work, worship, Laborem exercens and the United States today', *Logos* **5** (2002), pp. 25–48.

Schumacher, C., *God is work: Discovering the divine pattern for work in the new millenium*, (Oxford: Lion UK, 1999).

Second Vatican Council, *Pastoral Constitution on the Church in the modern world, Gaudium et Spes*, (1965) (available at www.vatican.va/archive/hist_councils/ii_vatican_council/documents/vat-ii_cons_19651207_gaudium-et-spes_en.html, last accessed on 13th July 2009).

Shareholder ownership: A report on ownership of shares as at December 31, 2004, Office of National Statistics.

Shleifer, A. and Summers, L., *Breaches of trust in hostile takeovers*, (Cambridge, Mass.: National Bureau of Economic Research, 1987).

Singer, J., 'Jobs and justice: rethinking the stakeholder debate', *University of Toronto Law Journal* **43** (1993), pp. 473–510.

Smerdon, R., *A practical guide to corporate governance*, (3rd edn), (London: Sweet & Maxwell, 2007).

Stabile, S., 'Workers in the vineyard: Catholic Social Thought and the workplace', *Journal of Catholic Social Thought* **5** (2008), pp. 371–411.

Stapledon, G., *Institutional investors and corporate governance*, (Oxford: Clarendon Press, 1996).

Sun, J.-M. and Pelkmans, J., 'Regulatory competition in the single market', *Journal of Common Market Studies* **33** (1995), pp. 67–89.

The Takeover Code, (9th edn, 2009), (available at www.thetakeoverpanel.org.uk/wp-content/uploads/2008/11/code.pdf, last accessed on 20th July 2009).

Tavis, L., 'Modern contract theory and the purpose of the firm', in S. Cortright and M. Naughton (eds.), *Rethinking the purpose of business. Interdisciplinary essays from the Catholic Social Tradition*, (Notre Dame, Indiana: University of Notre Dame Press, 2002), pp. 215–236.

Tiebout, C., 'A pure theory of local expenditures', *The Journal of Political Economy* **64** (1956), pp. 416–424.

US Conference of Catholic Bishops, *Economic justice for all*, (1986) (available at www.usccb.org/jphd/economiclife/pdf/economic_justice_for_all.pdf, last accessed on 13th July 2009).

Vagts, D., 'Reforming the "modern" corporation: Perspectives from the German', *Harvard Law Review* **80** (1966–67), pp. 23–89.

Vann, G., O.P., *Morals and man*, (London: Fontana Books, 1960).

Vischer, R., 'Subsidiarity as a principle of governance: Beyond devolution', *Indiana Law Review* **35** (2001–2002), pp. 103–142.

'The morally distinct corporation: reclaiming the relational dimension of conscience', *Journal of Catholic Social Thought* **5** (2008), pp. 323–369.

Waddington, J., 'What do representatives think of the practices of European Works Councils? Views from six countries', *European Journal of Industrial Relations* **9** (2003), pp. 303–325.

Lord Wedderburn of Charlton, 'Companies and employees: Common law or social dimension', *Law Quarterly Review* **109** (1993), pp. 220–262.

Employees, partnership and company law', *Industrial Law Journal* **31** (2002), pp. 99–111.

Weigel, G., 'The Church's Social Doctrine in the twenty-first century', *Logos* **6** (2003), pp. 15–37.

Werlauff, E., 'The development of Community company law', *European Law Review* **17** (1992), pp. 207–231.

'Using a foreign company for domestic activities', *European Business Law Review* **10** (2000), pp. 306–313.

Wheeler, S., *Corporations and the third way*, (Oxford: Hart Publishing, 2002).

Wilber, C., 'Economics and ethics: The challenge of the bishops' pastoral letter on the economy', *Notre Dame Journal of Law, Ethics & Public Policy* **2** (1985–1987), pp. 107–124.

Williamson, O., 'Corporate governance', *The Yale Law Journal* **93** (1984), pp. 1197–1230.

Wojtyla, K., *Person and community. Selected essays*, (T. Sandok, O.S.M trans.), (New Jersey: Peter Lang, 1993).

Wouters, J., 'European company law: Quo Vadis?', *Common Market Law Review* **37** (2000), pp. 257–307.

Zumbansen, P., 'The parallel worlds of corporate governance and labor law', *Indiana Journal of Global Legal Studies* **13** (2006), pp. 261–312.

INDEX